The Road to Waterloo

Jacqueline Everett

The Road to Waterloo

Jacqueline Everett

Published by The Other Albion Press

A CIP catalogue record for this book is available from the British Library.

eBook also available from www.endeavourpress.com

ISBN 978-0-9932772-0-7 (Paperback)

Book layout and cover design by Clare Brayshaw

Front cover image from an original oil painting by William Sadler

Prepared and printed by:

York Publishing Services Ltd
64 Hallfield Road
Layerthorpe
York YO31 7ZQ

Tel: 01904 431213

Website: www.yps-publishing.co.uk

Dedication

In memory of my parents, Joan and Ken Everett,
who first speculated on the French connection
and
Thomas Cooper my great-great-great grandfather,
who fought at Waterloo

About the author

Born in Lancashire, Jacqueline Everett now lives in Yorkshire. She is currently writing Waterloo Man, the second book in a planned series of interlinked novels stretching from the Napoleonic Wars to the Second World War, exploring big events through the lives of ordinary people. Waterloo Man will be published in 2016.

jacquelineeverett.co.uk

About the book

The Road to Waterloo is the first book in this series. Set during the last ten years of the Napoleonic Wars, it was initially inspired by the authors discovery that her great-great-great grandfather fought at Waterloo, as a serjeant in a light dragoons regiment. The Thomas Cowper in the book, though, is completely fictional.

Contents

1

The Son of Beelzebub

March 1805, Burton Lazarus, Leicestershire

It was not a good day to bury a child, let alone *The Chosen One*. The more Thomas Cowper tried to console his mother, the more she sobbed. 'Fear not, Mary: for thou hast found favour with God.'

Thomas heard enough voices of his own to know the Archangel's words should not be spoken aloud but muttered, 'Of course, Mam,' for there was little point in saying anything else. She'd lost her wits after each of her children's deaths, though this time was worse and with Grandma Cowper and now Michael gone, he was the only one left to shield her from his father's rages and their neighbours' scorn.

If only he could take her away from all this; the winds over Melton Hill, the earth clarting their boots, the springs drenching Main Street in day-long weepings, and the constant talk of Frenchmen ready to storm through every last house in every village in the land. Thomas stroked her bony hand, its skin as rough as a farm cat's tongue. None of them had eaten well that winter.

Yet, convinced as she was Michael had been *The Chosen One* come again to save their souls, there was no gainsaying her. So much so, his father had reluctantly agreed to process with Michael's coffin around the village for all to mourn His passing. Thomas and his mother were to walk ahead, whilst his father led the horse with stony-faced Hannah and the little ones wedged firmly inside the cart, for the morning's deep frost made it perilous underfoot. Thomas glanced at the Burnabys' cottage as they passed. No sign of Grace. His mother liked Grace and Grace his mother. There were few enough girls willing to walk out with the son of a woman given to losing her mind. Suddenly he felt her pulling away from him, trying to free his grip.

'Michael's calling me,' she insisted, her eyes searching the horizon.

Thomas took her hand and tucked it under his. 'No, Mam. Remember. Michael can't … not anymore …' Thomas once again saw Michael lying bleeding at the foot of the apple loft ladder, and felt zig-zag shafts of light skewering his eyes, a foul taste rising in his throat. His mother tugged harder. Thomas tugged back.

'Hold tight or you'll fall and hurt yourself,' and he tried to ignore the voices that whispered louder and louder: ' But you're glad Michael's dead, aren't you?'

~

And so they struggled on until they reached the bottom of Hollow Lane, where Blenheim stopped. Thomas sighed. The horse could be as stubborn as his father. At last they succeeded in urging the black dray forwards, holding its neck steady as the cart creaked up the hill.

Thomas willed himself not to slip, counting off every turn in the road until they reached the church, with the dankest corner of its graveyard reserved for those villagers obliged in death, as in life, to huddle too close to their neighbours.

As they approached the lych gate, Thomas saw Grace and her sister, Sarah, waiting by the churchyard wall. Moving closer, he whispered, 'Grace, about Michael …'

But Grace put her forefinger to her lips and shook her head. 'Not now, Thomas,' and she turned to his mother, gently touching her hand, to explain 'We're just waiting for Squire Rearsby's party before we go in.'

~

Back out again in the cold air, waiting for the parson to lead them to the grave, Thomas tried to avoid Sarah catching his eye, for Grace's sister had much too sharp a tongue for his liking. Every morning as he left Home Farm's stables, he'd meet its dairymaids hurrying up Main Street, Grace and Sarah skittering ahead like young foals, their pattens scraping loudly against the ice-hardened wheel ruts; and every morning Sarah would find another way to embarrass him.

But Sarah was not to be ignored. She twisted her thin lips into a half smile, and challenged Thomas's gaze with her dark grey eyes. 'Well, there'll be a fair few village lasses weeping over their one and only true sweetheart today.'

Grace picked up her skirts. 'Sarah!

Sarah smiled. 'Well, you know what he was like.'

Thomas tried to hurry his mother away. This wouldn't be something she'd want to hear about her precious Michael, even though everyone else knew he had flirted, and more, with all the village girls. He and Grace used to laugh about it; until Christmas just gone.

Sarah turned to Thomas. 'Still, it leaves your way clear with our Grace.'

Grace's face blanched. 'Sarah, that's a wicked thing to say.'

Sarah now turned her gaze upon Grace. 'My wickedness, as you call it, has nothing to do with what happened to Michael.'

Thomas saw his mother's face pucker. She began to sob and grabbed his arm. 'God will punish us all for killing The Chosen One.'

Thomas felt his stomach judder but he spoke as calmly as he could. 'Mam, it was an accident.' He placed his hands over his mother's icy fingers.

She pulled them away. 'Gabriel warned me about Satan's other son.'

His mother's obsession with Satan was new. When he was younger, her demons had taken the form of monks from the leper hospital which had stood in Burton hundreds of years ago. Hooded figures in black, who punished you for your sins.

'Mam. It was an accident – nothing to do with Satan.'

His mother flung back her head and wailed.

Thomas told himself it would pass. 'Let's get Michael buried, eh?' He put his arm around her shoulders and eased her towards the heaped earth in the far corner under a yew tree.

She was sobbing again. 'Fear not, Mary: for thou hast found favour with God.'

'Mam. Come on.'

But still she wailed, 'You killed Him. You killed The Chosen One and now none of us will be saved.'

As they reached the graveside, Hannah snapping at the little ones, his father busy with the coffin, his mother became even more agitated. She stared at the mourners. 'He said Beelzebub would have his disciples out in force.'

'Mam. For Michael's sake. Shh'.

His mother began to beat her fists against his chest. 'It should be you in there, Beelzebub's son in that grave, not our Michael.'

Thomas heard the frenzied beat of wings, felt the icy sweep of powerful wings shattering the air. He couldn't breathe – his own mother accusing him of murdering his brother. He grabbed her arms and held her close.

'Have I not been a good son to you?'

She spat in his eye. 'The son of Beelzebub is no son of mine.'

Thomas, his face running with sweat, felt the icy sweep of powerful angel wings shatter the air.

He heard himself yell, 'It's you who should be in that grave, not me, not Michael, but you!'

He heard himself curse the day she married his father; he saw himself pin her arms behind her back and push her towards the pit. All it took was one last shove, to tip her, screaming, into its freezing emptiness.

'Don't you ever, ever say that again,' Thomas shouted after her.

He began to run and as he did so, he heard the unmistakable voice of his father, roaring, 'I'll kill you; I'll bloody kill you!'

~

Thomas didn't stop running until he reached the fields beyond Melton Hill, when he fell down next to the hedge of the topmost field. Surely no one, not even his father, would risk chasing him any distance over these frozen mires? Maybe he could just stay here? But almost as soon as he had leant back against the ditch bank, he felt his stomach contract, his entire body retch, pitching him forward onto his knees until the last dribbles of snot-green liquid ceased, till once again he could hear his mother's voice ringing in his head, her rough hands scrubbing away the foamy froth from his mouth.

'That stomach of yours will be the death of you.'

Thomas wiped his mouth clean on the underside of his smock. No. His mother would be the death of him. Born only six weeks after the wedding, he was surely the only reason why his parents had married, so why wouldn't she curse the day he was conceived? Sometimes he too thought he could hear the voices that visited her, their high-pitched taunts, their scolding and relentless accusations. As for his father, schooled like himself by Grandma Cowper to read and write, surely he could have chosen better for himself? He might have been a less ill-tempered man if he had, though Grandma Cowper insisted, it was only after Thomas had been born that his mother's wits began to loosen. Thomas grimaced: yet another reason for both his parents hating their first-born.

He tried to imagine crawling home, to rehearse something they might say to each other. But the words wouldn't come. Exhausted, he threw himself under the hedge's lowest leaves, covering himself as best he could, until, just before the sun started to drop in the sky, he woke to the sound of men talking. He heard Bailiff Strutt's booming tones drift up from the lower field, before catching the higher pitch of an angrier second voice – his father's.

'I don't think there's much point in pursuing him further, Tom,' Bailiff Strutt pronounced, slightly out of breath.

His father sounded more threatening than ever. 'Wait till I get bloody hold of him.'

Thomas began to panic. He was hardly well hidden. What choice did he have? To be thrashed like he'd never been thrashed before, or to resist but still fail to knuckle his father to the ground?

The voices were moving closer, magnified in the clear air.

'... Mistress Cowper is ill, is she not?' Bailiff Strutt spoke like he understood such things.

Thomas heard his father protest, 'Aye, but only on account of our Thomas treating her the way he does.'

Bailiff Strutt sighed. 'But would you not consider just a temporary committal to an asylum?'

'Then what am I supposed to do with three lasses to look after if she's locked up? Send them away to the poorhouse?'

'Your Hannah is almost grown and wise beyond her years.'

'I don't need that kind of help from a ten-year-old lass. I need a son who's not driving his Mam into an early grave.'

Thomas heard his father slap a horsewhip against a tree, much as it would soon be cutting into his own flesh.

His father moved nearer. 'Just wait till I get my hands on him. She's ten times worse than she was this morning. If he hadn't lost his temper with her, she'd have settled down once we'd got the burial nicely over and done with.'

Thomas heard a rustle, felt his heart stop, looked up and saw Bailiff Strutt on the other side of the hedge peering through leaves at him. Bailiff Strutt put his finger up to his lips and turned away, back towards his father, gesturing towards the village.

'Tom. We're wasting our time.'

His father disagreed. 'He'll be here somewhere, I warrant.'

Bailiff Strutt persisted. 'Perhaps you're best shut of him. Let him get hired by another estate, till Mistress Cowper settles down. You don't want her getting worse and those young lasses of yours ending up in the poorhouse, do you?'

Thomas heard his father mutter under his breath, 'Aye, you're right. I'll have to think of the lasses from now on.'

With that, they were gone. Bailiff Strutt couldn't have made it any clearer to Thomas. He was to put his old life behind him. Yet as darkness fell, it was the happy memories not the sad ones that kept him awake: dancing with Grace at the Harvest Festival; squinting at the roof carvings of musicians who seemed to be attending to the parson's sermon more intently than the parishioners below; following the hunt back to Great Dalby Cross, the hounds with their brindled skins thrown loosely over their lean frames and lanky legs, at rest but forever watchful, tails moving like so many divining rods, the dowsers of the kill. But now he was the quarry.

He clasped his arms round his knees and shivered. He felt dizzy. What was he to do? Thomas nursed his frozen hands and tried not to think about Grandma Cowper dead last year, her old cottage in Stathern given up five or more years ago; but he felt the tug of his grandmother's sturdy arms pulling him up from tangled stream banks, teasing him out of briar hedgerows as they searched for yarrows, thistles, alder, nettles, strawberries, and ferns for her great stock of remedies; the cures she told Reverend Crabbe about so he could write them all down in a book; the nettle and fern, he remembered, being especially good for stomach cramps.

Curate Crabbe. Thomas closed his eyes, remembering Stathern church high above the village stream, its yellow ironstone tower perched above roads mired in so much mud they could be cut off for weeks in their own Kingdom of Heaven. He pictured the churchyard: angels cut into pale headstones, their wings beating as violently as moths in a jar; he heard the clock in the nave ticking; he fingered the tracery of the many-sided stone font, where his mother had seen him baptised by Curate Crabbe himself, yet could still declare Thomas to be a child of Lucifer. His grandmother would have known exactly who to blame for further addling his mother's wits, filling her head full of Judgement Day torments and the Fallen Angel Beelzebub – their parson in Burton Lazarus.

Yet when she lived in Stathern, the Widow Cowper had been devoted to Curate Crabbe, who, like her, knew the power of herbs and stories to heal souls as well as bodies. It was only after the curate had left Belvoir Vale that she was persuaded to abandon its low-lying pastures and join her son on Burton's wind-scoured hilltop.

Thomas remembered the sticky clay that made ploughing the land so difficult that most of it was left to the cattle; the soft grasslands; the smell of the milk, which the Vale's dairymaids turned into soft crumbling cheese. He felt his heart pound as if once again struggling to the top of the narrow escarpment dividing the Vale of Belvoir from Melton. Thomas wondered whether he would ever again look out over the vale he loved.

For, above all, he remembered love. His grandmother's love.

2

Lady Day

Thomas woke up nithered. It'd been a cold night and the morning was little better. If only he didn't have such terrible dreams. Feeling tears beginning to form, he rubbed them away and stumbled downhill through the middle fields, creeping into East Farm's stable yard to take his leave of the horses. Although it was long before the start of the working day, his father might well have been waiting for him so, as he lit the tallows, he was relieved to see only Blenheim and Ramillies dozing in the darkness.

Bending down, he grasped one of Blenheim's hooves and lathered its feathers with lard. 'Don't want folk forgetting about them, eh?'

The black carthorse gently shifted his weight as Thomas rubbed the fat onto each leg in turn. Thomas at last pulled himself up and laid his head against Blenheim's broad neck, while Blenheim whinnied his usual encouragement. But then Ramillies began to neigh and snort, so Thomas moved into her stall, picked out an overlooked piece of grit from her mane and stroked her nose. Ramillies threw back her head; she always could read his mind. Satisfied he could do no more, he banged the mud off his boots against the stable wall, rinsed his hands in the trough and grabbed an old hay net to take with him, to advertise his trade.

Pale clear moonlight over the frost-stiffened pastures promised another cold day. No time to waste. Leicester was a good three to four hours away. He wiped his dripping hands on his smock and blew through his fingers, his breath spiralling up against the first rays of light coming over the ridge. He was running late.

He walked briskly up Pepper Lane and then out towards the Oakham Road by the churchyard. In this strange half-light, he could just make out the church's pale edging stones, though its ironstone bell-cote was almost invisible. Time to go. But something still held him there, thinking about what used to be. Even if he did not intend to say his good-byes to the living, he surely must to the dead.

His grandmother's grave was just off the main path. He took care not to squash the scattering of yellow flowers underfoot. Aconites. Poisonous. In the end they had buried Grandma Cowper, one of the parson's most vigorous critics, right under his nose by the porch, in a plot paid for with her own money and marked by a rough-hewn cross. Grandma Cowper would be spoiling for a fight with so many in the after-life that his mother had thought the cross a wise precaution.

Thomas had often noticed Grandma Cowper muttering her own thoughts during the sermon and used to worry that the parson or even God Himself would surely find her out. The parson didn't suspect she spent Sunday afternoons in the company of others inclined towards Methodism, discussing the Holy Book more intently than they ever listened to him. Thomas and Grace would usually tag along too and copy out improving texts, hunched over Bailiff Strutt's rough-hewn kitchen table. Thomas often felt more at ease with his Grandmother's God than the parson's, not that he would ever say so. After all, he lived in an estate village, where it wasn't wise to go against the religion of the parson or the squire.

Thomas looked towards the end of the churchyard. He walked over to the heap of newly dug earth and bent his head. He whispered one of his grandmother's prayers. 'God is in your heart and His works in your works, and His love in your love of your neighbour.' Suddenly his stomach began to tighten as if his mother's fists were once again drumming on his chest. He felt some of yesterday's anger return. Didn't she have enough children left to take some comfort from them? 'For God's sake,' he mouthed the silent blasphemy.

But what was he to do about Grace? With parents' permissions given, he and Grace could have become betrothed, and then all would have been allowed, until either a baby or the offer of a cottage brought the marriage forward. Yet, much as he would have liked to lie with Grace, something had always held Thomas back. Maybe it was the sight of his own mother worn down by too many children dead and alive, and his father toiling all day in the fields but scarcely making a living. Thomas knew that was what families did. They made you unhappy. But he couldn't tell her that. Could he?

He stamped his feet and blew on his hands. He had one more thing to do before he left.

3

Promises

So he was gone. Grace leant against the cowshed wall, shooing the other girls in ahead of her. She just wished she hadn't cried in front of Bailiff Strutt. But then Bailiff Strutt turned back to speak to her.

'If he's any sense, he'll be on his way to Leicester hiring fair by now. Mind, I reckon he's not long left off seeing to those horses of ours, so it mightn't do no harm looking for him in the churchyard. You know how much he thought of Widow Cowper.'

As Bailiff Strutt waved her on her way, Grace ran up the lane as fast as she could towards the churchyard. Did Bailiff Strutt know something she didn't? What had Thomas been trying to tell her yesterday when she'd shushed him? That moment yesterday when Grace saw him racing out of the graveyard, she knew something had happened that would change their lives forever. Only Bailiff Strutt still had a good word to say about him. Everyone else thought mother and son both mad. Sometimes Grace wondered about that too. She remembered when Thomas was younger, you could be talking to him and it was as if he wasn't there. Just for a moment or two. But no, he wasn't mad and she couldn't let him go without making a fight of it.

~

As Grace entered the churchyard she could hardly bear to look, but sure enough Thomas was there, standing under one of the great yews by Michael's grave. She was just about to go to him when she saw him kneel down and scrape up a small clod of earth.

She drew back into the porch, and it was only after Thomas had finished pressing the soil into a small cloth bag that she ventured closer.

'Thomas.'

He turned sharply. 'Grace?'

She felt herself beginning to babble. 'You wanted to talk to me about Michael.'

Thomas reddened. '... Not any more ... not after ...'

Grace tried again. ' It seemed important.'

Thomas shook his head. 'It was nothing.' His eyes were nearly as red as his face. 'I know it wasn't right, what I did to my mother.' He looked down at his feet, then looked up. 'Mind, it wasn't right neither, Sarah saying all those things about me and you and Michael.'

Grace blushed. 'She was just trying to make mischief for us in front of your mother.'

Thomas nodded. 'She did that all right, but I've no choice now but to go to the hiring fair.' He reached for her hand.

Grace put her hands behind her back. 'But what about us?'

Thomas looked into her eyes. 'I'll come back for you as soon as I can.'

She shook her head. 'When?'

Thomas leant forward and touched her cheek. ' Soon.'

She put her arms around his neck and pulled him close to her. 'Take me with you, Thomas. And when we're settled, we'll ask our parents if we can be wed.'

He kissed her forehead but slowly began to remove her arms from around his neck.

'I can't, Grace.'

She felt a stone drop into her stomach. He was leaving Burton Lazarus. He was leaving her and that was that.

When she still said nothing, he took her hands in his. 'I will send word.'

Grace looked down at her feet, anywhere rather than at him. 'But what if I leave Burton too, then what?'

Thomas leant closer. 'I'll still find you.'

She felt the momentary warmth from his hands drain away. 'Sometime, never?'

He squeezed her hands. 'A year or two, maybe.'

Grace knew it could be foolish to ask for an understanding, but nevertheless found herself saying, 'Promise.'

He smiled and kissed her fingers. 'Promise. When these troubles are behind me.'

Grace tried not to cry. 'I suppose I must wish you well.'

Thomas kissed her on the mouth with such triumph Grace could hardly bear it. She picked up her skirts and ran back towards East Farm, back towards Sarah's scorn and Bailiff Strutt's set expression. Running down Pepper Lane, past its high walls and bedraggled hedges, she was dizzy with rage. She had tried her best, but for all Thomas's fine words, she had to wonder: would he ever be back?

Well, if Thomas Cowper were abandoning her, she would not pine away. She picked up a couple of ice-coated stones, gripping them hard until she felt calm enough to make any vows count. She swallowed her tears, promising herself never to cry over him again. She pitched one of the stones hard at the first thing she could see. It bounced against the smooth grey bark of the beech tree clinging to the bank that sloped down to the village, and then rolled away spent, deep into the drifts of leaves.

'I hate you, Thomas Cowper. I hate you!'

As she approached the wall, she tossed the other stone from hand to hand. 'Don't think I can't do just as well without you, Thomas Cowper.'

So with that promise to herself, she threw the last stone slap into the wall, wiped away her tears on the back of her sleeve, and set her face towards East Farm's mucky cattle byres. She too, Grace Burnaby, had plans.

~

Thomas knew it had been a reluctant blessing but brushed his hands firmly across his eyes, stamped his feet and felt his toes recoil in pain. He should never have stood about for so long. He struck out south down the turnpike, and then crossed the road and walked past the field that bordered the old leper hospital ruins close by the Hall. He decided to cut across the meadows and go straight on to Great Dalby, skirting the lower lake.

At last he was on his way under an open sky turning to blue, though still grey on the horizon, with touches of pink in the east. He began to feel free, experiencing everything as though for the first time: the fine lines of beech branches like besoms brushing the heavens; orange-beaked blackbirds strutting about with twigs, nest building; scuffed autumn leaves of oak and beech sprinkled with silver dust; the shimmering stone-capping on a wall; the cold slicing against his face, his feet making a dull thud; the cawing of rooks; the cooing of wood pigeons; the frost lighting up last year's brambles. Then, as he raced down Sandy Lane, as the hill positively tumbled him onto the Dalby road, he was stopped in his tracks by a lakeside willow, thrusting high in a great pyramid, glowing red in the low sun. A burning bush. A vision of the Promised Land. Good enough for Moses; and for Thomas Cowper.

~

Thomas realised he was lost. He sat down, leant back against a chestnut tree and wondered how far away the Hall would be. There was always a Hall where there were chestnuts; they were no use to man nor beast otherwise. He looked around him but there was no one to be seen. It must be one of those deserted villages he'd heard tell of, houses and churches still standing, but with not a soul left living there to work the land. Sometimes the land seemed to be worked, but, people would ask, by whom? 'Ghosts,' the grandmothers would reply, 'ghosts of all them families thrown off their own bits of God's earth.'

But if there were a Hall, there would be somebody he could ask. Once he'd rested a while, once he'd warmed up a bit. He'd begun to nod off when he saw Grace standing next to him, her long auburn hair catching the winter sun, her dark eyes smiling, reaching out to him, but then she was gone as suddenly as she'd appeared. He tried to stand up to shout after her but the words wouldn't come. He felt a great heaviness in his body as though the chestnut branches were pinning him to the ground, their curling limbs bending low to trap him like a fly in a web, their buds dripping a stickiness which left him helpless to escape. He heard bells in the distance and began to make out a procession of dark hooded figures carrying Michael, blood still running from his mouth, moving closer and closer. Thomas told himself it was just another one of his bad dreams, one of his absences, but he started to run, half- expecting to see more wraiths digging out the lane's side ditches.

~

He was striding towards Leicester by its grandest route and the closer he got, the more his spirits were lifted by the great panorama of the city walls and church steeples piercing the bright blue sky; but as he came clattering down the paved street just outside the walls he was knocked back by a great stink, a terrible miasma, seeping out of the muddy stream running alongside. It was worse than Melton after market days, when blood and shite mingled freely in its ditches. He retched. He, who could pile dung heaps as high as a house, was to his shame fetching up like a feeble mouser, fur and bone sticking in its craw after too much hunting. His head began to spin. What if his mother was right? What if he had killed Michael?

4

The Roll of the Drum

March 1805, Leicester

Thomas told himself everyone knew his mother had lost her wits. Why should he, or anyone else for that matter, believe anything she said? His or hers, the voices aren't always right, are they? How could he have had a hand in Michael's death? Michael was already dying when he found him. He wiped his hand across his mouth and tried to remember the directions to the hiring fair.

'You want to get yourself to Coal Hill. If there's anybody needing a farm servant, that'll be where you'll find them.'

So where was Coal Hill? He looked up and down the broad street of stone setts lined by grand houses, but all he could see was blood, Michael's blood running down its gutters. He closed his eyes till he felt the vision finally pass before setting off again. There was still no sign of a hill, but as he moved closer to the town centre he heard the clattering of horses' hooves and a thump, thump, thump together with a great number of huzzas, moving towards him. It was like nothing he'd ever heard before. He quickened his pace. He began to make out the sound of a trumpet as well as the thud of a drum beating out a regular rhythm. He hurried on till he came to an open square where the whole of Leicester seemed to be assembled. A recruiting party was out in force.

Thomas took his place amongst the crowds waiting for a great spectacle. He was not disappointed.

About half a dozen men on fine horses with short nag tails were soon processing down the main street towards them, led by a drummer. Thomas pushed in closer. He could see an officer riding a dark chestnut gelding, its hindquarters muscular, chest sturdy, neck long and curved, eye clear and bright, and head beautifully balanced. Its back was covered in a blue cloth edged in gold flowing over its rump, a brocaded crest beneath embroidered white feathers above some initials he couldn't quite make out. It was as fine a horse as he'd ever seen. The officer too was just as handsome with his powdered hair tied back by leather thongs, sitting bolt upright on a sheepskin-covered saddle, his waist emphasised by a crimson sash between blue trousers and a jacket with embroidered cuffs and collar. The jacket was threaded across with so many white loops Thomas thought they looked like a woman's stays. Thomas marvelled at everything: the officer's helmet layered in cloth close to his head, the leather headpiece topped by a crest of fierce fur, his curved sword hanging by his side.

The soldiers were hardly less grand, their horses almost as splendid as the officer's. Thomas began to imagine himself in their place. Suddenly he noticed the officer smiling; his plump pink face was smiling at him. Thomas then felt a tug at his elbow. He turned and saw a skinny, ginger-haired lad pointing in the direction of the officer, muttering something Thomas didn't catch at first; not that Thomas had time to respond before the young man continued.

'I made those boots.'

Thomas wasn't sure he'd heard right. 'Boots?' he repeated.

'For Captain Dickenson there. Two pairs in finest leather. See.'

Thomas looked again in the Captain's direction but his heart was beating so fast he scarcely heard anything else the skinny fellow was saying.

'Captain Dickenson's very particular about his riding boots. We've made them for years now – his family have an estate round here.'

'You're a shoemaker?'

The young man nodded. 'Will Freer of Peacock Lane.' His face fell. 'Till yesterday...'

Thomas looked this scrawny Freer fellow up and down. Probably older than him. Maybe twenty or so. Face pale and freckled, red hair curled and untidy, blowing in the wind. He had the kind of expression you might guess was usually cheerful but there seemed to be no stopping his prattle.

The red-haired fellow was still talking by the time Thomas had gathered his wits; ... 'and it's exactly on account of this Bailey my master and I have just parted in the most unhappy of circumstances. You see when Captain Dickenson told me the 36th were recruiting, I said to my master, 'I've a mind to go for a soldier, show Boney what we reckon to tyrants who get themselves crowned emperors. So what do you think my old master said to me? "There are tyrants aplenty at home to fight without you going and joining their army." Well, then we started. All night we argued. About the rights and wrongs of the war and whether the French and the Americans are the only upholders of liberty left. I pointed out Boney wasn't even French and whatever he had believed in he'd clearly forgotten, marching into every capital in Europe bold as brass, till things became so heated my master tore up my indenture papers, threw down my tools and told me to find myself another master and somewhere else to lay my head.'

Thomas had scarcely followed a word the shoemaker had said, but gathered he too was jobless and homeless.

Thomas felt the relief of confession. ' Thomas Cowper from Burton Lazarus ... till yesterday. I am also without work and somewhere to lay my head.'

Freer nodded and gently touched his arm. 'Then we're two of a pair.'

Thomas felt the warmth of Freer's brotherly sentiments. 'So it would seem.'

Freer tightened his bag over his shoulder. 'So you're on your way to the hiring fair?'

Thomas hesitated. 'I suppose I am. And you?'

Freer shook his head. 'Nobody's going to hire an apprentice shoemaker with no papers to his name.'

'Mind, I've an inclination to go a-soldiering myself,' Thomas found himself saying.

Freer pulled a face. 'I too had a mind for it, but whether I have the heart for it is quite another matter.'

'But if we are both so minded shouldn't we just...?'

Freer raised his hand. 'Most certainly not. Let us behave like the rational creatures we're supposed to be and have a drink before we decide on anything.'

Thomas laughed. He liked this Freer fellow in spite of himself and fell into step behind him as Freer wove his way through the crowds, gesticulating as he talked. Freer waved briefly towards the two inns opposite each other on the corner.

'The Lion and Lamb, where gentlemen Whigs meet and chew the fat in comfort about the necessity of reform.'

Reform of what? Thomas wasn't sure he dared ask.

'The Three Cranes, where the country squires are agreed, without exception, parliamentary reform would mark the end of our fine nation.'

Ah. Parliamentary reform. Thomas had heard talk of that.

They had, by now, reached an even finer coaching inn with a grand porch close by a watering pond for its horses.

'Want the latest news from London? Just ask the post boys at The Three Crowns,' said Freer.

Thomas stopped. He noticed something wrapped round one of The Three Crowns' broad plaster pillars. He walked over to inspect it. It was a printed notice; he carefully traced out the words.

'The Thirty-Sixth Regiment of Light Dragoons seeks young Fellows whose hearts beat high to tread the paths of glory where each Young Hero, on being approved, will receive the largest bounty allowed by the government.

Come forward then and enrol yourselves in a regiment that stands unrivalled and where the kind treatment the Men experience is well known throughout the whole Kingdom.

Must be over 16 years of age, over 5 feet 6 inches tall, active and well limbed with no ruptures. Apply to Serjeant Fallowfield, and then blocked boldly in another ink, *at The Blue Boar, Leicester, by Tuesday next.*

NB. Smart young Irishmen taken.

Thomas felt his heart leap at the very notion of being a hero. Freer, glancing at the poster over Thomas's shoulder, muttered, 'So we've till tomorrow to make our minds up.'

Thomas shook his head. 'Not if I have to find another master before the end of the fair.'

'By today then. We've the rest of the day.'

Thomas nodded. We? Yet it felt natural to throw in his lot with this carroty- haired scarecrow of a man, as though the two of them would be able to meld the shoemaker's head to the ploughboy's heart, and act as one.

~

It was as they approached The Black Bull overlooking the open meadows that Thomas's resolve begin to waver. With its low roof and rough airs, it reminded him of The Royal Oak at Great Dalby. It reminded him of home.

Maybe he should still go to the hiring fair? Then after a couple of years, he could return to Burton, his mother's accusations forgotten, him forgiven. He stared across the river at the cattle chewing steadily, oblivious to everything, and began to see his own life unfold without hope of any future forgiveness, though for what he wasn't sure.

Thomas rubbed his eyes till they hurt. He couldn't believe that Michael, wrenched out of Death's grasp at birth, had been reclaimed so easily at just sixteen years old. With his blue eyes and fair complexion, his mother had always referred to Michael as her gift from Heaven, unlike the earth-bound Thomas with his dull brown eyes, red cheeks and awkward ways. Maybe Grace had thought his younger brother a better match, after all? He stopped to catch his breath. No. Grace's Sarah is just a mischief-maker. Pure and simple.

'Cowper!' Freer was shouting to him, signalling him to move closer to the river. 'Look. This is the exact same place where Master Bailey taught me to swim.'

~

Will Freer stared into the swirling waters and remembered being tied to a rope, while Bailey encouraged him from the side.

'Now splash those damn legs of yours! Come on; no one's lame in the water.'

Freer felt his stomach flip as he remembered his master's last words to him. 'There are tyrants aplenty at home to fight without you going and joining their army.'

He turned and saw Cowper with his farm worker's hands, fresh face and dark brown eyes gazing intently into the river. Freer sighed. He would have to explain.

'I'll certainly not get work with Bailey again, but the problem is,' Will Freer pointed to his feet, 'this leg's shorter than the other. That's why I was put to shoemaking by the parish in the first place. Mind, the first thing Bailey did was to build up my boot. '

Cowper frowned, 'You're lame?'

Will saw Cowper hadn't grasped the possible consequences. 'So the army doctor may well refuse me.'

Cowper threw up his hands. Then I shan't go if they don't take you as well.'

Will's spirits began to lift. ' Let's drink to that at least.'

Thomas smiled but then gestured towards The Black Bull, turning his gaze resolutely away from the meadows. 'Can we go somewhere else instead?'

~

As they approached The Blue Boar, Thomas noticed some lads with leather aprons loitering by its entrance. Freer must have seen them too for he promptly tugged Thomas up the next lane till they reached a brick building set back from the road. It seemed to be some kind of chapel. The Great Meeting, Freer had called it.

Freer quickly pulled Thomas inside.

'Best keep out of the way of those idle apprentices whose master laid a charge against Bookseller Phillips for selling Tom Paine's books.'

Thomas tried to remember if he'd come across this Tom Paine before, whilst Freer sat down and stared into the darkness.

'Just because we Unitarians and the followers of Tom Paine believe people should be free to think for themselves, the government are as fearful of us as of the Tyrant himself. So they bribe mobs and persuade layabout apprentice boys to declare men of reason, and Liberty itself, to be their enemy.'

Freer paused before looking up. 'What about you? What do you believe in?'

'Me?' Thomas realised he didn't know what he believed in, but Freer turned away, apparently not needing a reply and sat twisting his hands together as though wringing out every last minute of time. Suddenly he stood up. 'Well, Cowper, what's it to be then?'

5

The Recruiting Serjeant

By the time Thomas and Freer returned to The Blue Boar, there were more lads hovering about the yard entrance. There was much talk about the bounty and the fine uniforms, though few of them seemed to know a great deal about horses. One of them seemed a little older than the rest. Peter Quilley, he called himself, a tall man who seemed well informed about the military life. Soon they heard the steady beat of the drum of the returning soldiers, with another smart fellow heading the party, a huge dark-haired man with a face the colour of over-ripe damsons.

'The recruiting serjeant,' Quilley whispered. 'Always the one to watch out for…'

~

Serjeant Jack Fallowfield was pleased with himself; they might even pick up a few country boys from this crowd and all. But then one of them dared to push forward and run his hands down the neck of Jack's horse. Fallowfield dismounted.

'What's your name, lad?'

'Thomas Cowper. And you, sir?'

Fallowfield swallowed hard. He was the one supposed to ask the questions.

'Serjeant Fallowfield of the 36th Dragoons.'

The lad turned his attention back to the horse.

'Bit of a head shaker, ain't she? Trouble with her ears?'

It was true enough his wretched mare had been shaking her head more and more since they'd left Nottingham. The boy was probably right. Not that Fallowfield was going to say so.

The boy was now peering into her ear.

Who the hell does this boy think he is? But Fallowfield thought of the lad's bounty and tried to look encouraging.

'It would take more than a bit of head shaking to trouble one of our hardy troopers here.' Fallowfield tapped his fingers hard against the horse's nose to emphasise his point. 'She's a beauty, eh?'

'Aye, she is that, sir.'

Fallowfield leant forward. 'Fancy riding one in a few weeks time?'

The lad looked up. 'Like her?'

Fallowfield paused. He nearly had him.

The lad began to stroke the mare's head again. 'Just like her?'

Fallowfield thought even harder about the lad's bounty money and forced a smile.

Be reassuring, Jack, he told himself.

'Oh, aye.'

Cowper took a minute to consider this. 'Our parson says the army is always on the lookout for country boys.'

'Did he now?' Fallowfield liked them too. He found them easier to bend to his will, though possibly not this one.

Jack Fallowfield forced himself to smile again. 'Like your parson says, we're in need of men like you.'

It was true, of course; they needed every last one they could lay their hands on. If they were going to fight off an invasion, not even fools would be turned away.

'I tell you what. Let me buy you a drink. Talk to the rest of the fellows here; they'll tell you what makes a good cavalryman. Bring your friends. And if you decide it's the life for you then it's but a short trip to the magistrates at the Town Hall to claim your twelve guineas.'

Fallowfield paused for effect. 'Twelve guineas, lad; more money than you've ever clapped eyes on, I warrant.'

Cowper looked doubtful.

Go steady, Jack, let's not lose this one, Fallowfield said to himself.

'Now you don't have to take the King's shilling to enjoy a fine afternoon's conversation, though my friends here will vouch for the life we have travelling the world fighting for King and Country.'

Fallowfield was all too aware of how for the last ninety years the Dragoons had been used mainly as border troops; fighting the Jacobites; dealing with the odd English mob or two; garrisoning bloody Ireland. His heart began to race – bloody Ireland. He took a deep breath. So, so much the better if they could parade the prospect of foreign enemies in front of any young men willing to listen; and good stories they were too.

The Cowper youth turned and signalled to a ginger-haired lad standing under the arch into the courtyard and watching the proceedings as carefully as a man on picquet duty.

'Freer, the serjeant here is going to buy us a drink.'

Suddenly the courtyard filled up with a dozen or more fellows who'd been hiding in the shadows.

Fallowfield smiled. If they couldn't persuade all of these lads to sign up then Corporal Dermot Murphy would have truly lost the gift of the gab.

Fallowfield paid the landlord to charge the party's tankards, and soon Murphy was revived enough to tell the story of when in 1793 the 36th had acted as dismounted dragoons at the Siege of Toulon, touching on the cunning of Napoleon's gun emplacements and the subsequent retreat of the navy. 'If only they'd stopped the man in his tracks there and then …'

~

Aye, Thomas thought through the haze of particularly strong ale; if only; if only he and Michael hadn't fallen out over Grace; if only Michael hadn't decided to take himself off yet again to sleep in the apple loft; if only Michael hadn't slipped; if only Thomas could believe he wasn't to blame for everything. Saving his country from Boney was the least he could do to make amends – so long as Freer enlisted too. He looked across at Freer and smiled as encouragingly as he could.

~

Murphy's tale of this lost opportunity to stop the Tyrant in his tracks made Will Freer's heart skip several beats. That's all it might have taken if someone had had the foresight to nip the whole Emperor business in the bud. He glanced across at Cowper, who was nodding at him. If Cowper still had the heart to fight, Freer wasn't going to see his new friend march off to face Boney without him.

~

Jack Fallowfield peered around the gloomy Town Hall rooms above the Square and couldn't have been more content. A dozen of them were about to take the King's shilling for almost certainly the usual reasons. Murphy may have stirred their hearts with tales of adventure and patriotism, but what brought them into the fold was the want of money, the lack of a proper home, the desire to escape from an irksome apprenticeship or to escape the law. Not that Jack Fallowfield cared.

Fallowfield drummed his fingers, waiting for the doctor to declare them fit enough to be marched in front of the magistrate to swear their allegiance to King and Country. 'And obedience to Jack Fallowfield,' he muttered to himself as he saw that Cowper fellow walk in.

~

As Thomas and Freer entered the dark wood-panelled courtrooms, Freer whispered, 'You wouldn't want to be on the wrong side of the law in here, would you?'

Thomas grunted and began to sweat. The thought hadn't entered his head before, but what if his father had believed his mother and was intending at this very moment to lay a complaint against him with the magistrates? For murder? True or false, he was surely a marked man. His only hope was to leave with the regiment tomorrow; then he'd be safely on his way to face Boney instead.

He wiped the sweat off his face. The doctor might declare he had a fever and that would put an end to everything. But the doctor seemed more concerned to discover ruptures than fevers.

'So, you're fit enough to die for your country, young man.' The old doctor scribbled something on a piece of paper, handed it to Thomas, and pointed in the direction of the magistrates. Thomas, his stomach sore from the pummelling the doctor had given him, still managed to speak up clearly enough for Will to hear. 'I'll wait for my friend first, sir.'

The doctor shrugged and beckoned to Freer, whose shortened leg was now quite plain to see. He took one look at Freer, cleared his throat and pronounced him unfit for service. Thomas's heart plummeted, but Will stood his ground and waved his boots at the doctor. 'I can walk as well as another man with these on.'

The doctor ignored him. 'I said you're dismissed.'

Freer shook his head. 'So I'm not to be a soldier after all, my friend,' he said to Thomas. He reluctantly put his boots on again whilst Thomas gathered up all their belongings.

Thomas began to sweat again as he remembered his promise to Freer that they'd stick together, whatever happened at Freer's medical. But now? Thomas's face was burning. Just when he'd thought he'd soon be away, out of reach of the Leicestershire magistrates.

He breathed deeply in and out like his grandmother used to tell him, felt a coolness returning to his cheeks, wiped his kerchief across his eyes and smiled. 'I told you, I'm not enlisting without you.'

Suddenly, out of the corner of his eye, Thomas saw Fallowfield striding towards them. He'd clearly noticed Freer's dismissal.

Fallowfield rounded on the doctor, waving away his explanation. 'We're the cavalry, not the bloody infantry. It's the horses who do the marching.'

The doctor, his flabby face pale with anger, grimaced and commanded Freer, 'Walk across there, first with your boots on and then without 'em.'

Thomas could hardly bear to watch Freer hobble, whilst Fallowfield stood guard over the doctor's shoulder. The doctor grunted and summoned Freer back to pummel his abdomen for any evidence of ruptures. Then Thomas again saw the doctor scribble something and give it to Freer.

'Doubtless you'll make just as fine a fighting man as the rest of 'em.'

Fallowfield smiled.

~

Once they'd sworn their oaths in front of the magistrates, Peter Quilley sidled up to them.

'Come with me and I'll show you how a man might hold on to his bounty money for longer than a night in spite of yonder recruiting serjeant's best efforts.' Thomas whispered to Freer that he thought Quilley a good-hearted fellow, but Freer muttered that he wasn't so sure; there was something about him that didn't ring true.

~

The recruits had come back with their twelve guineas and Corporal Murphy had recounted more tales of daring and adventure; now it was time for Jack Fallowfield to make his move and relieve them of their bounty money, gathering up as much as he could for his unlisted 'necessaries'; as well as fripperies for the recruiting party's sweethearts and wives, and the evening's fund for ale.

As Fallowfield quickly slipped the landlord yet more of the recruits' cash to fill up their tankards, he signalled Murphy to continue. Since the war started, Catholics like Murphy had swelled the ranks of recruits from Ireland no end. He was definitely the man to tell the story of the regiment's Papal blessing, treading the delicate path between holy reverence and earthly enthusiasm. Fallowfield had hand-picked his recruiting party, born spinners of yarns the lot of them.

Now he'd been given the nod, there was no stopping Murphy. He described the scene as though he had been there himself: a party of officers from the 36th Dragoons, kneeling like the repentant Protestants they were, eyes fixed on the Pope blessing them and their men in all their battles against the monstrous French Hydra.

Fallowfield could see it was almost enough to turn an old war-horse like Murphy soft in the head in just the telling of it, never mind the new recruits. Visions of gilded rooms drenched in sandalwood and cedar incense mingled with the bitter, sharp reek of ale. They wanted more. Fallowfield called the landlord over, ordered more ale and took over the tale telling. Surely they must have heard the story of how only four years ago these very men had sailed to far-away Egypt and had captured a complete French convoy without losing a single man or horse? His listeners leant forward as one and toasted the good health of the heroes sitting in front of them as Fallowfield handed round his leather Tarleton helmet.

'See this badge here with the Egyptian Sphinx on it?'

He didn't expect any man in The Blue Boar to have heard of such a creature, but they all seemed to catch the respect in his tone.

'Part lion and part man, made of stone and as big as a church, guarding these temples and them even bigger than a church, bigger than anything you're ever likely to see anywhere.'

Fallowfield too was starting to feel overcome with the memory of it. He pulled himself up sharp but as he looked round the room to check on his listeners, he noticed one of the recruits sitting alone and obviously sober. Sparrow – yes, that was the lad's name. But where were those three friends of his? Now who were they? Quilley, Freer … and that damned Cowper.

Fallowfield banged the table with his fist. The whole lot of them were doubtless as sober as Sparrow, maybe only on their third pint of ale, no more; saving most of their bounty money for their own pockets rather than his. How could he have missed that? How was it he hadn't spotted they were cheating him? Now he remembered: when he'd gone round to collect their money for the first round they'd all tipped in, but then, for the second, only one of them was there to pay. The others were nowhere to be seen though their tankards were still on the table, half-full. And the same for the third round. Bastards! It would have to be Cowper who'd thought it up. It must have been him who'd put the others up to it. They'd keep on doing it too if he let them get away with it. No. Not for one more bloody minute. Fallowfield rose from his chair and clenched his fists.

~

Quilley had insisted they needed a fourth person to make it work and had co-opted the youngest recruit to join in his scheme, even though, from Sparrow's expression, Thomas guessed he had little idea of what was going on. But Sparrow seemed happy enough taking Quilley's orders. All they had to do was this: all four of them would pay for the first round and stay sober enough to take it in turns to pay for the next round while the others left the table for a while, and in that way they would preserve much of their twelve guineas intact.

It was going well and Thomas, out of sight in a dark corner, was busy stuffing ten guineas back in his boot when he glimpsed Fallowfield bearing down on Sparrow, who was due to pay for the next round. Seeing the expression on Fallowfield's face, Thomas guessed the serjeant had just noticed their deception and planned to make Sparrow pay for it, even though the lad was the least culpable of them all. Thomas dived forward. He was too late; Sparrow was already on the floor. Thomas knew how to take a beating, the best way to roll with the punches, how to protect your body from the worst of it. There was only one thing for it. He threw himself between the bewildered Sparrow and the enraged Fallowfield.

~

By the time Freer returned from the jakes, it was as if Fallowfield had put a spell on all the men in the room. It wasn't even a proper fight. One man set against another over some grudge or imagined insult was simple to understand, easy to join in with, but not Fallowfield's merciless attack. Freer guessed the reason for Fallowfield's wrath but could see it would take more than him to stop the man.

Freer hurried over to Murphy, claiming a rather stronger acquaintance with Captain Dickenson than he could have justified, but it was enough to stir the Corporal into action. That done, Freer quickly found his fellow recruit, Josh Tranter, former bare-knuckle fighter, and pointed to where Fallowfield was attacking their friends.

Arm in arm they pushed closer to Fallowfield. From his own observations, Freer knew that cunning and the agility to throw your opponent off balance were just as important as any pugilistic skills. Tranter understood the situation and grinned, toothless as the day he was born. They sidled up behind Fallowfield and Tranter, with a deft flick of his foot, tripped the Serjeant, who fell heavily to the ground. No one, least of all Fallowfield, knew how it had happened, or – fortunately for Tranter – who among the crowd had brought down the big man. By the time Fallowfield was ready to resume his assault Captain Dickenson had sent Murphy back with his orders, which the Corporal now trumpeted over the din. 'Serjeant Fallowfield, Captain Dickenson requires your attendance. Immediately.'

Fallowfield, jaw still tight as a cat's arse nodded, dusted down his uniform and without a backward glance hurried out into the night to find Dickenson.

~

Jack Fallowfield cursed. 'Bloody Captain Dickenson requires his cover serjeant to escort him to the bloody Assembly Rooms.' Being a cover serjeant was a position of trust on the battlefield; defending your officer's life was a regimental honour, but to nursemaid Dickenson in the middle of bloody Leicester was not living the military life; and just when he was sorting out an outbreak of insubordination. It was the final straw. Never mind Captain Dickenson playing the country squire, teaching his men to ride hunting style. Well, that was up to him; but he, Jack Fallowfield, had to teach his men to obey his bloody orders.

~

When Thomas woke up he realised his right eye was swollen shut, his ribs throbbed and his jaw was as sore as the last time his father had punched him to the floor for answering back. He wasn't sure how long he'd been insensible, but long enough for someone to have stripped off his clothes and put him to bed. He could just make out a figure moving in the darkness and tried to speak but his lips were too swollen to make any sound other than a grunt. He felt around with his tongue, checking for broken or missing teeth. Miraculously they still seemed in place.

The shadowy figure turned out to be Freer, swishing a cloth about in a bowl of water, but on hearing Thomas grunt, he turned round.

'Awake eh?'

Thomas grunted again.

Freer wrung out his cloth, came over and began to wipe Thomas's face.

'You've come off a lot worse than Sparrow, but that's what you meant to happen, wasn't it, to protect the lad?'

Thomas nodded. To shield Sparrow had been his first impulse, but afterwards through the pain, he had told himself he was just paying his dues.

Thomas began to drift off to sleep again. It was hardly a good start to his new life. Still, he couldn't expect the Recruiting Serjeant to be happy at losing his chance to cheat them out of their bounty money. But as Thomas had to work under the man, maybe he could find some way of proving himself worthy to be a dragoon, and maybe, with his friend Freer at his side it would all turn out for the best.

All he had to do now was to break the news to Grace …

6

Bounty Money

Leicester, March 26th 1805

Dear Grace,

If you are reading this, then William the carter from Melton has fulfilled his promise to deliver this to you on his way home from the fair. He also brings another package for you, in addition to this letter, which I urge you to take the greatest care of. I will explain why later.

But firstly, I have many things to tell you. I arrived at Leicester in time to see the most excellent marching parade of soldiers on horses.

As it happened, there was another lad standing next to me, by the name of Will Freer and he, like myself, needing also to start his working life afresh. So Freer and I decided there would be nothing better than to take the King's shilling. The magistrate, in front of whom we had to swear the oath and sign our papers, was most encouraging and said the country needed more young men like us as the government fears Boney will threaten these shores once again this summer. But they say too the war could be over within a year or two, if only Britain and our Allies can stand firm together.

Thomas hesitated briefly. Best not to mention the beating inflicted by Fallowfield.

So take the greatest care when opening the package, as I have enclosed seven guineas from my bounty money to keep safe, though please do use it to pay for postage costs when I send you letters, and if my mother requires any additional comforts.

Thomas paused. Nothing could now change what she had said, what he had done.

I hope my mother has recovered her wits by now. I hope you too are well. I assure you I have not forgotten my most solemn promise to you. I will write again soon.

Yours, Thomas.

Thomas laid down his pen, amazed that his fingers remained largely unscathed, and sealed the two letters as securely as he could.

~

Grace threw Thomas's guineas across the room with such force it brought Sarah scurrying in.

'What's the matter?'

Grace told herself to stay calm. It would be round the village soon enough, but for the moment she couldn't bear Sarah quizzing her like this.

'I dropped some bobbins.'

Sarah clearly didn't believe her.

'Shall I help you pick them up?'

Grace tried to sound measured. 'No thank you, Sarah. I can manage perfectly well without your help.'

'It doesn't hurt to be civil, Grace.' Sarah flounced back downstairs.

Grace burst into tears. She still believed that if Sarah hadn't brought up the matter of Michael in the cruel way she had, then Thomas's mother wouldn't have become so distraught and things might not have turned out so badly. Yes; the more she thought about it, the more she was inclined to blame Sarah for the entire mess. And now he's gone a-soldiering. She wanted to howl, shout and stamp across the floor. Instead, she began to gather up the coins from the far corners of the room and gave herself a serious talking to. Upset she might be, but she was not going to be so foolish as to squander Thomas's money, perhaps one day *their money*.

By the time she'd made sure she'd retrieved all seven guineas and rolled them up in her linen inside her small pine box, she had calmed down enough to go downstairs and attend to her chores before retreating to bed.

But hard as she tried, she couldn't sleep. The whole village would know by tomorrow that William the carter had delivered two sealed letters to Grace Burnaby; everyone already knew that Thomas had abandoned her, though most considered it a blessing. She too must try to consider it a blessing, but now he'd sent her this money to keep; what did that mean? That she was just a trustworthy person or that he meant to keep his promise to come back for her? But how could he come back now he'd gone and enlisted? How could he come back at all after what had happened between him and his parents?

She recalled how Thomas's father used to rant and rage at him if he so much as answered his mother back, even as she'd cling to Thomas, sobbing that she'd brought forth an unfeeling, heartless creature. Well, perhaps his mother was right after all. Perhaps Thomas did only care for himself, and if that were true then she would be doing no more than her duty by looking after his money.

But as she sat up yet again, huddled into her shawl against the night air, she suddenly heard Thomas's mother wailing from across the lane and then Thomas's father's raised voice sharp above her cries. Grace crept to the window and opened the shutters. The tallows were still lit in the Cowpers' cottage and she saw Mary Cowper, wild-eyed, with young Hannah tugging at her mother's shift whilst old Tom Cowper shouted, slapped his wife's cheeks and pulled her back inside their cottage. Grace had never seen old Tom hit Mary before. It had always been Thomas he'd set upon, never Michael or the girls.

Michael, the golden boy. She wiped away a tear. Of course she'd been fond of him; but she knew better than most how a handsome young boy who can do no wrong can turn into a young man who won't take no for an answer.

As for Mary, Grace couldn't remember her losing her wits for such a long period before. Old Tom Cowper blamed Thomas, but now most of the village was beginning to avoid both Mary and old Tom. Grace though still remembered late summer days in the Cowper orchard up on the ridge picking apples, when Mary would comb the broken bits of twig out of Grace's hair, teasing out the knots so gently, she could recall the sensation of it to this day.

As for old Tom, he'd threatened to horsewhip Thomas should he come anywhere near him or his mother again. It was not an idle threat. Sometimes she thought she understood why Thomas was as he was. She remembered how they used to imagine running away together to start their lives afresh, but after Michael died it was like he'd died too.

For sure, Thomas would never be back. Staring dry-eyed into the darkness, she decided to ask Bailiff Strutt to put in a good word for her with Squire Rearsby's housekeeper at the Hall. She would have to start her new life without him.

7

Bastards and Gullions

March 1805, Nottingham

'Bastards, gullions, bastards, gullions, bastards, gullions … '

Thomas glanced around in vain for a friendly face, but although some of the women were merely solemn or just pointing to their bellies, most were jeering, spitting, and chanting.

They'd no sooner passed the large church and turned up into these narrow lanes, when Thomas had noticed the groups of women in clusters further up the hill. His heart had begun to swell with pride again as he remembered how they'd been sent on their way from Leicester in a flourish of drums, amidst the hearty cheers of well-wishers. He'd directed his gaze towards the womenfolk of Nottingham, ready to smile and look the part of a brave soldier. But now he was closer, he realised the women were chanting contemptuously, not welcoming them.

'Bastards, gullions, bastards, gullions, bastards, gullions, bastards, gullions!'

'Happens every bloody time we come.' Corporal Murphy muttered oaths over Thomas's head. 'Talk about bearing a grudge.'

Thomas was puzzled. 'Grudge?'

'Bloody food riots a few years back. Had to knock a few heads together.'

Murphy made to ride off. 'They're bloody lucky they aren't in Ireland.' He tapped his nose. 'The Serjeant and I could tell you tales about our time there that would make your hair stand on end.'

Thomas turned to look at Freer but he was nowhere to be seen. Then Thomas caught sight of him buying ribbons and lace from a pretty young woman standing aside from the main groups with a hawker's tray. Suddenly Freer's expression changed. By the time Freer had caught up with the rest of the party, Fallowfield had spurred his horse right up to the edge of the crowd.

'Good day to you, ladies. So where are all your brave fellows then? Hiding under your petticoats?'

Suddenly the women started throwing the contents of piss pots and every other foul-smelling container they had with them before disappearing as quickly as they had arrived down narrow ginnel ways.

'Bloody whores.' Fallowfield shrugged and carried on up the hill.

Thomas, wiping his face clean as he could with his kerchief, turned to see how Freer had fared. Freer's face had scarcely a stain on it but all the colour had drained from his cheeks.

'What the hell did that girl say to you?'

Freer lowered his voice. 'She said … How did we feel about killing women and children?'

~

It seemed an interminable time before they reached the barracks. At last, passing through the gateway in the stout wall, they came into a spacious yard.

'Everything you could possibly need,' announced Murphy. 'Hospital, food stores, exercise yards, all safely tucked away from those biddies out there.'

Murphy next marched them into their quarters, a large draughty room with cribs one above another and side by side with scarcely enough space left to climb onto the straw palliasses. There was even a crib placed under the large table in the centre of the room. The room seemed full of men already; Thomas wondered how the new recruits would ever be able to squeeze in. Murphy wasted little time before taking them to a vast wall cupboard, to pick out blankets and a couple of sheets. He then set about folding them straight as a knife-edge before tucking the blankets and sheets interleaved into a mattress roll. It was all accomplished in what appeared to be a few seconds as he commanded them to follow his example. As Thomas struggled to achieve the necessary crispness of fold, he thought he could smell a beef stew. Hard to tell through the fog of pipe smoke and stench from the large piss tubs in the corners, but surely…? He turned to Freer and wrinkled his nose. They were sorely in need of a good meal. Murphy saw Thomas's nose twitch and laughed.

'Don't think you'll be getting any of that, my lads. You'll be collecting your own rations from the sutling house and making a good wholesome pot yourself before the evening's out.'

Sparrow looked blankly at Murphy. 'But cooking's women's work.'

'Not in the army it isn't. Wives are in short supply around here. As for the womenfolk in these parts, they can do plenty of other things to provide comforts for you young soldiers, but cooking isn't one of them.'

It was clearly an old, much-rehearsed joke; the veterans roared with laughter.

'These men here'll show you.' Murphy smiled, turned and left them to the mercy of their fellows.

A very tall dragoon, powerfully built, emerged from the clouds of pipe smoke close to Freer. Freer, tall but thin, looked positively insubstantial beside this great hulk, who took one look at Freer and stretched out an arm as though he might hit him but merely let his hand fall upon Freer's ginger locks. He tousled Freer's hair vigorously enough to snap his spine.

'You'll not be needing all that after tomorrow,' he said. 'Look here at how we dress our hair.' He pointed to his own head. 'Wait till Murphy's missus gets hold of them curls.'

Thomas hardly dared look. This wasn't a man you'd want to risk staring at without being asked. The soldier's hair, scraped back into the regulation queue and flecked with traces of white powder was a faded ginger, but which might once have been as red as Freer's. Thomas wasn't quite sure whether the man wanted to humiliate Freer or engage in comradely banter.

Suddenly Quilley stepped forward, smiled as only a man suddenly blessed with good fortune can, and produced from under his bundles a flagon of ale.

'Then we can enjoy his final days as a red-haired soldier with you all.'

Portions of stew were provided from the soldiers' own feast, strictly on the understanding that the recruits' rations would be collected later to supplement tomorrow's meal.

But what was now clear to Thomas was that from now on, caught between whoever ruled the barrack-room roost and the iron fist of Fallowfield, his life was still never going to be his own.

8

Rouse About! Rouse About!

March 1805, Nottingham Barracks

'By Bob's rattle, the Sun's burning holes in your blankets. Rouse about! Rouse about!'. Murphy opened the barrack-room door at five sharp. It was still dark.

His night disturbed by snoring, farting and cries from the veterans, Thomas had slept only fitfully.

'Did you sleep?' he whispered to Freer.

Freer pulled a face. 'Give me my own company curled up snug beneath Bailey's workbench any day,' and with that he rolled out of bed.

'To the stables.'

Freer and Thomas dressed as quickly as they could, aware that lateness would not be tolerated. But then Thomas noticed that Quilley still lay abed.

'Hey Quilley.'

Thomas moved across the room to shake him. But Quilley wasn't there.

Thomas could hardly suppress his shock but immediately threw the blanket back over the hump of bedding. He looked around. Nobody seemed to have noticed except Freer. Sparrow and Tranter were pulling on their boots and, as the stables trumpet call had just sounded, all of the seasoned troops had already left. Freer nodded and put his finger to his lips. Thomas didn't wish to be implicated in any deception. What should he do? They hadn't even served a week. This could be nothing but a calculated desertion, Quilley's bounty being more or less intact. Thomas had scarcely crossed the room back to his own bed before Murphy returned.

'Follow me.'

Thomas made as much haste as he could to obey, hoping an eager and speedy response would stop Murphy noticing they were a man short.

As they crossed the courtyard, still in darkness, Freer whispered, 'No wonder Quilley was determined to hang onto his money.'

Any further conversation was cut short by Serjeant Fallowfield, who greeted them as they arrived at the stables block.

'So, Johnny Newcomes, you want to be dragoons, eh?'

It wasn't really a question, but the four recruits shuffled awkwardly as a token of assent, Thomas all the time praying that none of the others would comment on Quilley's absence. Fortunately, Fallowfield seemed far too preoccupied with explaining his rules of conduct to be followed in stables to notice he was one recruit short, but it surely wouldn't be long before Quilley's absence was discovered.

'Without a horse to ride, you're not a dragoon; you're worth less than the lowest infantryman. So unless you look after your horse, it'll not serve you well when you most need it, and it'll be my duty and my pleasure to flog anyone who fails in this task.'

Thomas thought this advice was reasonable enough but was troubled by the threatening tone Fallowfield now routinely adopted.

Fallowfield quickly led them to the far end of the stables where there were five horses waiting. As Thomas cast his eye over their mounts, it was clear some would be less biddable than others. He noticed too that each horse had a number branded on its flank. Fallowfield stepped forward. 'Each horse has its own regimental number. Make sure you remember it.'

Thomas could hear Freer shifting his feet. Both men suspected that neither Tranter nor Sparrow knew their letters or numbers.

Fallowfield paused and glared at the four men.

'Where's Quilley?'

Thomas felt compelled to fill the silence. 'Still in the barracks, I expect, Serjeant.'

Fallowfield cursed and turned on his heel, then swung round and pointed to the stalls. 'These better be mucked out before I'm back.' He set off at a quick march.

Tranter tapped his head. 'That man Fallowfield has a foul temper on him.'

'Aye. And if we don't get these stables cleaned out, he'll have us all flogged,' Sparrow agreed.

Thomas knew that none of them, except for him, had any experience of dealing with horses. It was going to be well nigh impossible to achieve anything in time to avoid Fallowfield's threatened punishments. Their assigned horses also seemed less than willing to co-operate and had started to neigh and fret in their stalls.

Freer turned to Thomas. 'You better tell us what to do then.'

Thomas moved towards his own horse and quickly explained the separate tasks needed, gesturing to pieces of equipment to illustrate his points.

'Oh, and move your horse. Like this'.

Thomas whispered into her ear, 'What's your name, my beauty, eh?' and then leant firmly on her rump to get her to shift position.

Soon they were all working at a steady pace and by the time Fallowfield returned all the stable bedding had been changed and the horses were ready to be fed. But Fallowfield was in a worse mood than before.

'Don't bloody tell me none of you knew Quilley had deserted. Don't pretend you're the bloody innocents. Desertion is punishable by death; eh, Sparrow?'

Thomas was relieved that he and Freer had been able to keep Quilley's absence from the others, who were clearly astonished at this news. Thomas knew himself to be a bad liar and felt his very existence to be yet again at the mercy of an unforgiving man. Perhaps that was why Quilley had absconded; perhaps he'd foreseen his fate.

Fallowfield signalled them to follow him past the dung pits into the forage barns and granaries.

'Horses are to be fed strictly according to army regulations, morning and evening. Daily allowances fourteen pounds of hay, ten pounds of oats and four pounds of straw.'

Fallowfield suddenly stopped and walked over to Thomas, breathing heavily straight into his face. His breath was as foul as the rest of him.

'So, Cowper, you'd better take greater care of your forage than you did of your friend, and if you think I don't know you had a hand in Quilley's disappearance, then you're very much mistaken.'

Thomas once again felt himself to be a marked man.

9

Haircut

March 1805, Nottingham Barracks

'I've heard tell of you and your friends.'

Thomas, sitting down on a low chair, knew immediately that this was not kindly meant. Bonnie Murphy, wife of Corporal Murphy, was a short, broad-backed woman with arms as muscular as any soldier's, which she now rested on Thomas's shoulders. Bonnie Murphy was the designated hairdresser for the regiment.

'A word in your ear, Johnny Raw. I don't take kindly to my man not fetching me a few ribbons, after all his trouble looking after you.'

Thomas clutched the requisites which had already been charged to his account – powder bag, powder puff, soap, and candle grease – even tighter; as though they might offer some protection against her ill temper.

Bonnie seized his hair, tugging it violently and began cutting it so close to his skull that he was left with what felt like a rat's tail dangling down his back. She quickly moved on to knuckling his head with the candle grease as firmly as if it were a ball of dough. By now Thomas felt like begging for mercy, but before he had time to draw breath to protest, she took up the pot of foul-smelling soap, lathering his head and remaining hair as thoroughly as she had kneaded his skull. He tried not to retch with the smell. Unmoved, she seized a queue pad filled with sand and shoved it against the back of his head, then, with a lace, pulled his hair so tightly around it that tears came to his eyes. Not content with this torment, Bonnie registered her displeasure, just one more time, by dismissing him from the barbering with a forceful slap on the back. She smiled broadly.

He began to wonder what it was about him and women that they found him so hateful and a convenient object of their wrath.

'There, young man. Let it not be said that Bonnie Murphy doesn't know how to turn out a soldier whose hair will be a credit to his regiment until the day he dies.'

Now it was Freer's turn. He'd been busy, as instructed, sweeping up the remnants of Thomas's hair and solemnly presented him with a few locks. Thomas stuffed them away before Bonnie inflicted yet more pain in the name of regimental requirements. Freer had heard Bonnie's complaints about her lack of ribbons and finery, which she'd expected from Murphy's share of their bounty money, and he was not going to be caught out. So, before getting any closer to the barbering chair, he pulled out the lace and ribbons he'd bought from the girl in the crowd the previous day, the same ones, as he'd told Thomas the previous night, he'd been intending to send as a peace offering to Bailey's daughter.

'Mistress Murphy,' he said, smiling, 'I can see that this has been a most disappointing day for you, but Cowper and I would have no wish to distress you further, especially when your husband has been such a good fellow to us from the very start of our acquaintance.'

Bonnie Murphy picked up the bundle of trifles that Freer offered her, turning them over as though they were gold, picking out in particular an edging of white lace. Thomas had only ever seen lace adorn the cuffs of gentlemen before, and this was almost as pretty a piece.

'Well, of course, you're a couple of fine fellows yourselves.'

She sat Freer down as though he were royalty, cutting his hair as gently as she could, with the cropping of Freer's curls regretfully undertaken in the line of duty. At the end of her work she gathered these up as tenderly as any mother. Thomas hurriedly gleaned a few to give Freer, as his friend had done for him, for the sake of their former lives, and sweethearts, present and future.

But before Thomas had chance to speak to Freer, he was scooped out of Bonnie's way by Murphy, who planted a kiss on his wife's cheek before marching Thomas off to the tailor's dark and sour-smelling room. The tailor, a short, dark-haired fellow with a faint moustache, sized him up by eye and signalled him to exchange the clothes he stood in for one of the standard-issue uniforms.

Thomas had scarcely time to retrieve his few possessions from his discarded clothes before being dismissed and sent on his way. He clutched the small bag of soil taken from Michael's grave, together with the additional items of uniform required, trying not to drop locks of hair in a trail behind him. Suddenly the tailor called him back to refasten the leather-stiff stock around Thomas's neck, which promptly gave him even more of a headache. By now Thomas had come to realise just how much tribulation had gone into making the members of the recruiting party look the smartest people in Leicester, and sorely wished he might trade in his thumping headache for his old clothes.

By late morning, the four of them almost looked the part of cavalrymen and, changed back out of their newly issued stable dress to their undress uniform, they were marched out of the barracks gates for their first lesson in horsemanship.

10

The Riding School

'Don't suppose they ever let you ride the buggers though,' Serjeant Fallowfield replied, sharp as a sword thrust, to Thomas's admission that he'd worked with horses since he was twelve years old.

Thomas was surprised by the large number of recruits, including Freer, who knew next to nothing about horses, and hoped his reputation would rise on this, their first day at the riding school. He thought Fallowfield would be pleased to have a new recruit who understood horses. But when Thomas looked at Freer and saw him shaking his head he realised his admission was another mistake.

'So, Private Cowper, show us how it's done,' Fallowfield commanded.

Thomas decided it might be best to deny everything. 'But I wasn't allowed to ride them, Serjeant. I'm just like anybody else, Serjeant, new to riding'.

This wasn't true. Besides, Fallowfield was having none of it. 'Cowper! Mount and ride. That's an order.'

Fallowfield called for the dark chestnut mare with a small white blaze on her nose that Thomas had noted earlier to be one of those less biddable. She was led in by Corporal Murphy; her eyes were bright and ears alert. In his dealings with the mare so far, Thomas had judged her to be only just broken in but now he would have to ride her in front of everyone.

Thomas knew he would require every skill he possessed to show this mare he was not afraid. Clearly Fallowfield expected the horse to protest and throw him as soon as he climbed onto her back.

'What the bloody hell are you waiting for, Cowper?'

Thomas moved cautiously towards her. She was not even saddled and was equipped with only with the most rudimentary halter bridle, probably designed to stop a novice from raking the horse's mouth. Of course, a cavalryman had to learn to ride using his legs to control his mount, for one hand had to be free to wield a sabre.

Corporal Murphy offered to give him a leg up onto her back. Thomas shook his head, and stroked the horse's neck before running his hand up to her ears. He spoke to her in the same way he'd always spoken to Ramillies and Blenheim, especially Ramillies, whom he'd helped grow from being a weak, neglected foal into one of the most dependable plough-horses he'd ever come across.

Just behind him Fallowfield's voice was quietly menacing. 'Private Cowper, get on that horse. Now.'

Thomas pretended to begin to obey, but knew it was more important to stay calm and to convey this to the mare. She was already tugging to be released from Murphy's grip on her halter. Still speaking softly to her, Thomas carefully swung himself onto her bare back. He relaxed. This mare and he would eventually come to an understanding, he felt sure.

He allowed himself to look up as they passed Fallowfield and the other lads. Fallowfield seemed displeased Thomas had managed to stay on; he immediately ordered Corporal Murphy, who was leading the mare on a lunge rein, to increase the pace. The mare broke into a trot, which tested Thomas's skills to their limits as they bumped around the ring. Fallowfield now ordered Murphy to play out the lunge rein to signal to the mare to move to a hand gallop. The riding school walls whirled past, and Thomas felt every muscle in his body harden and tense. Surely, he was bound to fall. But no. At last he was instructed to halt. Murphy was almost smiling. Thomas had managed to stay on. Maybe, maybe even Fallowfield would be satisfied, offer him some praise.

Fallowfield walked over to him and looked him in the eye. 'When I ask you a question, Cowper, I don't expect to be told a pack of lies.'

Thomas wanted to protest, deny he'd ever been on a horse's back, claim only native wit, but thought better of it.

'Yes, Serjeant.'

'So don't pretend to me you've never ridden before.'

'No, Serjeant.'

'The mare's yours, anyway.' Fallowfield began to walk away. 'There's a bit too much Arab in her. She needs a firm hand. Like her rider.'

~

Captain George Dickenson hadn't felt so pleased with himself for a while. Four new dragoons twenty minutes into their first lesson and only two of them had fallen off more than three times. Of course, these were good and steady fifteen-handers. He'd picked them himself last year. Steady but spirited and responsive. If only the same could be said about the usual run of recruits. Not that the men cost the army forty-five pounds apiece. But then, where would a cavalryman be without a good horse under him?

At least none of these recruits seemed terrified of their mounts. That would come later. Yes, he had to admit that these lads from Leicester had something about them, though most of them were still at the first stage, bumping along, with no sense of finding the horse's rhythm, hanging on as much to the manes as to the reins. But that friend of Freer's had already found a half-decent seat, with his hips square and thighs and knees snug against the horse's body.

So Fallowfield had chosen well again. The big man certainly cut a fine figure in his uniform and rarely failed to impress the country boys they badly needed. He also seemed to have the knack of shedding the useless ones to other recruiting parties; Dickenson sometimes wondered how he managed it, and what favours he demanded in return. But, in these times, it was every regiment for itself. A good thing it was agreed that the 36th Dragoons should retain primary rights in Leicester, where the immediate problem wasn't Napoleon but the able-bodied men of the Shires who'd so far declined to enlist.

Pity he found a useful fellow like Fallowfield the most unsettling subordinate he'd come across in all his years of service.

11

Nothing but a Gentleman's Residence

Thomas wondered if he might be safe now he was beyond the reach of the Leicestershire magistrates. After all, he'd not seen any wanted notices, or hue and cry on the streets of Leicester. With only the accusations of a mad woman to go on, perhaps his father had thought better of involving the law. He decided to risk writing to Grace again.

Nottingham April 1805

Dearest Grace,

We marched the thirty miles or so in relative ease, as we are all fit men, for they will take no other, though my friend Will Freer has a slight limp. One of the other recruits in my barracks room, Tranter, used to make his living as a fairground fighter. You may even have seen him at Melton Fair. Sparrow, who's almost the same age as me, he thinks, flits about quieter than the bird itself. But Quilley, who helped Freer and me to preserve our bounty money deserted on our first day here. This has made for some difficulties with our Serjeant.

We have been sent to Nottingham because the Gentlemen Yeomanry built a fine riding school for themselves which they are now obliged to let us cavalrymen use. Freer says, it's only because they know that we will be the first to be sent to fight Boney, whilst they stop at home to defend their own fields and estates. The school is built snug into the crook of the castle walls, not so far from our barracks, which are in a corner of the castle's parklands. The castle is scarcely a castle. For all its sturdy walls it is nothing but a gentleman's residence perched on the edge of the cliff. The cliff is hardly more substantial, for it is made of the softest red stone, not as sturdy as our own ironstone and quite riddled with holes and caverns as if giant rats have been carrying away mouthfuls of it for centuries on end.

I have been allocated a newly recruited remount. She is high-spirited but not shaken by either the loudest of noises or the sight of flames, which we use to test our horses' nerves. I have therefore called my sturdy mare Fearless and hope she will prove true to her name when she and I are called upon to do our duty.

I must finish, for the trumpeter is sounding the evening's retreat, a warning to us all to stow ourselves safely upon our beds before the next half-hour is out. I hope this finds you well. I will write again when we know we are moving south.

Yours, Thomas

I hope you are safely in receipt of the seven guineas bounty money I sent from Leicester with William the carter.

12

Stable Talk

Thomas had never been happier. The day was filled with stable duties, morning and evening and riding lessons and drills on foot or on horseback. When he'd ridden before, bareback on Blenheim and Ramillies, they'd been steady-as-you-go dray horses, more used to plough harnesses than a young lad's weight slithering across their backs. Still, it meant he understood the movement of a horse, the feeling that vibrated through every bone, how to bend your body to its body whilst bending its mind to your mind. In this spirited mare, with her purposeful long strides, he sensed her power and pace would be checked only by his ability to control her and to remind her of her schooling. He took a vow there and then to become worthy of his horse.

So, by the end of their first week in Nottingham, Thomas was beginning to feel that he'd born to be a soldier, and the more time he spent with the horses the more he felt at ease. In spite of everything, he'd settled down better than Freer, who seemed to be having second thoughts about his decision to join the Army. Freer, his precious copy of Tom Paine's *The Rights of Man* stuffed inside his stable dress, talked about his doubts far too freely for Thomas's liking. Even walls could carry reports back to Fallowfield. Besides, Freer needed to concentrate on learning how to manage his own horse, Libby – short for Liberty, not Elizabeth, he'd explained solemnly to Thomas – who was still far too frisky for him. But there was no stopping Freer once he'd warmed to his theme.

'You see it's not governments that give us rights; it's nature itself.'

Thomas grunted, 'First things first. Can you remember how to take the bridle off?'

'Course I can. Like this, isn't it?' But Freer was not to be put off. 'You see we are all born with rights.'

'What rights?' Thomas ran his hand over the horse's neck. 'Noseband, then throat-lash.'

Freer turned round. 'That's what I mean; we haven't got any rights now but that's not how it should be.'

'So how should it be then?' Thomas said. 'No; now ease the headpiece forward over her ears like so. But watch her mouth. Slowly! Don't wrench; allow her to let go of the bit.'

Freer smiled one of his disarming smiles. 'Got it. See, it's not those that govern us who should be the only ones with rights – to money and power. We should all have them.'

Thomas was taken aback. 'The same as the King and his ministers?'

Freer nodded. 'Exactly. All men should have equal rights and our leaders should be chosen for their talent and wisdom, not because they're members of the aristocracy.' Freer swung around. 'Done that. Now what?'

Thomas waved towards the set of hooks behind them. 'Hang the bridle up there. Wipe the bit first! But hold on a moment, Will, what about the King? How should we settle who should govern us without a king?'

'But don't you see, Thomas, any fool can inherit a throne. It could be easily settled if we all had the right to vote.' Freer turned back to his horse. 'So I loosen the breastplate next?

I remember Fallowfield saying something about loosening the breastplate.'

'And the crupper.'

'Right. Stand still, madam. You see, if we all had equal rights and our leaders were men of reason then we should all be treated decently and offered a proper education with a fair wage for our work, whatever we did.'.

'Steady. She's going to blow,' Thomas cautioned.

Freer laughed. 'Bollocks.'

Thomas tried to look serious. 'I mean it. Watch her arse!'

Freer struggled with the crupper. 'The damn thing's stuck.'

Thomas moved closer. 'Here, give it me. Gently girl, gently does it. You'll feel a lot more comfortable like this. Right, now we can get everything else off. Here, I'll pass them to you.'

Thomas removed all the equipment and passed it to Freer as carefully as if he were handling priceless treasure. But as Freer was putting it away, still muttering about justice and equality, Thomas heard a sound at the far end of the stables and quickly put his finger to his lips.

Freer stopped muttering and responded – a bit too loudly, Thomas thought. 'So, one valise, one cloak, one waterdeck, one carbine, and one pistol safely stowed.'

Bending over to pick up some handfuls of straw, Thomas pointed behind him. 'Now we need some litter.'

Freer signalled his thanks. 'How much, do you reckon?'

Thomas leant his head against Fearless. 'Just enough for under her feet, like this. Easy, girl. Now let's wipe you down with this little bit of straw, round your ears and that chin of yours. Eh, you like that, don't you?'

Freer began to wipe Libby down. 'You treat your women as well as your horses?'

'You treat yours like you treat Libby?' Thomas joshed.

Freer looked down at the floor. 'Never had any complaints.'

'Really? This one doesn't look too happy.' Thomas moved Fearless out of the way. 'Right, madam, let's turn you round. Steady, steady. Let's hitch you up here. Nearly done now.'

Thomas bent down again. 'Now we twist the straw into a decent-sized wisp and finish off with a good massage under the belly. Here, have some more. Don't be afraid to rub hard, like a washerwoman.'

'Like this?' Freer attacked Thomas's back with some straw.

Thomas laughed and turned his head towards the door, trying to stop the straw going down his neck. Silhouetted in the doorway, he caught sight of a familiar figure. Fallowfield. Had he been there all the time? Thomas prayed he'd not heard what Freer had had to say about the idiocy of kings.

13

Load your Bloody Weapons First

Thomas grimaced. No sabre drill today. They were learning to use the regulation-issue carbine and Fallowfield's rapid instructions soon took on a preacher's fervour.

Fallowfield pointed out that they were now holding, even if not correctly, the very latest of the Board of Ordnance-approved carbines.

'You can forget the Brown Bess. A broad-arsed musket is for massed lines of infantry, not for us dragoons. I repeat, we're cavalrymen and a cavalryman is not an infantryman on a bloody horse. By the end of today you will know this weapon better than the back of your own hand.

'Your carbine been made shorter in the barrel so you can reload whilst mounted.'

Fallowfield adopted his most resigned and disgruntled tone.

'Which means carbines are less accurate than the rifle ... '

Thomas remembered now about rifles. Freer reckoned it'd been the American colonists' hunting rifles that had done for the British Army.

'... and less lethal than a musket volley, but that's what the Board of Ordnance has recommended to Horse Guards and that's what we're issued with. So we'll have to make the best of it.'

Thomas suddenly began to realise that Fallowfield, in spite of appearances, did not believe in upholding the authority of his superiors, only his own.

'… examine every inch of your carbine as closely as if she were the finest whore in Nottingham.'

Thomas ran his fingers over the sturdy wooden stock, the brass plate snapped over the hidden cache of tools, and every other part of the weapon.

Fallowfield continued. 'It might not look shiny and smart but do *not* scrape away that dull brown colour covering your barrel unless you want to alert the enemy to your position.'

Fallowfield paused to let the warning sink in.

'Any of you fire a gun before?'

Thomas glanced around to see if anybody had, but the rest of them were looking at their feet.

Fallowfield was getting into his stride.

'All eyes on Corporal Murphy, who's going to show you what to do.'

'First. Preparing to aim. Look over the top of the barrel, flip up that back sight and look through the notch, keeping the foresight – that's this point at the end of the barrel – in line with your target.'

Thomas raised his weapon, looked through the sights and then raised his carbine as though to fire.

Fallowfield was damning.

'Lower that bloody gun, Private Cowper! Now, all of you, look at the vent at the end of your barrel. This is where your priming charge sparks your carbine's main charge. So, if you don't keep it clear with the wire pick the Board of Ordnance has thoughtfully supplied in the handle, you'll have spiked your own gun. Understand? Your carbine is never going to fire. And if you don't keep the rest of your bloody carbine as clean as a whistle, your bullet's going to foul or blow back on you.'

Thomas knew about keeping tools clean and well maintained, and what was a gun but a soldier's tool?

'Next. The ramrod. Don't pull at it, Sparrow! Never detach a ramrod from your weapon in the field. It will do the job without being removed from its mount.

'So you have powder in your powder horn, and shot stowed away, greased and ready for ramming down your barrel. Pity the poor infantryman who has to bite his cartridges open, eh.

'Next. The flintlock. That's the thing that looks like a cock with a bit of stuffing in its mouth.'

Murphy pointed to a piece of extravagant metal work.

Thomas quickly ran his fingers over the flintlock whilst Fallowfield continued. 'Right now it's uncocked. Pull the trigger once and it's half-cocked. Pull it again and it's fully cocked, ready to fire.'

Thomas's fingers were itching to pull it. Only yesterday, he'd seen a few veterans practise their drill with live ammunition.

Fallowfield added, 'If you want to stay alive, keep your flint sharp.' Murphy now pointed to the flint screwed tightly into place. 'Knap it and renew it altogether after sixty to eighty firings.'

Fallowfield pointed again to the flintlock. 'You see that long piece of steel sticking up in front of the hammer? That's the frizzen. After the flint strikes it to make a spark, this spark lands in the now open powder pan – are you following me, Sparrow? – setting off its charge through the previously mentioned vent, igniting the gunpowder in your carbine barrel to send its little lead ball on its way straight through the eye of the nearest crapaud.

'Now you're thinking, how the hell am I going to remember all this?

'Simple. You're going to do exactly as I say and do it again and again until you can do it in your sleep or under fire, and in less time than it takes me to count to thirty.

'Position your carbine.'

The carbine was heavier than it looked; about the weight of small sack of flour, Thomas estimated, but his hands moved rapidly through the drill again and again. He smiled and forgot his worries over Quilley, the way Fallowfield constantly picked on him and Sparrow, the lack of news from Grace. This was why he'd enlisted, to protect his country from Boney, the biggest tyrant of them all.

But when Thomas next looked up, he caught a glimpse of Fallowfield's blood-red face staring at him, his mouth twisting into what seemed to Thomas a silent prayer of hate. The Serjeant's eyes were as intent as a cat's, biding its time, waiting to pounce on its prey. And he, Thomas, was the prey.

14

Running the Ring

Thomas knew this would be his first and last chance to impress Dickenson with his sabre skills. The recruits had been taught well over the past twelve weeks. Their instructors, using Le Marchant's manual, had taken them through each graduated exercise, firstly on foot and then on horseback. But now they had to prove their ability to run the ring, one of the most demanding of Le Marchant's exercises. Once they passed these tests, their days in Nottingham would soon come to an end.

They were to rehearse their full range of skills that afternoon, each taking his turn. Every man's performance would be scrutinised by Captain Dickenson in consultation with Serjeant Fallowfield; Corporal Murphy would stand by to adjust the targets after each man's demonstration. Thomas would be the first to ride. As he waited for Dickenson's command he cast his mind back to the training they'd had. How many times had Fearless run at that edge post and he'd sliced away the willow wand? – and yet his heart still thumped as vigorously as the first time.

~

On Dickenson's command, Thomas launched Fearless through the maze of targets, keeping his eye fixed on the wand, slicing it with ease, then swerving round towards the turnips mounted on posts; swooping, dodging and diving, he managed to inflict cuts on them all. Now Dickenson ordered him to get his horse ready for running the ring.

Thomas fixed his eye on the small ring the size of a crown, hung like a rigid noose from a miniature gibbet. He cantered slowly into position, gradually increasing Fearless's pace to a gallop as they took two circuits of the riding school before, head down and elbow tucked in, he thrust his sabre point into the ring. At the same time his legs commanded Fearless to halt before the sword was yanked out of his hand.

~

Sparrow, the last one to take his turn, looked his usual worried self and his horse too seemed uneasy, but as they galloped towards the ring Thomas saw that something was amiss. Sparrow was twisting in the saddle, and then flew off sideways in a confusion of skewed girths and frayed leather and sprawled as if lifeless on the floor. Thomas once again saw Michael's broken body, bleeding, lost to the living.

Fallowfield yelled, 'Sparrow, get up! Right now! Corporal Murphy, examine the horse for injuries.'

Thomas shook his head to get rid of the memory. Sparrow was stirring. He wasn't dead. Thomas dismounted, threw his reins over to Tranter, ran forward and pulled Sparrow to his feet, but the lad was still dazed. As Thomas gently edged him towards Fallowfield, he wondered which of them would be the more severely punished, him for breaking protocol or Sparrow for the fall. Not Sparrow, he hoped. He noticed Freer also dismount and go over to Murphy, then examine the saddle whilst Fallowfield resumed his tirade.

'Private Sparrow, if you've damaged that horse or saddle I'll dock your pay and have you flogged for good measure.'

But now Murphy stood up. 'Serjeant, this saddle's not fit to be on a donkey. It's falling apart. No wonder the lad came off.'

Dickenson sighed; he seemed ready to wash his hands of the whole business.

'Corporal Murphy, can it not be repaired?'

Murphy shook his head. ' I'm not sure it would be worth paying a saddler to try and mend it, sir. Then again, I'm not sure we have any spare saddles with us.'

'Order another saddle, Serjeant Fallowfield,' said Dickenson. 'Immediately.'

Now Freer spoke up. 'Sir, I should be able to patch that up enough till a new saddle arrives.'

Dickenson paused for a moment, then nodded.

'See what you can do, Private Freer. See what you can do.'

Thomas glanced at Fallowfield, who had seemed strangely pleased when Dickenson had ordered him to purchase a new saddle. The Serjeant was now deep in thought. Thomas suspected that they hadn't heard the last of this saddle business.

~

Jack Fallowfield disliked Freer. He often found him insolent without being able to prove it. And Freer was clever too, wheedling his way yet again into Dickenson's good books. Fallowfield had already tried to warn the Captain that Freer was spreading sedition in the barrack-room with his talk of that traitor Thomas Paine. But Dickenson hadn't wanted to believe it, and even if he had believed it, he was too spineless to do anything. So Fallowfield didn't see the point of reporting to him unless he could present more solid evidence. But having identified another troublemaker in the ranks he didn't intend to give up now.

~

Thank God for a willing boot maker! George Dickenson rode back to his quarters counting up the cost of the day's exercise. Like everything else needed to equip the regiment, new saddles didn't come cheap. As the quartermaster was constantly reminding him, this war had already cost the nation dear. Even their Colonel was having to dig deeper into his own pockets just to keep the Regiment looking smart. Dickenson set his jaw. When would this damned war be over?

15

Heart of Oak

Bonnie Murphy's face was bright pink. 'Dermot says I was to run and tell you. It's Quilley. The 67th caught him in Derby trying to run off with their bounty money and all. Fallowfield's cock-a-hoop.' Bonnie smiled and crossed her arms. She hadn't forgotten the loss of her ribbons.

~

It was the news Thomas had been dreading, though he wasn't quite sure why. After all, ever since Quilley's desertion, Fallowfield had held him and Freer personally responsible for his absence. As if they'd have stayed to take the blame, Freer would grumble. Surely now Fallowfield would call a halt to his constant sniping. Only yesterday he'd stopped Freer from taking Sparrow's newly patched saddle to Captain Dickenson for inspection even though the Captain had specifically ordered Freer to do so. It was a trivial enough incident, but a reminder that Fallowfield had not forgiven them.

Fallowfield soon had all the recruits marched down to the parade ground to watch the bedraggled, unshaven Quilley hauled in leg irons to the officers' block for his court martial. Freer was concerned that Quilley would be persuaded to give evidence against them in return for fewer lashes of the whip. Then another rumour spread through the barrack-room.

'It'll be nothing less than the firing squad for Quilley,' Murphy whispered.

~

George Dickenson took the view he'd rather have one of his recruits half-alive than dead. A public flogging would have been quite enough. After all, they lost enough men to injuries and disease. But as the commander of the 67th, who was senior to him, had demanded the ultimate punishment, Dickenson had reluctantly ordered Fallowfield to choose a man from their own company to include in the firing squad.

~

Jack Fallowfield was happy enough to see Quilley dispatched in the manner he deserved. If he'd been an ordinary deserter, he would have been flogged. But as Fallowfield had suspected, Quilley's trick was to join a new regiment in every town, taking its money and deserting. Now Fallowfield was pretty sure Freer and Cowper must have known about Quilley's plan to pocket his bounty money and then desert. They'd been as thick as thieves back in Leicester and had obviously succeeded in keeping most of their own bounty with Quilley's help. So which of them should he choose to take part in the firing squad?

~

Bonnie Murphy stood back to check that her Dermot's queue was as neat as she could make it; it wouldn't do for Private Quilley to be summoned to meet his Maker by a regimental drummer less than impeccably turned out. She crossed herself at the thought of it. But now Dermot was blathering as if Quilley had been his best friend, not the rogue who'd robbed them both of a fair share of his bounty money.

'I know the man's a thief and a deserter, but you can tell Dickenson would rather have had him flogged and kept him under lock and key for a while.'

Bonnie sniffed. Sometimes she thought she'd have made a better soldier than her Corporal. 'You got to set off as you mean to go on, make it clear once a man's taken the King's shilling that's it and deserters will get what's coming to them.'

As usual, Dermot wasn't really listening. 'Fair enough, but Fallowfield's gone and ordered the Cowper lad to join the firing squad and shoot the only friend he's ever had in the regiment.'

Bonnie wiped her hands firmly on her pinafore. 'Nonsense. That red-haired fellow's Cowper's friend.'

'You know what I mean.'

Bonnie dusted the last flecks of hair powder from Dermot's shoulders.

'So it will be our God-given duty to get Cowper as drunk as a lord and help him forget about the whole damn business.'

Dermot kissed her. 'A wake's a wake to be sure it is.'

~

Thomas wondered what he could have done to deserve this. As they marched, like the well-drilled soldiers they'd become, into the courtyard where all the available men were assembled to watch, Thomas felt sick.

Murphy drummed solemnly, men marched, trumpets sounded and Quilley, in the centre of it all, stood tall and nonchalant, as if this was a game. Thomas had liked Quilley, but he could see now Quilley had used him and Freer to conserve his own bounty. It was lucky that Fallowfield could prove no other connection, or Thomas and Freer too might be facing a firing squad. Quilley had put them both in danger; he deserved to die and Thomas would do his duty. Boney would never be beaten if recruits just took their money and deserted.

But Thomas's mind would not settle. He felt his stomach churn, cursed his guts and wished he had some of his grandmother's remedies to hand. He saw again the cool, deep-banked stream that ran along the lane by Stathern church, the sturdy white gravestones, the raised mounds of the dead. As the squad went through its drills, memories of Fallowfield's instructions rang in his ears.

'Bring the rifle to full cock.'

'Line up your sights.'

'Aim.'

'Fire.'

Thomas smelled death, heard the steady rattle of the officer's preparatory orders, closed his eyes and fired.

~

Quilley's face was untouched, almost tranquil in its composure. Thomas saw the officer step forward to administer the final shot. He could have been shooting rats.

~

Bonnie Murphy thought the day had gone much as she'd expected. Quilley had acquitted himself well enough, and her Dermot had drummed as only an Irishman accustomed to week-long wakes could. For sure, the Regiment had done right by God and King George. But, like Dermot, what she didn't hold with was arse-faced Fallowfield making young Cowper shoot his friend. That was a trick, a dirty trick like the rest of his mischief. All this nonsense about Cowper being the best shot.

As for Bonnie, who prided herself on being as tough as any soldier, a great survivor, a looter and plunderer from enemy and friend alike, she was not one to hold a grudge for long. She'd even prayed to the Virgin Mary to grant Cowper Her forgiveness for depriving Bonnie of her ribbons. So she insisted Tranter, Sparrow Freer and Murphy take Cowper down to the river, to the old pilgrims' tavern and get the lad to drown his sorrows. After all, Brewhouse Yard, tucked under the Castle Rock, was the first resort of people down on their luck.

~

Thomas felt nervous to be down Brewhouse Yard. Until now he and the others had kept well away from here in case they ran into more hostile locals. So what the hell was Freer doing trying to befriend the landlord?

'No one tell you about you lot putting down the bread riots then?' the landlord responded, slamming a couple of tankards down on the counter.

Freer persisted. 'Aye; well, soldiers should never be used to suppress the protests of those merely claiming their basic right to food and shelter, but that'll be the heavy cavalry for you. All brawn and no brain. We light dragoons are meant to think of the consequences before we act.'

Thomas, dizzy with ale and guilt, gripped the side of the bar next to Freer and prayed for sobriety.

The landlord smiled.

'That's as may be, but it was men of the 36th who put down the bread riots here. For which some of us were grateful.'

Freer turned red and made to leave, but the landlord pushed two tankards of ale in their direction.

'Some stupid buggers have to fight Boney, eh?'

~

Freer raised his tankard. 'Death to the Tyrant and full bellies for the good citizens of Nottingham.'

Cooled by the wind blowing gently across the ancient water meadows, gardens and orchards, the soldiers swung their legs back against the low yard wall and watched the evening sun drop low in the sky; all seemed well with the world, until Tranter decided, in a fit of patriotism, to sing *Heart of Oak*, loud enough for all to hear:

To honour we call you, not press you like slaves

For who are so free as the sons of the waves?

It was one of his fairground tricks Tranter boasted about; if he sang a patriotic song before a fight the crowd invariably favoured him. But Freer had had one tankard of ale too many and was in a bellicose mood.

For who are so free as the sons of the waves?

'What freedom?' Freer shouted.

Tranter, astonished by the interruption, stopped singing, letting Freer take the floor.

'Have we forgotten the good men and women of Nottingham who've already lost their lives in the cause of Liberty? How is a man to fill his belly if he doesn't demand his rights?'

Thomas's head began to clear. He moved across the yard. Their drinking companions might not be friends either of Liberty or of Freer. Thomas had noticed an ill-kempt fellow taking a close interest in Freer's words. Elbowing a couple of other drinkers out of the way, he tugged at Freer's arm.

'Shh, shh; how many times have you warned me about government informers desperate to earn their pieces of silver, by fair means or foul? Tranter, another verse!'

Tranter began once again and Freer's next words were drowned out by the rousing chorus;

Heart of oak are our ships, Jolly Tars are our men…

Soon Freer was joining in as rowdily as the next man. To Thomas's relief, the ill-kempt fellow seemed deep in his cups. Thomas prayed that by tomorrow the fellow would have forgotten the fiery ginger-haired soldier, proclaiming the rights of the citizens of Nottingham.

~

As they staggered up the hill back to the barracks, Thomas was still the soberest of them all. Suddenly he glimpsed the ill-kempt fellow disappear into a pool of shadows outside the Riding School. Thomas motioned them all to halt and put a finger to his lips. Another figure then came into view for a moment and vanished into the shadows. He was very tall and had the upright bearing of a soldier but otherwise it was impossible to make out any details. Yet there was something very familiar about the way the man walked; but then again, weren't they all now like peas in a pod?

16

Stathern

July 1805, Leicestershire

It was on the first day of their march south to Romford, three days after Quilley's execution, when Thomas decided to desert. Seeing the long wooded ridge that overlooked his grandmother's old village in the Vale of Belvoir had unsettled him even further.

Thomas had relived the moment of Quilley's death ever since. The dead man's face reproached him constantly and Thomas no longer cared if he too were to suffer the same fate.

The only question was where and when to go. Here on the open road wasn't the place, but sometime when beyond the reach of Leicestershire magistrates but before they left the Midlands completely. Once again he glimpsed Michael's face; heard his mother shouting, '… now none of us will be saved.'

Although Freer had pointed out that Quilley's actions could have damned them all, even Tranter and Sparrow, Thomas had seen the colour rise in Freer's face, his knuckles turning white when he heard Quilley had been sentenced to death.

'Punishment should be proportionate to the crime,' Freer had later declared. 'That is the sign of a society based on justice and reason.'

'Aye, and pigs might fly.' Tranter had spat onto the floor.

Thomas sighed and tried to keep his eyes on the way ahead, not letting them wander towards the hills. 'The Fosse Way,' Captain Dickenson had told them, 'was built by the Romans for their own soldiers.' But the more Thomas tried not to look, the more he found himself staring at the distant Vale.

He recalled his grandmother's complaints about the Vale's miasmas, the villagers' petty cheating and lies, and the new ways. Grandma Cowper could not abide the so-called improving landlords and farmers who hired men and women by the day to suit themselves, and the parsons with their glebe lands and tithes were no better. So when, as a young woman, Grandma Cowper reckoned up all that was wrong with her world, she declared herself unreconciled to any authority less than Christ Himself. Her songs were laced with indignation:

They hang the man, and flog the woman,
That steals the goose from off the common;
But let the greater villain loose,
That steals the common from the goose.

The more Thomas's thoughts turned to his grandmother's sense of outrage, the more Fearless began to edge away from the column, as though she too had had enough of the military life. Thomas pulled her back into line and tried to control his own impulse to run, but Fearless was having none of it and tugged him away yet again from the main body. Thomas now let her have her head, willing her to bolt, to carry him off into the woods, but Freer immediately came up from behind and forced the restless Fearless back into line.

Freer moved closer. 'The bugger only did it to break you.' Thomas glanced at the bugger in question. Fallowfield was currently occupied with Sparrow.

Freer whispered, 'You take the King's bloody shilling and that's it. 'S only the same as being under the thumb of the parson, the squire, the magistrates, and the bloody town council or corporation, for that matter.'

Thomas whispered back as fiercely as he could, 'But we'll never be free of Fallowfield as long as he's our bloody serjeant, will we?'

Freer leant over and slapped Fearless's saddle.

'So we must get ourselves promoted to be serjeants as well then.'

Thomas adjusted his stirrups and pulled his *what the hell are you talking about now, Freer?* face.

Freer was not deterred. 'Look, Cowper, if enlightened men get the chance, one day, maybe, it will be different. In the meantime, as long as we're private men, Fallowfield will have us by the balls, so let's face him together.'

Thomas, trying to calm both himself and Fearless, ran his hand along the mare's neck. He felt her muscles relax. That was good.

Freer persisted. 'Besides, let's say if a man runs off and doesn't find work they'll only send him straight back to his village of settlement, and that man wouldn't want that, would he?'

Freer knew enough about Thomas's situation to understand there had been some kind of serious falling out.

Thomas looked at Freer. 'Not unless that man wanted his father to whip him to within an inch of his life. Or worse.'

Freer looked shocked. 'Worse?'

Thomas blinked. Of course there was more to tell, but who'd want to share such a secret, even with a good friend like Freer?

He turned away and fixed his gaze ahead, along the Fosse Way, which had brought them from Nottinghamshire to Leicestershire, knowing it to be as indifferent as it had always been to soldiers marching far away from home. But to have left Grace behind as well had been, he was beginning to think, just plain foolish of him.

17

The Receiving House

July 1805, Romford, Essex

Having been in Romford for nearly a week, Thomas now made his way to the town's receiving house at The Cock and Bell. If only Grace would reply to his letters. Apart from a note in May to say she'd received his bounty money, he'd heard nothing.

The landlord had no sooner told him it was his daughter, Miss Louise Young, who dealt with all the mail, than she appeared. She signalled Thomas to follow her into the next room, where a substantial set of divided shelves filled the opposite wall. Taking down various bundles and placing them on a table she ran her fingers over them, before looking up.

'Thomas Cowper, you said?'

'That's right.'

'Sweetheart or family?' she asked.

'Neither, exactly,' he faltered.

'But only officers get other kinds of letters, and they're mostly bills from their tailors or other such creditors.' The fair-haired girl looked up again and smiled.

'I wouldn't know about that.' Thomas blushed and tried again. 'Are you quite sure there's nothing?'

She glanced through the letters again. 'Nothing.'

Even in her curt note acknowledging receipt of the bounty money, Grace had indicated she would write again. Or so he had thought.

Thomas's disappointment must have been obvious as the business-like Miss Young turned to put her bundles of letters back in their place.

'You can't make people write to you.'

Thomas stammered, 'I know that well enough.'

She leant across the table. 'But if you keep writing, perhaps she will write back … one day.'

Thomas suddenly felt hopeful. 'Do you think so?'

'As long as you live as an honest man and can write as an honest man, why shouldn't she, unless she's already found another?'

Thomas, although initially heartened by these remarks, now felt the conversation venturing into dangerous territory. He drew himself up to his full height and thanked Miss Young for her time and said that, doubtless, he would be seeing her again soon.

'We keep a tidy alehouse here too,' she replied. 'I may see you again perhaps before you write that letter of yours.'

'Good day, Miss Young.' Thomas bowed his head and left.

Thomas felt strangely encouraged by this encounter and promised himself to write to Grace again the very next day. When he finally sat himself down, he could still hear Miss Young's strong and confident voice snapping at his heels.

As long as you live as an honest man and can write as an honest man, why shouldn't she, unless she's already found another?

~

Romford July 25th

Dear Grace,

Thank you again for your note. Thomas wondered what he could possibly say next. Again he heard Miss Young's insistent voice echoing in his head. Write honestly. *He stared at the paper for some time, slowly chewing over his words like the end of a pencil.*

I fear that my enlistment has upset you, though there are many loyal soldiers here who have wives and sweethearts, even though it is not encouraged. Once we have defeated Boney, I will be back. My promise to you is not forgotten, Grace. But what is to be our duty in these times? They say that England is so short of men now that young fellows like me, with no means to buy ourselves a substitute, will be drawn, sooner or later anyway, to serve in the militia. Is it not better instead to choose a fine regiment such as the 36th Dragoons?

You would like our home depot, Grace, for Romford is much like Melton. Our barracks are just beyond the High Street but eight hundred or so additional men give the town the air of a permanent market day, all of us jostling for space between the animal pens with drovers from Scotland or Wales bringing in their beasts for the London butchers to buy.

We are mustered here ready to protect London against any French force that might slip up the Thames, though Lieutenant Webster, our new officer, who's just transferred into the Regiment, is of the opinion that Napoleon is losing heart for an invasion this year. So we wait and watch, keeping ourselves in readiness by training on the many heaths around the town.

Our journey here was very straightforward – write honestly; write honestly – *though it was a difficult time for us all before leaving Nottingham.*

You remember I wrote to you about the man Quilley, who helped us preserve our bounty but then deserted. Just before we left Nottingham he was captured, brought back to our barracks and then punished most severely.

Thomas hesitated. What could he say without either sounding cruel or pitiful in his account of the affair?

It was a day that has left its mark on all of us, especially myself, as I was ordered to join the firing squad which was to end his life on this earth. Quilley was brave enough but I have been sick at heart ever since.

I am sorry to be so melancholic. If only you were here with me, Grace, I should be much cheered by your presence.

Ever Yours, Thomas

More honest; but so long as he was unable to admit to Grace that his mother's accusations might be true he could never write as an honest man.

~

When he made his way back to The Cock and Bell with his letter, Freer insisted on joining him, wishing to acquaint himself with the forthright Miss Young, whom Thomas had described in such detail. It was Freer too who first noticed the picture. It was hanging in The Cock and Bell's back room, where only Landlord Young's most sober customers were permitted; though, miraculously, Freer had persuaded Miss Louise Young within minutes of meeting her that two humble dragoons might also qualify for this privilege.

Freer moved closer, peered at the painting and turned to Louise.

'What's this place? I've never seen the like of it before.'

Louise looked up from her accounts. 'I don't expect you have. It's a cathedral in Paris, but don't go telling my father that or he'll have it off the wall and straight onto the fire.'

Freer examined it more closely. 'A cathedral. Where Napoleon was crowned Emperor? That cathedral?'

Louise smiled. 'You'll have to ask Lieutenant Webster.'

Freer turned round. 'Lieutenant Webster?'

Louise stood up, moved closer to Freer and pointed to the right hand corner of the picture. 'See. CRW. Charles Robert Webster. That's his full name.'

Freer was puzzled. 'You mean he painted that picture from life? He's much too young. The war's being going on for years now.'

Louise smiled. 'But he tells me that after the Peace of Amiens, all kinds of fashionable people took the opportunity to visit the old royal palaces, see the latest fashions, drink French brandy.'

Freer looked at Thomas and laughed. 'That's our plan when we get there, eh?'

Louise sat down again with her accounts.

'The only trouble is, Lieutenant Webster has almost bankrupted himself painting so many scenes from his sketchbook; he's had to give me this to cover the carrier's bill for his last purchase of paints and canvases. But don't you go telling my father that either. He wouldn't understand. Anyway, it's only till the Lieutenant's sister visits in a few weeks. You know what these young officers are like. But Lieutenant Webster says I can keep the picture even so.'

Freer seemed positively animated. 'So that is where it all began.'

Louise frowned. 'What began?'

Freer bowed solemnly. 'When we lovers of Liberty realised Napoleon was our Enemy. As Thomas Paine says, we fight not to enslave but to set a country free and to make room upon the earth for honest men to live in ...'

'And honest women too, Private Freer!' chided Louise.

Freer held his hands up, begging forgiveness. 'And honest women too, Miss Louise Young.'

Thomas smiled into his tankard. Freer had at last met his match.

18

Hounslow Heath

September 1805

Thomas was sad to leave Romford. That summer he'd almost been happy. His hauntings by Quilley and Michael were slowly beginning to fade, but most important of all, Fallowfield had been away with Dickenson on another recruiting mission, leaving just a young cornet and the amiable Lieutenant Webster as their company officers.

They were leaving the Thames in order to protect the main route between London and Portsmouth, for there was much loose talk about what the Navy might have to do next. Although Freer would occasionally indulge in threats to give the Tyrant a bloody nose, Thomas could see his friend was unhappy. Thomas guessed this was entirely due to his enforced parting from Miss Louise Young.

They'd been on the march now for several days. Their cumbersome baggage carts were slowing them up as the whole regiment moved in stages closer to the south coast. Last night they'd camped on the edge of Hounslow Heath, where autumn breezes shook them to sleep in their great bell tents, but this morning they'd woken to the unmistakable stench of rotting flesh. The wind must have changed during the night. It was Freer who claimed to know what was causing the stink. 'It'll be the gibbets,' he said confidently.

But it was all Thomas could do to stop himself puking, chiding himself much as his mother used to when he gagged over the mould in his bread at the end of the week. It was unnerving; the further south they moved from Burton, the more he found his mind returning to her. The more he tried to ignore what she'd said, the more it upset him. Everywhere he turned he saw her frightened face. He pictured her trying to ward off evil spells, repeating again and again the old sayings and prayers, all mixed up together, like the good Christian pagan she was. 'I don't care what the smell is,' Thomas grumbled, 'It's foul.'

'Just you wait and see,' Freer said.

Freer was right. Once they'd struck camp and resumed their journey along the main coach road they began to see posts like way-markers ahead. Soon their path was darkened by highwaymen and footpads paying the usual penalty of their trade, hanged on the town gallows and then put to rot in gibbet cages at the scene of their crimes. Like dead crows strung up to frighten off the other birds, thought Thomas, as the cages swung and creaked in the breeze.

When the first gibbet came into view, Thomas found it impossible not to stare at the remains still recognisable in the midst of the putrefaction.

'He'd have been better off joining the cavalry,' Tranter joked.

Another wit joined in; 'Should have got himself a faster horse.'

But Freer, though pleased to be proved right about the source of the stink, suddenly became angry.

'Poor bugger probably had an empty belly and a family to feed. Give the fellow a bit of respect.'

Fallowfield was riding down the column when he heard Freer's remarks. He reined in his mount. 'Since when do common criminals deserve respect?'

Thomas now realised there was little point in trying to please Fallowfield. He would have to try and out-manoeuvre him.

'We were saying, Serjeant, maybe we should show these poor sinners some Christian charity.'

Another voice joined them. 'Indeed, Serjeant; as good Christians we should all echo that sentiment.' The voice paused. 'God have mercy on their souls.'

Sparrow spluttered an obedient 'Amen,' as Thomas turned to see Lieutenant Webster, who had halted behind Fallowfield.

The Serjeant's face turned a deeper shade of puce. As soon as Webster was out of hearing, he sneered. 'Why the hell does he think they're here? Because they didn't deserve a Christian burial in the first place.' Fallowfield looked at Freer and Thomas as though he had something else to add, but then flipped his reins across his horse's neck and trotted off.

~

Serjeant Jack Fallowfield slapped his sabretache. Inside was a sworn statement from one of the regular informers who frequented Nottingham's old pilgrims' tavern, as well as a report from the landlord confirming that Private Freer had not only besmirched the reputation of the King's forces with seditious talk but had also spoken wildly about the Tree of Liberty. Any loyal subject would know Freer for a revolutionary, maybe even a spy. It was merely a question of biding his time. As for Webster, Fallowfield would soon find the soft underbelly of this so-called officer who spouted pieties in front of the men ... Jack Fallowfield's men.

~

Lieutenant Charles Webster soon realised it had been a mistake to cross swords with Fallowfield. But Webster had been distressed by the sight of so many unshriven corpses, and, like Cowper, thought they deserved some respect. He admired Cowper and his friend Freer for standing up to Fallowfield; not that he should, since insubordination and familiarity paved the road to ruin. Some of the men might have been joshing, but he had felt for the sake of all their souls he should offer up a prayer in spite of Serjeant Fallowfield.

~

'Bloody Fallowfield,' Freer said, speaking more quietly, as the serjeant rode back up the column. Thomas smiled; his stomach had finally adjusted to the stench, and doubtless Freer would now explain how greater equality between men would not only increase the sum of human happiness, but would also remove the need for gibbets strung along the public highway. Thomas wished he had Freer's faith in the perfectibility of Man. These doubts unsettled him, though not as much as the threat of being examined on Judgment Day and found wanting.

What was it Freer had said yesterday about Thomas Paine reckoning the world was under the government of both superstition and the sword? Not that Thomas thought this Paine fellow right in all his opinions but he'd have wagered a day's pay that the man must have had a mother much like his own.

~

After crossing the iron bridge at Staines and with the steely gleam of the Thames well behind them, they made their way steadily south, past wooded valleys and over another stretch of sandy scrub, its slender pines and birches swallowing the fading afternoon light, until Captain Dickenson at last instructed them to dismount and see to their horses. Only five miles or so to go and they would be at their final destination, Guildford, at the foot of the North Downs, where, Dickenson told them, they were to await further orders, orders which would depend entirely upon Napoleon's next move.

19

Jacob's Ladder

September 1805, Guildford

As they rode into Guildford the autumn sun was already low in the sky. Their barracks were in the grounds of a large mansion in the lower part of the town. The high street loomed up in front of them, as steep as a Jacob's ladder. Dickenson thought they would probably be moving on again quite soon; probably to the South Coast, for the rumour now abroad was that Napoleon's Grand Army had merely decamped from Boulogne and was regrouping elsewhere in order to effect his invasion of England. But Freer was not so sure. According to the more sober patrons of The Cock and Bell back in Romford, Boney had taken a beating already, what with the weather and the stout defences Englishmen were building everywhere. They reckoned his spies would have scuttled back to France with their tail between their legs once they had witnessed the nation's determination to defend its shores.

Coming to a new town, Freer now made it a habit to seek out all those who were well connected to the intelligence networks: manservants, cobblers, tailors, artisans; all those who could interpret what the packing of valises or the ordering of goods might signify in the broader plan for the defence of England. So when Freer came back with his latest news, everyone stopped to listen. He had it, on good authority too, that Nelson had recently dined in Guildford on his way back to his country estate in Merton. That, Freer concluded, was surely proof there would be a peaceful winter if the great man himself judged it safe to leave his fleet over the coming months.

Thomas no longer knew what to think. Quilley's ashen face was fading from his dreams but now his mother's friars were invading his nights.

That night one friar, with a face like a walnut, tried to grab him, shrieking and wailing as loudly as his mother when she'd denounced him as the Son of Beelzebub. He sat bolt upright. He pulled the blanket off his bed, planted his feet firmly on the ground and tried to establish if he was awake. He was having a nightmare. That's all it was; but not like his mother's ones, he told himself. She used to stumble round the cottage, bumping into the few bits of furniture they possessed, sobbing she had to find her children to warn them to stay away from the lepers' bells. His father had long ceased to reason with her. He would slap her cheeks, shake her awake and tell her he was back off to bed, leaving her on her knees, muttering to some god or other known only to her. Thomas wondered if night terrors could be passed from mother to son.

The next morning Freer commented that Thomas looked excessively pale. Thomas laughed off the haunting by blaming the strength of the local ale. That afternoon he made some excuse to leave Freer and the barracks behind him and wander alone up The Mount. He didn't know what he hoped to find other than some distraction to lift his spirits.

As he approached the Guildhall and its huge overhanging clock he caught sight of a sign depicting a Bible and paused. Maybe the shopkeeper would know if any Friars used to live in the town?

The bookseller clearly thought Thomas an unlikely antiquarian; but Thomas persisted and as he did so, Lieutenant Webster walked through the door.

After Thomas's hastily paid compliment, Webster confirmed what Thomas had been worried about.

'Our barracks are indeed built in the grounds of an old Friary.'.

'What did the friars do there, sir?'

'I suppose they did what most friars did. They took the message of the Gospel to the people, reaching out to ignorant and lost souls.'

'But did they dress in black, sir?'

'I suppose they must have done, for they were known as the Black Friars.'

Thomas's heart skipped several beats and he quickly excused himself.

'Thank you, sir. That was very interesting, sir.'

Ignorant and lost souls. The phrase ricocheted round Thomas's head as he rejoined the crush on the High Street. It was Tuesday and the market was in full flow. He decided to make his way to The Crown, where he and Freer had already made the acquaintance of Oliver and several other ostlers. They were good for gossip and news from those passing through the town. Gentlefolk, coach passengers, even drunken sailors returning home from their ships added daily to the ostlers' store of information.

Thomas hurried through the archway into the stable yard, past the carts and carriages to the horses. Greeting Oliver as he went in, Thomas grabbed a pitchfork and gestured towards the last of the stables requiring mucking out. Once the steaming dung had been shifted onto the cart ready to be taken away, Oliver sat down to share his beer and bread with Thomas.

'Word has it that the fleet will be on the move again soon.'

Thomas leant forward.

'I thought Nelson had gone back to London.'

'There was a post-chaise through last week, they say, bearing orders for him to return.'

Oliver took another sip of his beer. Thomas could hardly contain his excitement.

'You mean Nelson will be coming back through Guildford?'

'This isn't called the Sailors' Road for nothing. But he's not been through yet.'

~

That night was as fretful as the last. This time, rather than a friar begging him to join their number, Thomas saw his mother beseeching him to return, crying out to him to come back to her. Her face was paler than he'd ever seen it, but her voice was just as penetrating and plaintive as he remembered. She begged him to speak to her. He couldn't. He tossed and turned but he couldn't break free of her hands grabbing his. Suddenly his mother turned away, looked back just once, wiped her face clear of tears and said she should have left him in the poorhouse alone and without a mother's love. She moved away without a moment's more conversation or accusation. He woke up weeping with the words still in his head: *without a mother's love.*

He'd never even considered that some of his mother's anger might stem from love rather than hate. He took out a pencil and paper from the pocket book under his pillow. The desire to write something, to make some kind of peace with his mother was overwhelming. No point though. No point in even thinking about writing. His mother couldn't read. That would have to be an end to it. He looked round the barrack room at the sleeping figures and suspected most of them thought little about their souls, though they were still prepared to die for their country. It was Thomas who was the ignorant and lost soul.

He knew what he could do. He would write to Grace. Thomas took out his pencil and pocketbook once more and moved closer to the light of the lantern. But could he admit to Grace that not only had his mother accused him of murder but that his mother might possibly be right? He sighed. The friars and Louise Young had spoken... *Write as an honest man.*

Thomas began by asking Grace to speak to his mother, to tell her that although he didn't know when he would return, he thought of her often and hoped she was thinking of him. But he also needed to know why his mother had accused him of killing his brother, for he remembered nothing except finding Michael bleeding at the foot of the ladder.

Was it enough? Was it true? Was it honest to say this to his mother when he'd spent the last six months so angry with her? He scribbled a few more lines, wishing Grace well and begging forgiveness for asking her to undertake this task. He promised to write again to her directly and tell her of the many interesting things to be found in this town. He hoped that she too was in good health.

~

The next day, after drills and stable duties, Fallowfield announced they were to move out of the barracks to make way for another regiment due to arrive that evening. Their troop was to move to The Crown and a second troop would be billeted at The White Hart.

'At least we're not at The White Hart.' Freer smiled, knowing that inn to be the favoured drinking place of the followers of Prime Minister Pitt and all those opposed to Liberty. Besides, Freer took a decidedly practical view. The evenings were already chilly; the barrack room was severely overcrowded. The stoves, which he'd taken care to inspect, were clearly going to be inadequate, and The Crown kept good fires on its lower floors, so their rooms would be warm even though they were still waiting for their fuel ration allowance. Thomas just hoped he'd sleep once he'd left the ghostly friars behind him.

The Crown owed some political allegiance to the Whigs. This made the billeting of troops less agreeable to the landlord; not only were rates less favourable than those charged to travellers, but the current conduct of the war was not popular in Whig circles. But by Friday, Freer and Thomas, largely by virtue of their efforts in the stables, had become friends with the reluctant host; so much so that Thomas decided to ask the landlord what he thought of Oliver's report that sailors were no longer to be seen rolling drunk to London but were now returning to Portsmouth. Also, Oliver reckoned, Nelson himself had been visited by one Captain Blackwood and ordered to return to his command of the Mediterranean Fleet. 'What do you think, landlord?' asked Freer.

'If I were a French spy,' said the landlord, 'which I'm not,' he added hastily, 'I would watch out for a post-chaise speeding south on the Portsmouth Road, perhaps overnight, and doing its best to avoid attention.'

20

The Funeral

24 December, 1805, Guildford, Surrey

After Thomas sent his letter to Grace, his spirits began to lift. Grace was a favourite of his mother's and if anyone could persuade her to talk about Michael's death and maybe forgive Thomas, it would be Grace. He had no idea how long the post would take to reach Burton, but as it had only taken two or three weeks from Romford he had high hopes he would hear from her within the month; the end of October, at the latest.

The rest of September passed quickly enough. There was news confirming the rumour that Nelson had rejoined the fleet; much was now expected of the English men-of-war, but after the initial flurry there was only silence. Then in early November, with every stagecoach carrying a naval man, who would stop to dine at The Crown, the desire for news reached a new frenzy. Oliver even reported that a Lieutenant Lapenotière, travelling in a post–chaise from the West Country, had only that Guy Fawkes Day been seen to change horses in great haste on the turnpike across Bagshot Heath. But the hearty protestants of Guildford were far too busy drinking to the downfall of all things popish for this intelligence to excite much attention at the time. Everyone was sure that any naval bulletins would have to travel through Guildford. No one suspected this might be the very man entrusted with Collingwood's despatches to the Admiralty that told of both the nation's great victory and its greatest loss. Though later, in the light of this news, the Bagshot ostlers remembered most clearly they had definitely remarked on the Lieutentant's melancholy yet elated state. It was a story that every ale-house and coaching inn in Guildford later examined, drew its own conclusions from and lamented. England had been saved, but at what a cost.

In late November Thomas took to visiting the Receiving House every day. Surely Grace must have talked to his mother by now? By Christmas he'd given up hope and so, when on Christmas Eve a letter finally arrived, he felt faint with anticipation. Freer fortunately had not accompanied him. Thomas broke the seal and saw the letter contained three sheets in Grace's rather cramped hand.

~

December 6th 1805

Dear Thomas,

As I write this I can see across the lane to your parents' cottage under the clearest full moon Burton has known these last few months. If only I could lighten your spirits as much as the moonlight is illuminating your old home.

I am the bearer of sad news. Your mother was taken ill in church last Sunday. Your father and Bailiff Strutt carried her home, then your father went to Melton for the doctor as soon as he could. Your father could not have been more attentive to her needs, although it must have cost him dear. But she could not be saved, though the doctor came daily, partly at his own expense, they say. By Wednesday he could do no more, and today, Friday, she was buried.

Your father tells everyone it was an apoplexy brought on by the vindictiveness of others, her nerves already weakened by these long months of grieving. The cause of her death is no longer of consequence, you might feel, but it seems to matter greatly to your father, who threatens revenge on us all except myself and a few others who kept faith with her, whatever misapprehensions and fancies took her. I fear that in his present state he will refuse to communicate with you.

Thomas read the letter's opening lines again in disbelief. His mother was scarcely thirty-six. As for his father being consumed by grief, he really couldn't imagine that. No. He couldn't see how a man who despised her ignorant and superstitious ways would have sacrificed more than a week's wages to try and save her. Ploughmen had their own tried and trusted remedies, without recourse to some quack they could ill afford.

He shoved the letter inside his jacket, resolving not to read any more until he'd found a place to be alone. He pushed his way through the press of people clustered around the market stalls and made his way down the hill, turning right at the carrier's until he came upon the old churchyard, looking almost as gloomy as he felt. He leant against its gnarled flint walls and took out the letter. His breath steamed in the frosty air and his cold fingers fumbled to unfurl its thin sheets once again.

Now that the initial shock had worn off, he began to worry about everything else. Had Grace read his letter to his mother? Had she begged her to put aside the bitter words she and Thomas had exchanged? Had she been able to ask for an explanation of her accusations? He tried to reckon the time this letter had taken to reach Guildford and how long his last letter would have taken to arrive in Melton. Then again, how long might Grace have waited to go to her? He calculated that she had had all of October and November to talk about his letter with his mother. He looked at the first page again to see if he could divine any other meanings.

But all he saw was his father angrily declaring his wife had died of the apoplexy brought on by the malice of others, especially Thomas's. Didn't they understand a woman might become mad with more than grief, her mind unhinged by disturbing visions? 'And how is your poor mother today?' the villagers would say whilst muttering under their breath, 'Why old Tom Cowper don't send his Mary to the madhouse, I'll never know.'

He began to read the rest of Grace's letter.

> *Once the sun was up, your father led the cart with your mother's coffin through the village up to the church, the little ones perched like angels guarding her coffin all the way, Hannah walking.*

Thomas grimaced to think of his young sisters as angels. His parents had buried too many babies just like angels, his father carrying the small bundles on his shoulder, as if sacks of grain. He went back to Grace's letter.

> *Bailiff Strutt kept your father company at the head of the procession.*

Thomas saw himself once again at Michael's funeral walking past the gable ends of East Farm, the barns stretching to the far rump of Burton village where the land drops away steeply to the fields below. He could hear the creaking of the cart as it made its way through the lanes, its sides brushing against the winter twigs and saw Hannah and the little ones lurch as it slowly moved towards the church. He saw himself once more standing on the curve of the lane, looking past the Oakham road into the far distance.

We said prayers by the graveside, standing quietly together, each of us with our own memories. But the wind was blowing most bitterly, and we did not linger long for fear of the girls catching a chill. You will remember where Michael is buried. She is buried with him.

Thomas pictured it exactly. He remembered the last time he'd been there; the pale headstones engraved with smiling suns and words of remembrance; the huge stone pyramid edged by cannonballs that nudged so close to the path there was hardly room to pass by; he was once again walking through the grass to the upturned sods piled upon Michael's grave.

He untied the small cloth bag from his neck and stroked the sticky soil, then brushed the earth back into the bag and closed it.

I fear I can write no more tonight. This day has been a hard one for all of us who loved your mother and watched her sadness these last few months.

Yours, Grace

She had said nothing about his letter, nothing about his mother's accusation about Michael's death, nothing about forgiveness. Had his mother died still cursing him?

Thomas's jaw tightened; he crumpled the letter in his fist and kicked the wall several times before letting himself slide slowly down, his back scraping against the uneven flints. The sun was beginning to drop in the sky.

21

Lost

Where the hell is he? On a night like this and all. Will Freer pounded up the High Street. He'd try The White Lion first.

~

No bloody sign of him at The Swan or The Angel either. Maybe it was time to stop and have some ale. Think about what to do next. Will fingered his tankard, tapping its sides like a drum, not a whit calmer. Where the hell could he be? Freer's heart suddenly missed a beat. Surely, knowing Fallowfield would be watching his every move, surely Cowper would never desert? Not now. It didn't make sense. Once away from Nottingham, Cowper's spirits seemed to have been restored, and Guildford was a decent enough place. They'd arrived just in time for the great fair on St Catherine's Hill, with the old chapel ruins high above like a country squire down on his luck presiding over the general merriment. In early October there'd been a giddiness in the air, as though they were still only playing at soldiers.

It was about then that Cowper had started trailing up to the Receiving House for letters that either never came, or he never told Freer about. But he'd always come back to barracks to see to his stable duties. Not this afternoon, though. Freer had had to lie for him, tell Fallowfield he had the shits. The Serjeant clearly didn't believe him, but fortunately he was distracted by Sparrow, who'd just discovered his horse was lame. Still, Freer never thought he'd see the day that Cowper neglected Fearless.

So where next? The Red Lion? Unlikely, but Freer carried on up the hill and put his head round the door. No sign of him. Damn it. Where was he? It was Christmas Eve. It was only when he reached The White Hart at the top of the hill, and his enquiries were met with a singular lack of interest, that he finally lost his temper. He kicked some mud off his boots onto the landlord's newly swept floor and left.

Retracing his steps, Freer calmed himself down at The Three Tuns and told himself not to lose heart. Of course, The King's Head! He hurried down the hill towards Star Corner, but as he turned along Quarry Street he could just make out a figure, knees drawn up to his chin, slumped back against the churchyard wall, staring into the twilight.

Freer wasn't sure whether to shout with relief or annoyance at the dance that Cowper had led him.

22

And Found

Will Freer moved steadily closer, as though approaching a halter-shy horse, till he got within a foot or so of the wall.

'You'll catch your bloody death. Here.'

Freer leant forward and stretched out his hand. But Cowper went on staring into space, his fist clenched around a crumpled piece of paper.

Freer squatted down next to him. He didn't seem to be drunk. 'What's happened? What's the matter?'

'My mother ...'

It was the first time that Cowper had ever spoken of his mother. Freer had always assumed that she was long dead, like his own mother. Perhaps it was about the girl, Grace, Cowper used to talk about to Louise. Maybe the mother had written to say something had happened to the girl. Maybe this wasn't about Quilley at all. First things first.

'Come on, shift yourself. I'll buy you a drink at The King's Head and ...'

Freer trailed off. He looked again at Cowper, offered both hands and pulled him to his feet.

The King's Head was warm, crowded and noisy; a place that conspired to drown out most normal conversation, and anyway Cowper was still reluctant to speak.

Eventually Freer understood: Cowper's mother had died and there had been a great quarrel between them. Freer could scarcely remember his own mother or father, and when he heard this he leant forward and put his hand lightly on Cowper's left arm. He was relieved to hear it wasn't the girl who was dead, though he did manage to keep this thought to himself.

'Doesn't your father have other family at home?'

Cowper swirled his ale in his tankard, scrutinising its depths.

'I've three sisters still living.' Freer, who possessed neither brother nor sister, ruminated silently. He looked at Cowper's face and recognised the same expression his friend had had when ordered to join Quilley's firing squad; as if to say what else can a man expect? This is what I deserve.

How could he possibly shake Cowper out of this? Freer set his own tankard on the table as gently as he could.

Cowper paused and swirled his ale a little more vigorously. 'I left on bad terms with both my mother and my father.'

'So what did you argue about?'

Cowper sank back against the settle and stared into the fire.

'After my brother Michael died, just before we quarrelled at his funeral, she took it into her head that the Archangel Gabriel had told her Michael was The Chosen One, the new saviour of the world. And then at the funeral, she said I'd murdered him and I was the work of the Devil, or the son of Beelzebub to be more precise.'

Freer checked Cowper's expression. He wasn't joking. It was now as though the sluice gates had opened. He couldn't seem to stop himself.

'You see, you can't argue with a mad woman. I shouldn't have argued with her. I can see now it wouldn't have hurt to ignore her and stay calm.'

Freer decided he had to ask. 'But why did she say … what she said?'

Cowper looked up. 'What do you mean?'

Freer took a deep breath. 'Why did she say you'd murdered your brother?'

Cowper shook his head and looked intently into his tankard.

Freer placed his hand on Cowper's arm. 'Did you?'

Cowper drained his tankard. The fire flickered low in the hearth, its logs slowly collapsing into embers. Ordinarily, Freer would have put another log into its fading flames but he didn't dare move. He didn't want to disturb Cowper more than he had to.

Cowper shook his head again. 'Who knows? I don't. I just remember hearing Hannah scream, and then my mother, and then there was Michael lying on the ground at the bottom of the apple loft ladder, blood everywhere.'

Freer gripped his arm. 'Don't you remember anything else?'

Cowper pressed his hands against his temples. 'Only the arguing and fighting with him about all kinds of things … him laming one of the plough horses, pestering Grace for kisses, him telling tales and then my father braying me across the room instead of hitting *him*.' Thomas sighed. 'I'd forgotten that. Now that would have been bad, because though he was only a year younger than me, he'd not a bit of spare flesh on him. My mother said he could have died several times over when he was born; that's why she thought he was special, the only child of hers who really did come back from the dead.' Cowper threw up his hands. 'The truth is I don't know what happened. But I got so angry at her saying all those things. Then I started to worry that maybe I had ... somehow ... though not knowingly.'

Freer tried to clear his head. '... not knowingly?'

Cowper tugged at his collar. 'I have these strange spells ...'

Cowper seemed to be finding some relief in telling his tale, so Freer inclined his head closer towards him.

Cowper went on. '...when I see and hear things that aren't there.'

Freer held his tongue and nodded encouragingly as Cowper hesitated.

'I'm really a bit too much like my mother for my father's liking. He blamed me for her losing her wits after I was born. Well, it was more the start of her losing her wits, after every confinement and every death. Even then she thought I was possessed; or so my grandmother told me. But she said my mother couldn't help it.'

Cowper paused again and wiped his brow.

'That's why I stayed behind with my grandmother in Stathern. When I was born, she tried to drown me; my mother, I mean. She thought I was the Devil and had come to kill her. My grandmother reckoned my mother had been poisoned in her wits when she was a child by one of the rectors in Stathern. My grandmother called him Reverend Maggotface. She said he was a fearful fellow who talked of nothing else but Hell and Damnation just so he could terrify his flock into obedience.'

Cowper put his hand over his eyes.

'If only she'd stopped having babies ...'

He rummaged in his overalls, found a rag and blew his nose.

'Maybe my mother was right and I'm destined to do the Devil's work, not God's. After all, I might as well have killed her. As for Michael, some days I really believe I could have done.'

Freer had never had to deal with such complications of family life. It had been hard enough adjusting to life with a master, never mind anything like this. As for God, he could feel his cheeks beginning to burn red with the injustice of it all. Suddenly the church bells started to ring throughout the town. Christmas. Freer could see it was time to make a stand, take on the Almighty Himself.

He lowered his voice. 'What has God or the Devil to do with any of it? That's nonsense, Thomas. You know it is.'

Cowper nodded, but without enthusiasm.

Freer pressed his case harder. He was ready to cast off all the shackles of faith, even the rational God of the Unitarian Great Meeting, the rock of his childhood.

'We're free men, Thomas. Free to follow our own path without bringing God into it, or the Devil, for that matter.'

Freer leant back against the settle and looked closely at his friend. He hadn't won this battle yet, let alone the war. But an affirmation of Man's capacity for Reason and Common Sense was the only rallying cry to the colours he could think of.

He bent down to pick up a log and placed it on the fading embers. The fire spluttered into life once again. But Freer had an uneasy feeling that his friend's unhappiness was going to take more than fine words and a pint of ale to cure. He would have to be vigilant for some time yet. What little he could remember of his own parents was how his father's grief at his mother's early death turned into melancholy and that into death by his own hand.

23

The Road to East Blatchington

January 1806, The South Downs

Freer was first with the news. 'It's a good seventy miles away. Four days' march, they reckon, with baggage trains, though why the hell would the Tyrant want to invade in weather like this?' Freer continued to grumble as he and Thomas packed the baggage wagons high with bell tents. Thomas cursed too as they struggled to adjust the frozen ropes. 'Hope they're not expecting us to spend the winter in these things.'

'Of course not. But like Webster says, the Regiment has to take all its baggage with it whenever it changes depots. Before you know it, we'll be tucked up in some cosy barracks.'

So Webster was his source of information. Thomas smiled. Of course.

Lieutenant Webster was a decent subaltern who treated his men far better than Serjeant Fallowfield. He seemed to have a soft spot for Freer, sending him on occasional errands when perhaps, by rights, it should have been Fallowfield or at least a Chosen man. Perhaps Webster distrusted his Serjeant as much as the rest of them.

'Huh. I'll believe that when I see it.' Thomas clapped his hands together for warmth.

'But then what's to do when we do get there? Do they think the Tyrant's going to slip his army in under the fog and find his own way to London? We can't even find our bloody way to the river.' Freer yanked the ropes harder.

It had been a long January of thick white fogs lingering most of the day in the bottom of the valley where the barracks were. Though the officers were warm enough in the big house, the men had come to detest the chill and dampness that seeped through every cranny. Thomas couldn't abide the place and regretted ever admiring its High Street and panoramic views. What was it to him where they were posted next?

They headed south before the dawn had fully broken, keeping the chalk pits to their left and St Catherine's Hill to their right, and Thomas wondered again at his foolishness. How could he have ever enjoyed the blood and gore of the bearbaiting and cockfighting at the fair? How could he ever have thought death was a game?

Beyond the alder trees of the Tillingbourne Valley, the trees seemed to be mostly oak, saved in readiness for the navy's shipyards, Freer pronounced. Their sturdy trunks and bare branches covered the hillsides with such grandeur and solidity, Thomas felt even more ashamed to be such a frail creature. He looked around at his fellow dragoons, who seemed more substantial, more real than he could ever imagine himself to be.

~

The next two days were clearer, with a chill wind, and after two more nights in tents there was endless talk of warm stoves and straw palliasses. Thomas too couldn't wait to leave these hills behind him... hills that folded, and rolled, seduced and enchanted. They could have persuaded a man to embrace them to the death. Thomas felt sure of that.

Not that Freer seemed to notice. He was far too excited at the prospect of seeing the sea. He'd hardly stopped talking about it. This, he asserted, was when they would really understand England was an island, though neither of them could imagine what the sea might look like. The Thames had appeared grand enough when they'd gone down onto the marshes below Romford, but they'd been told by Lieutenant Webster that even that great river was nothing like the sea.

The sun was already low on the horizon as they followed the track from the toll road into the village of East Blatchington. Thomas noticed a church with a squat tower at the crossroads to their left as they passed down the shallow incline. He caught sight too of a small street of decent brick houses just beyond the corner of the churchyard. By now Freer was beyond excitement.

'As soon as it's light tomorrow we should see it. Now that will be something to write to Louise and Grace about.'

Thomas sighed. He'd already written a letter to Grace, thanking her for letting him know the sad news and enquiring, as delicately as he could, whether she'd read his last letter to his mother. He dared not write again so soon.

24

The Seven Sisters

January 1806, East Blatchington, East Sussex

In the morning they woke to the intelligence that Pitt was dead; 'as dead as the Coalition against Napoleon,' declared Captain Dickenson, announcing the news to his men.

'What coalition's that?' muttered Thomas to Freer.

'Our allies abroad against the Tyrant, I think.' Freer whispered. 'Webster said he'd heard the Austrians and Russians took a beating from the Tyrant no one had ever seen the like of at somewhere called Austerlitz.'

Dickenson was trying to make the best of this news.

'We may well stand alone once more abroad, but at home we remain in the good hands of the King and his new government. So let our own vigilance not cease, whatever the empty chatter about reconciliation with France. This bay alone is wide enough to land the entire French army.'

Was there no stopping Boney? Even Dickenson didn't seem sure; the spectre he conjured up of the blue-coated French storming onto the very beaches beneath their feet made Thomas's spirits sink even lower; though the Captain did go on to promise them that within the next three days they would replace the regiment currently in occupation of the barracks and would once again enjoy the benefits of bricks and mortar.

'Look. Over there.' Freer poked him in the ribs. Thomas turned his head, as much as he dared, in the direction Freer indicated. The dark sky was streaked with so many different shades of blue and grey that Thomas had to scrutinise it for several minutes to distinguish between sky and sea. So that was the sea? Napoleon's enemy and England's only friend, but what a friend! As the morning progressed, Thomas began to feel his bones ache with its encompassing desolation, its emptiness.

Not that Freer seemed at all disturbed, and by the time stable duties were over, he'd already found out the best way to reach the sea. It was still daylight, in the period of grace between parades, inspections and evening duties, when Freer grabbed him by the arm and led him towards the cliff.

'Never mind the others,' he urged, as Thomas tried to look behind him. 'Over here.'

For a moment or two, Thomas thought Freer intended to scramble straight down the cliff face, but after stopping at its very edge, Freer looked about, as if for a path. Eventually Freer pointed vaguely westwards.

'Down here, to the right of the battery, there's an inn right next to the beach, further up. They say it's where the French last tried to invade, a couple of hundred years ago. But as it floods regularly, you can't always rely on it being open.'

Thomas couldn't imagine how Freer had had time to acquire this information, let alone find his bearings. Under Freer's tutelage Thomas was now reasonably good at finding his way, but Freer was still better. So leaving the rest of them behind, Freer and Thomas crept down the winding track to the sea. Thomas couldn't have imagined a more barren sight than the one that met him there. The beach was a stony, muddy place; the waves pressed against the beach like hungry pigs to the trough.

'Just wait till summer,' Freer said, 'when we can swim out to those rocks.' He signalled towards a distant blackness in the sea ahead.

Thomas studied the swirling water. 'I can't swim. Remember?'

'Well, perhaps not to those rocks, just yet.'

Freer continued to dodge and jump away from the water snapping at his feet.

'It's easy when you know how.'

'Never.' Thomas turned his back on the spectacle, and began to make instead for the low building further along the shore.

'I'll buy you a drink,' Thomas shouted back into the wind.

Freer stopped jumping, turned and waved. 'I'll see you there then.'

~

Shivering with cold from the biting winds, Thomas made his way as quickly as he could to the squat building ahead, Freer slightly behind.

As Thomas tugged open the door, they were greeted by a portly man with a jolly face which flowed down into a double chin.

'Landlord Jack Crouch of The Buckle Inn at your service.'

'Will Freer and Thomas Cowper of the 36th Dragoons, at yours.'

~

By the time Thomas and Freer paid for their third round of drinks, Landlord Crouch was musing further on the ups and downs of local politics.

'We've scoundrels round here selling rotten meat and bread to the army, making such a pretty penny out of this war they'll give us all a bad name.'

Landlord Crouch tapped his large nose and looked briefly around the low- ceilinged room.

'I know who they are and they know what I think of 'em but what can anyone do?'

He poured more ale into Freer's and Thomas's tankards, and both quickly handed over their coins, the better to keep the landlord's narrative flowing.

'Seaford's been in the pocket of its patrons for hundreds of years, and it's them, not us so-called voters, who send our two members of Parliament to London to represent us.'

Thomas noticed that the landlord drawled out the word 'represent' in a way that indicated he thought this was the last thing their members of Parliament did for the voters of Seaford.

'Just look at us, with less than a hundred Scot and Lot voters; and when our patrons own their houses, well, they don't have to tell their tenants who to vote for, do they?'

Crouch shrugged his enormous shoulders and carried on rinsing out tankards while he listed the various twists and turns of Seaford politics.

Thomas's head began to spin with the sheer number of names thrown into the ring as though he and Freer should know who they were. But Freer just smiled. He was making a much better fist of looking as though he knew what the landlord was talking about.

'... and like the rest of 'em, as a Scot and Lot ratepayer, I'm well and truly in my landlord's pocket'. Jack Crouch ran his hands as far as he could reach over his enormous belly, then smiled. 'Mind, it would have to be a big pocket to fit the likes of me.'

Thomas grunted and nodded his head vigorously pretending to follow the landlord's drift, but Freer sat in silence; he seemed to be weighing up what Crouch was telling him.

'So I'm not going to not vote for my patron, am I, whatever I think of the conduct of the war or his rotten meat?'

Freer leant forward. 'Of course not. It's our unrepresentative Parliament that is truly corrupt, not honest voters living under the thumb of their landlords.'

Thomas nodded again. In these matters it was better to defer to Freer's opinion rather than attempt to form one of his own. In truth, he wasn't sure he had an opinion. Besides, Thomas's mind was elsewhere. Nowadays, it usually was. Last night the sound of the sea had haunted Thomas almost as much the sound of the lepers' bells and the friars' prayers. He wasn't sure he'd ever learn to live at peace with the sea's restless emptiness.

~

On the following day Thomas reluctantly found himself making his way with Freer over to the signal station on Seaford Head, carrying important dispatches. They would be riding far too close to the sea for his liking.

Freer decided to take the road back up the hill towards Blatchington; Seaford Head was just visible on the eastern horizon. Turning right past the parish church, they paused briefly at the top of the village to survey its substantial dwellings of flint and brick, now lit by a bright sun, before slowly making their way down the icy hill. With Freer paying rather more attention to reading about local landmarks on Captain Webster's sketch map than the going underfoot, Thomas was much relieved to reach the ponds, arriving at the bottom without incident.

Once over the next hill, they were soon able to drop down into Seaford, passing The New Inn and the old harbour stranded behind shingle and marshland. Freer stopped to examine the Martello tower under construction. Whilst he exclaimed over the deepness of the dry moat and the strength of its walls, Thomas scarcely bothered to look. Now that Nelson was dead, by the time these fortifications were finished Napoleon could have stormed the entire coast three times over.

Thomas heard the mocking tones of the seabirds circling the great cliff, its whiteness folded and crimped tight like a shroud. For all that it was an unusually sunny day, the air was nipping his nose and Thomas was keen to deliver their dispatches before Freer found anything else to admire. But once at the signalling station on the cliff top Freer began to enthuse about how the system worked, both along the coast and inland towards London itself. Thomas thought it a flimsy and precarious business, especially considering the weather they were having this winter. But Freer stoutly defended the ingenuity of it all.

'Of course the weather's bound to affect it, just like it would the Tyrant and all'.

Leaving Freer in animated conversation with the one of the seamen manning the telegraph post, Thomas began to walk alone with Fearless back towards Seaford but, drawn by the sound of breakers, he thrust his sabre firmly in the ground, tethered Fearless to the grip and moved closer to the cliff edge. The gulls screamed and dived above his head as he stared at the whiteness of the surf breaking and beating against the chalk, Thomas breathing in the same rhythm as the waves rolling in from the great blankness behind, listening for every sound speaking to him from across the oceans. Thomas wondered if his head was really spinning or whether it was just the surf moving so quickly below him.

Suddenly he saw himself standing before a great altar with Michael in flowing white robes holding a golden cross beckoning him and Thomas immediately felt a great urge to let go, to jump, to fall into oblivion. He heard the rolling pulse of the waves calling to him, the chorus of birds mocking his puny efforts to seek forgiveness. It was not as though anyone would miss him. Not like Nelson; everybody mourned his passing. But what was he to anyone in the midst of all this jostling and noise?

The last time Thomas had known such peace was playing down by the brook in Stathern below the churchyard where whole families were laid to rest under the spreading wings of cherubim and angels. Then he saw his mother standing on the edge of Michael's grave and heard her cursing his very existence. But that was all right. He didn't mind any more. He didn't mind if he fell down into the deepest grave a man could find himself in. He heard the frenzied beat of wings, felt the icy sweep of powerful wings shattering the air. He knew what had to be done.

'Thomas, don't move. Stay where you are. I'm going to come behind you and I'm going to put out my hand, and you're going to hold onto it. Understand?'

Thomas heard his grandmother shouting at him and pulling him up from the stream bank back onto the lane. Yes, yes, he had to climb back up again to her. Thomas turned and smiled but she wasn't there. It was Freer who was grasping his hand and moving him as gently as a boy carries stolen birds' eggs away from the cliff edge.

'Don't you ever be doing that again to me, Thomas Cowper. Eh?'

25

Mutiny

Thomas was worried. It had been a long winter, with too many weeks spent under canvas, and three men and four horses dead already. The men were in a mutinous mood.

Affairs in their encampment were going from bad to worse, the soldiers drinking themselves into a stupor every evening. All it needed was another unnecessary death, another delivery of weevil-ridden bread and their resentments would explode, beyond any reasoned calculation of risk and despite the unlikelihood of success. After weeks of empty promises of warm barracks and decent food, Freer declared it a tinder-box waiting to be lit. And as Landlord Jack Crouch might have predicted, it was the supply of rotten meat and a death that finally lit the fuse.

~

It was at Private Wintergreen's funeral, just before his troop trudged uphill to the church in their best dress uniforms, stomachs bloated and limbs shivering under a bitter sky, when things came to a head. Wintergreen had been a popular soldier with a cheerful uncomplaining nature and many a friend saw his death from fever and dysentery as a judgment upon the army.

During his last days Wintergreen had been racked by coughing fits, unable to stand, hot and cold flushes making him shake uncontrollably. He'd lain curled up on his camp bed as cramps assailed his stomach and bowels, streams of watery shite running down his legs onto the floor. It was all Thomas could do not to retch. But the dragoon was in need of comfort as well as clean clothes and padded drawers.

'As soon as you've some clean clothes you'll feel like a new man again.' Thomas swabbed Wintergreen's face with a damp cloth. Thomas signalled to Freer, who was hunting for fresh linen.

'No. Pass me those rags; let's use the rags first.'

Wintergreen submitted himself to the rough cleansing of his body with hardly a murmur whilst Thomas encouraged him as only the living can with the dying.

'Don't give up, Wintergreen, don't give up now; your fever's passing.' But Wintergreen put his hand out to tug at Thomas's arm as though to tell him that there was no need to go on pretending.

His close friends blamed the rancid meat and the cold as they huddled together in their bell tents, waiting for the other regiment to vacate the barracks. But then a rumour started that both regiments had to stay put now that Boney had plans to land on the Sussex coast much as the French had raided Seaford two hundred years or so before.

~

It was Tranter and Sparrow who warned them. Thomas had never seen Sparrow look so worried. Sparrow whispered, 'Wintergreen's friend Miller reckons there'll be more of us following him to an early grave if we don't take matters into our own hands. He wants Tranter to join them.'

Tranter nodded. He found it difficult to whisper with no teeth and signalled to Sparrow to carry on with their tale.

'Tranter here being a man of great strength and fighting skills.'

Freer immediately put his finger to Sparrow's lips. 'When?' he asked. 'When?'

'During the funeral. Tranter and the men are to take the officers and lock them in the church whilst Miller's men march on the town to seize fresh supplies.'

Thomas gasped. 'But we're surrounded by other regiments who'll put down any trouble within the day. Men will be hanged.'

Thomas looked at Freer, the great champion of the rights of man, who had been saying for weeks it would all end badly, almost as if the hard-pressed soldiers might be justified in taking matters into their own hands.

'Will. That's right, isn't it? That's what happened last time?'

Freer looked uncomfortable but nodded. 'That's exactly what happened last time, so just keep well away from Miller and his friends. No point in us all getting hanged when there's still the Tyrant to defeat.'

Sparrow spluttered, 'But how can we not get involved ...?'

Tranter grimaced. '... seeing as how we'll all be there for the funeral, anyways.'

Freer looked thoughtful. 'So how many are committed, do you think?'

Sparrow hesitated. 'About twenty or thirty, I reckon.'

Freer looked from one to the other. 'Do nothing; just do nothing...'

Sparrow lowered his voice further. 'Nothing?'

Freer ran his hand across his mouth. 'Nothing ... till I say.'

The bugle sounded. Sparrow tugged Tranter's sleeve. 'We've got to go.'

Thomas hung back. 'This isn't just idle talk, is it?'

The bugle sounded again.

Freer motioned Thomas to follow him. 'It might be madness but it's bloody serious.'

~

Thomas glanced around him. The church was cold. The vicar was a thin, sharp-nosed man in ill-fitting, shabby clerical robes. He didn't look well and began to cough as he read the texts from the lectern. Wintergreen's friends seemed to take the parson's spluttering as the final insult to their dead comrade. They fiddled restlessly with their sabres and rattled their sabretaches none too quietly. They looked like men on the brink of losing their tempers but Thomas still prayed that good sense would prevail.

Freer, stationed next to him, looked grim. There could be no more conversation between them now.

~

Lieutenant Charles Webster was angry, angry at the waste of yet another of his soldiers' lives. He and Dickenson had pressed their case on several occasions that the 36th should replace the current garrison in the barracks, but to no avail. And now, seeing poor Wintergreen coughed over by an uncaring cleric, he was even angrier. If this were his living, well, he'd make sure the place was cleaned and polished till it shone with God's love. He couldn't wait for the damned war to be over. All he could see was men losing their patience; and once that happened …

~

Will Freer had never felt so helpless. However much he sympathised with the mutineers' cause, he thought their plans suicidal. But how to head off the ringleaders, whoever they were, before it was too late?

Freer quickly looked around him. Of course. They'll be the pall-bearers. It stands to reason. They were Wintergreen's closest friends. Freer noticed they were beginning to move up the nave towards the coffin where Cornet Wilde and Lieutenant Webster were standing. Freer whispered to Thomas, 'Where are Wilde's and Webster's cover serjeants?' Freer couldn't see them anywhere. He almost wished Fallowfield was back but he was away again recruiting.

'Move forward with me towards Webster,' he whispered. 'Tranter and Sparrow, stay close. This is what we'll do.'

~

Charles Webster had had enough of the vicar's spluttering. He raised his hand, moving towards the startled cleric. 'Would you mind if I said a few words regarding Private Wintergreen?'

The vicar looked almost relieved and concentrated on coughing.

Webster stood beside the coffin. 'In Private Wintergreen we have lost a brave young man, whose friends will miss him dearly. I am sorry, too, that he had to spend the last few precious weeks of his life shivering in a tent in this bitter winter, and ...' Suddenly Wintergreen's half-dozen pall-bearers had turned and surrounded him and Wilde, shouting. Everywhere men were stamping their feet and yelling.

~

Will Freer thought they would be too late, but when the pall-bearers saw Tranter they parted their ranks to let them pass. Tranter, Cowper and Sparrow immediately placed themselves between the officers and the pall-bearers. Tranter signalled the pall-bearers, who now seemed unsure as to whether the officers were being detained or protected, to stay put.

Freer now realised he needed to turn the mutineers' thoughts away from their planned march into the town. But how to get their attention? He motioned the priest to move aside. Sacrilege might just do it. He leapt up onto the altar and waited for the noise to die down as the men realised what he'd done. As soon as he could make himself heard, Freer shouted above the murmur.

'In God's name, listen to me. Standing here on this holy table, I am ready to risk His wrath to save us all from the gallows. You've all heard tell of the mutinies at Nore and Spithead – and you all know how they ended. So how far do you think you are going to get with this business? We're surrounded by other companies of soldiers. Just bloody think about it.

'Finish this now before any more harm's done, and whilst Lieutenant Webster here can still report this as a heartfelt outbreak of grief for a good friend. Let the Lieutenant report instead that we need to be housed in warm barracks and be fed like fighting men not parish paupers.'

Freer took a deep breath and placed his hand on his sabretache containing Paine's *Rights of Man.* 'Give me strength,' he whispered to himself.

'Thomas Paine, a man of great vision and wisdom, has written a book, *Common Sense,* showing how everything we do in this life should obey the laws of common sense. So I ask you, is it common sense to wage this war over a friend's death when it is certain that more men will die – and for nothing? Is that what our good friend Private Wintergreen would have wanted? Does that sound like bloody common sense to you?'

~

Tranter looked at the pall-bearers in the threatening way only a professional pugilist can. 'So are you lads going to carry our friend here out to his grave or not?'

'The six pall-bearers picked up Wintergreen's coffin and carried it out of the church followed by the vicar, trembling and coughing. Cowper and Sparrow brought up the rear, escorting Cornet Wilde and Lieutenant Webster.

As the men, quiet now, began to file out after the coffin, Will Freer climbed down from the altar, brushed some mud off the cloth, bowed momentarily towards the worn image of the crucified Christ and muttered, 'So, strike me down right now or just bloody forget about it.'

Freer walked slowly towards the door and looked on from the porch as Webster insisted on taking his proper place by the graveside to throw in the first scattering of earth. 'Good man,' Freer whispered to himself.

~

Leaving the church behind, Charles Webster resumed his position at the head of the column and tried to digest the morning's events. He had been as shocked as the rest, if not more so, when Freer jumped onto the altar, and had prayed to God that He would forgive Freer even as he commended Wintergreen's soul to His care. He knew he owed Freer and his friends a debt of gratitude, which would have to remain largely unspoken. He had already counselled the young cornet to say merely that the men had been angered by Wintergreen's death and that a few hotheads among them might yet cause trouble if grievances were not met expeditiously. The cornet had quickly understood that their army careers would not be covered in glory should they have to admit the day had only been saved by a loud-mouthed private who had had the temerity to jump up onto an altar and pronounce the virtues of Common Sense. But grateful as he was, Webster felt the whole business would merely add to his sense of dread as he woke up each morning.

~

Charles Webster was relieved to see Cornet Wilde speedily purchase a promotion into another regiment. Private Wintergreen's funeral had weighed heavily on both of them. Whilst he told himself that the men were openly grateful for their rapid transition to barracks living, satisfying both his and their sense of a promise honoured, Webster felt an insidious malaise creeping over his soul. He had little in common with the bluff Dickenson or the other officers in the other troops, who appeared perfectly happy with their lot. Perhaps he too appeared happy to the outside world. Yet he was greatly apprehensive that if he did not make a success of this, his allotted career in life, then his sister Jane and all his family would shake their heads and sigh, *what can anyone do with Charles*?

26

Blatchington Horse Ponds

A hard winter became a hard spring, though with their move into the barracks and a fresh supply of meat, the death rate dropped dramatically and regimental life settled down into a tolerable routine – the only flaw being that Fallowfield had returned from his recruiting mission cock-a-hoop with six new recruits to terrorise.

Thomas was never more grateful for a friend than during those bitter weeks, when Freer found all manner of excuses to watch over him. Then one day, summer suddenly arrived.

Freer stripped to his waist and looked around. 'So who's for a spot of swimming in the horse ponds?'

Thomas frowned. 'It's not that hot.'

Freer snorted. 'Or cold.'

When nobody stirred, Thomas guessed that, like him, no one else could swim; but Freer looked so dejected that Thomas weakened.

'I'll come but I'll not swim.'

~

When Thomas and Freer arrived at the ponds, Freer stripped off and waded with some care into the nearest one.

'Lesson one. Get in the water.'

The pond, fed by a stream, was clear, with vegetation fringing its banks and Freer was soon swimming across it, splashing, and paddling like a dog, his arms rotating like Blatchington windmill sails.

Thomas could scarcely believe it when Freer returned not only safe but happy.

'Come on in. Look, it's just up to your knees, this bit and only up to your chest here.'

Freer held out his arms to Thomas, pulling him through the water and back again to the shore. Then he plunged once more into the water.

'Kick your legs. Look, like this.' Freer kicked his legs up and down, making waves. 'You kick now;' and so Thomas did, until he found himself moving forward, half pulled by his own momentum and half supported by Freer's arms.

'Next trick is to float to prove you won't sink, and you'll find, if you stay calm and breathe steadily, you can't sink.'

Freer turned and lifted Thomas until he was on his back, and, resting on Freer's hand, Thomas duly floated.

'What did I tell you?'

But only for as long as Freer held his hand under the small of Thomas's back; as soon as Freer let go, he completely forgot he'd ever floated, and as his body began to sink, he panicked, kicking his legs so hard they dropped, pulling him below the water. But then he saw Freer's face, heard him yelling to stop thrashing about and before he could sink again Freer had towed him to the side. He pulled him onto the bank and thumped his back until Thomas felt he'd coughed up the entire pond.

Once Thomas had recovered, Freer pulled him back towards the pond.

'What did you used to tell me when I kept falling off Libby? "Get straight back on or you'll never learn;" so

Thomas Cowper, you get straight back in that pond, or else... But listen more carefully this time.'

They had about two hours before stable duties resumed, and Freer poked and kneaded Thomas into a swimming kind of shape over the rest of the morning. Just before noon Freer said,

'Now, like you did last time, but hold out your arms and your legs as wide as they'll go, like one of them starfishes.'

Thomas struggled, kicked his legs, and tried again, stretching out his arms and legs and found himself floating; floating away from his old self and his old worries, floating out of time, his head bobbing up and down in the clear water, his eyes fixed on the blue sky, counting the clouds drifting slowly into the distance. He felt his body melt away, his muscles unresisting. He stretched his neck and head further back, gradually spreading out his arms and legs as Freer had taught him.

He was burning ... bright ... like a star.

27

A Resort of Quality

Hythe, August 1806

Dear Grace,

I am promoted to Corporal, which means I am now on the path to fulfilling my hopes faster than I had ever imagined. My friend Freer too has been promoted, which is equally pleasing to me.

Freer and Thomas were sure that their new ranks had been proposed by Webster as an acknowledgment for their part in averting the threatened mutiny at Wintergreen's funeral. But Thomas harboured no qualms about the outcome; this was different from the Quilley business, as he and Freer had taken to calling Quilley's death. Their preventive action had carried the day and saved many lives – unlike the preventive men set on by the government to catch the local smugglers, Freer joked. Not that he intended to tell Grace now exactly why his promotion had been so rapid, but maybe one day…

We are now in Hythe, which is on the coast also, but in the neighbouring county of Kent. We were fortunate to take up residence immediately in well-appointed barracks in wooden huts built from overlapping slats, rather like the boats you find around here. This is a much bigger and pleasanter town than Seaford, with a multitude of places for the gentry to assemble, even a theatre. They say it was set to become one of these new sea-bathing resorts, before the war. For the present the beach is better stocked with fortifications and building works than it is with bathing huts. So I have yet to see one of those ingenious structures. One day perhaps I shall visit the famous Brighthelmstone.

In the meantime, the foreshore is filled with the noise of construction work of all kinds; hammering and sawing, the breaking of stones and the banging of bricks, for everywhere you turn they are building Martello towers.

They are also building, following General Moore's plans, a canal to act as a further barrier should Boney ever manage to cross these waters. So, whilst our patrols are small in number, we will be able to give such advance warning that the telegraph shutters will signal their messages all the way to London and back, before so much as one Frenchman can escape from his boat. So do not fear, Grace; these shores are fortified by the stoutest and boldest of men.

As he recalled the fierce debates Freer had had about the effectiveness of this canal, Thomas hesitated before writing this, but if the famous General Moore had recommended the canal's construction then he felt sure it would serve its military purpose. He turned back to his letter.

I send my regards and utmost reassurances that we will fight and do our duty and never let this tyrant land his men upon England's fair shores.

Thomas felt his face flush. He knew his last words to be as much of a copy of Dickenson's talk last week as he could recall. He remembered, though, how stirring the Captain's words had been. Then again, he remembered that the protection of the great shoreline was shared with local militia and yeomanry, and he'd seen the local militia practising their drill, some of them without flintlocks, some with only pitchforks. As for the gentlemen yeomanry, although he knew that they had fine horses, he could also see that they were not men used to taking orders. Still, it was said that men fight hardest to defend their own lands. This would be where the militia and yeomanry would have an advantage, for Thomas had yet to feel that this coast, protected only by sand and shingles, was truly his home. But where was home?

He slowly dipped his pen once more into the ink.

Perhaps one day you and I may stand on these shores as man and wife and see such wonders together. One day when all talk of Boney has long gone.

Thomas was surprised to find his declaration of future intentions to Grace flowing so easily onto the page and felt pleasure, or possibly relief, as he pictured her opening his letter, her unruly auburn hair falling across her forehead as she read it.

I look forward to any news regarding my family and my late mother, but also, of course, particularly about yourself, whom I hold in the highest regard.

Thomas had heard this phrase a few times; Lieutenant Webster had used it when speaking of his sister in Scotland. Thomas thought it a phrase worth bestowing upon Grace.

~

Walking up at first light to the most distant top field in Burton, Grace hadn't wanted to cry, but now, far away from Sarah's prying eyes, her resolve began to crumble. She hadn't ever wanted to feel sorry for Thomas, even when he told her about being in the firing squad which had killed his friend. Of course you'd feel upset if you'd had to do that, but as she told herself, what do you expect if you go off to be a soldier?

As for his mother, Grace had been glad to hear he'd been upset when she died. Otherwise she would have thought him a complete monster. But whether his mother had ever forgiven him she didn't really know. She'd spoken to her and done her best to convey Thomas's regrets over their last argument. Grace had also asked Mary directly about her accusing Thomas of killing Michael, but she had been even more absent in mind during the last few weeks of her life, talking to Michael as though he was still alive, saying no man or woman is born without sin, but only God knows if they are to be saved or damned. Grace had dismissed these further ramblings as those of a mad woman but there had been something about them that had unsettled her.

So how could she even be sure his mother had understood anything, especially that Thomas begged her forgiveness? Admittedly, Mary had smiled and stroked her hand whenever Grace had told her that Thomas loved her and had gone away to fight for his country, but Grace dared say nothing about Thomas to anyone else, even to Hannah, who had seemed more upset by Thomas's absence than Michael's death. As for his father blaming Thomas for his mother's death, she almost began to feel sorry for Thomas, though the way he'd treated his mother at the funeral was still unforgivable. So when she read his letters she tried her hardest not to let her heart linger on the page, for she had not the strength of character to put them away or burn them unopened, which was probably just as well, as Thomas had now sent her the rest of his bounty money.

Did he therefore consider them betrothed? To keep sending her letters regardless of whether she replied was just too difficult for words. She didn't want to love Thomas. She wished she didn't, and that there was somebody else better. But when she looked round the village, she could see there were none to match him. Only Michael that Christmas had come close to stealing her heart away from Thomas, but Michael had been a spoilt boy who thought far too much of himself; though sometimes it seemed Thomas too was cut from the same cloth. But she'd always loved Thomas, and just to see him once more would probably have melted all her resolve. But, at a distance, she could still stay cross with him, until his last letter when he wrote: *Perhaps one day you and I may stand on these shores as man and wife and see such wonders together. One day when all talk of Boney has long gone.*

She burst into tears and began sobbing so hard she understood how Mistress Cowper might have died of grief. She pictured Thomas in those distant barracks, patrolling the shores, longing for them to be together again.

She stood up, straightened her skirt, spitting on the back of her pinafore to rub her face clean. She would have to be presentable when she arrived at the Hall for her interview.

~

Bailiff Strutt had done everything he could to prepare her for the scrutiny she would undergo by the Squire's housekeeper, but she was still taken aback by Mrs Robert's air of open hostility. Mrs Roberts firstly took her hands, but not in welcome.

'Over the years I've found this to be one of the most reliable ways of judging a young girl's character,' she announced, turning Grace's hands over several times to examine them.

'I would naturally expect a dairymaid's hands to be kept soft and clean, but the number of times I've seen perfectly respectable girls let themselves down by the state of their nails: bitten down to the quick, indicating a nervous disposition; too jagged to handle delicate fabrics; too long to grip tightly what must be carried up and down stairs in a gentleman's household; or too smooth to show she has ever worked for a living.'

After several minutes of further questioning on Grace's understanding as to an indoor servant's work, Mrs Roberts eventually dismissed her.

'Well, Burnaby, all seems satisfactory enough. You will start as soon as Bailiff Strutt indicates when it is convenient for him that you leave your current duties. I have generally found Bailiff Strutt's recommendations to have been reliable enough in the past, but with men I find I have to be sure they haven't had their heads turned by a pretty young girl; and while I'm on the subject, Bailiff Strutt did assure me that you are not walking out with a sweetheart. That is one of the things which is strictly forbidden whilst you live under Squire Rearsby's roof.'

Mrs Roberts paused, clearly waiting to receive Grace's own assurances.

The Hall was probably far enough away from the village for Mrs Roberts not to have heard about Thomas, and as Bailiff Strutt had not mentioned him either ...

'That is correct, Mrs Roberts,' Grace nodded. 'Bailiff Strutt is right. I am not walking out with any sweetheart.'

28

Brought to Account

March 1807, Hythe, Kent

Thomas sighed and returned to sifting through the heaps in front of him. 'What a mess.'

Freer nodded. 'You can see why Dickenson ordered us to help Webster.'

'Aye, but he's hardly welcoming us with open arms.'

Thomas liked Webster, but when he'd spoken to them earlier Webster had seemed reluctant to accept their assistance. Still, Thomas could see why Lieutenant Webster might be wary of having two lowly corporals to help when Serjeant Fallowfield had clearly failed in the task, but Captain Dickenson had been emphatic that Webster had been allocated their help whether he wanted it or not. The winter equipment and provisions accounts were to be sorted out immediately, and as Dickenson knew for a fact that Freer had kept his master's books in a shipshape manner, that was that. Orders were orders.

Freer bent down to pick up a piece of paper which had wafted under the table. 'That's why I said quite plainly to Webster it would be better to leave us to it and for him to do something else until we needed to speak to him.'

Thomas was always amazed by Freer's confident manner around Webster. Freer was undoubtedly a favourite of the

Lieutenant's whilst Captain Dickenson continued to have every faith in his personal boot maker. So here they were, surrounded by bits of paper and half-filled ledgers.

To his right, Thomas had assembled all the dockets he could find which indicated expenditure on supplies and provisions, and to his left, Freer had piled any acknowledgements of goods received and distributed within the regiment. In the middle was a large sheet of paper, ruled across with columns and rows, which he and Thomas had carefully drawn up. Freer explained that his master had not only taught him his shoemaking trade, but also the keeping of strict financial records, and this would be the only way to rescue Lieutenant Webster's seriously muddled accounts.

Thomas sucked the end of a stubby little pencil, while Freer continued to look under the table for stray dockets. Thomas sighed again. Things simply didn't add up. The column of sums of money paid out, and for what purposes, were now written against each other side-by-side, with bundled receipts matching the sums neatly ordered and satisfyingly accounted for. But there were also some columns of figures imported from Fallowfield's accounts, for which there were no matching receipts. Thomas now marked these solemnly with a question mark, and on the other side of the table there were distressingly few dockets to indicate where some of these goods had got to.

'Freer. You come and have a look. I can't make them add up at all.'

'All right, so long as you look through these piles in the drawers again.'

Thomas took out the desk drawers to search more systematically through Webster's sheaves of drawings and sketches, looking for any receipts that might have become lodged between the sheets. But there were no more to be found.

Freer soon called him back to look at the accounts. 'Do you see what I see?'

Thomas and Freer stared at the remaining gaps in the columns. The major gaps had begun to develop at the very same time that Fallowfield had taken over the day-to-day management of the accounts.

Freer clapped his hands with delight. 'Well, kiss my arse. We have our answer. Fallowfield.'

Suddenly the door was flung open and Fallowfield himself walked in as though he had not a care in the world, clutching a bundle of assorted dockets. Thomas prayed that he hadn't overheard Freer's triumphant cry of discovery.

Thomas and Freer both stood up. Signalling them to sit down again, Fallowfield lobbed his bundle right into the middle of the table, instantly upsetting their labelled heaps.

'You'll be needing these too.'

Thomas hastily tried to rearrange their papers whilst Fallowfield stood watching with that expansive and affable manner he'd displayed at The Blue Boar. Yet from the intensity of Fallowfield's gaze, it was clear to Thomas that he was not as relaxed as he was trying to appear.

'If you happened by The Oak tonight, we could talk about various matters of interest.'

Thomas was still trying to digest what this might mean when Freer replied with a degree of caution Thomas rarely saw him exercise.

'Thank you, Serjeant. If we get finished in time.'

Fallowfield's jaw twitched. 'There are things about Lieutenant Webster you should know.'

Freer looked him straight in the eye. 'I don't think it's our place to know anything about Lieutenant Webster, Serjeant.'

Fallowfield smiled. 'Like Captain Dickenson should know some more things about you. Like the time you and

Cowper were down Brewhouse Yard, making yourselves out to be loyal subjects whilst all the time you were stirring up mischief and spreading sedition.'

Fallowfield turned sharply on his heel and left, slamming the door behind him.

Thomas picked up the extra dockets.

Freer was furious. 'Bloody man never does a thing without trying to blame someone, and now he's trying to get Lieutenant Webster into trouble too.'

Thomas nodded. Freer, in spite of his grumbles about the officer class, had a soft spot for Webster. Thomas could see Fallowfield had misjudged matters if he was trying to implicate Lieutenant Webster in any wrongdoing.

Thomas muttered, 'And us and all ...'

Thomas knew about the penalty for spreading sedition ... real and imagined. It was one of the many homilies he'd heard from Freer about the iniquities of Thomas Paine's death sentence for writing *The Rights of Man*. Freer banged Fallowfield's papers down. 'Just let him try ...'

But Thomas recalled the figures in the shadows in Nottingham and felt the chill of Fallowfield's threat slither down his spine.

'I told you there was this man there writing down what you were saying.'

Freer straightened up. 'What kind of man?'

'Does that matter?'

Freer sniffed. 'Course it does. S'only his word against mine if he ain't a pillar of the community, and no pillar of the community is going to admit he was down Brew House Yard on a night, is he?'

Thomas, having finished reshuffling the old heaps, shrugged his shoulders.

'Who knows? He could have been a spy.'

Waving away Thomas's concerns, Freer pounced on the neat piles. 'Come on. Let's start matching Fallowfield's pile of dockets against the figures.'

But they'd no sooner begun than Thomas became uneasy again. He wasn't exactly sure why, as they seemed to tally, but there had been one item in particular, the replacement saddle for Sparrow, now accounted for by one of Fallowfield's new dockets, which Thomas knew must have been fabricated. The certain knowledge that Sparrow had not been issued with a new saddle to replace the one Freer had temporarily patched over eighteen months ago started to cast doubts upon the rest of the dockets. Sparrow's saddle was certainly not newly issued and by now it was in such poor condition again it might just end up killing the man. That was not a matter he could ignore; and he would not do so. He began to examine the other receipts with even greater care.

There was a faint familiarity about the hand on all of these receipts, although efforts had been made to adopt a variety of different signatures. Thomas began to identify certain similarities; in the way the flourishes flowed, the way circles didn't quite close and the certainty of the downward strokes, which dominated the line in an identical manner. All suggested someone was trying to disguise the fact that the signatures were by the same hand. Thomas looked again at the items listed. Oats? Horses had been without oats now for over a week. Fallowfield had told the men that there had been problems of supply and that they would have do as best they could, as it was nearly summer. Thomas hesitated. The one thing that Fallowfield cared about was their horses. Surely he wouldn't have deprived their horses of oats? Yet here was the order and receipt to say they were paid for and delivered. It wasn't exactly proof of Fallowfield's ill-doing, but Thomas felt queasy they might be about to discover even more discrepancies.

'Freer, come over here and see what you think about these signatures.'

Freer sat down as instructed and scrutinised the papers Thomas handed him.

'They're by the same hand, aren't they?'

'I'd say so.'

'Fallowfield?'

'Probably, but who's going to believe us? Who's Webster going to believe?' Thomas doubted that anyone would want to think that this gap in supplies might be down to straightforward thieving, even before any of the less scrupulous dragoons got their hands on extra fodder to sell. Besides, they were so recently promoted and Fallowfield was a serjeant of such long standing, he continued to be sent on recruiting missions and to hold other positions of responsibility. Of course, like most recruiting serjeants he robbed his new recruits of most of their bounty, and Thomas now realised this went without saying. But to rob his horses and men of proper food and equipment, and so damage their battle readiness? They ought to tell Webster. But what if the Lieutenant had been party to this as well?

'Supposing he's right?'

Freer leant forward. 'About what?'

'Fallowfield saying there were things about Webster we should know.'

'That's Fallowfield for you. The only problem with Webster is ... well, he should have been a painter or a man of letters but never an army officer, and you know what Fallowfield's like. He'll just bluster his way out of it, accusing us of everything you can think of, and Webster will hardly get a word in edgeways.'

'So what do we do then?'

'Let's show Webster what we've found and let him decide.'

Thomas was surprised. This didn't sound like the combative Freer he knew, who once would have wanted Fallowfield court-martialled, at the very least.

Thomas sat staring at the piles of paper, then picked up his pencil and began to ring the similarities of handwriting on the dockets Fallowfield had brought in. So they would merely bring to Lieutenant Webster's attention that the last six receipts appeared to have been written by the same individual, as shown by the pencil marks, without any obvious connection being made with Fallowfield.

29

What's to be done?

Lieutenant Charles Webster stared at the piles of dockets in front of him. All Dickenson had asked Cowper and Freer to do was to tidy up the papers enough to present a passing resemblance to some order, not launch a hunt for exactitude. And now they expected him to deal with this as well.

'So, what is it that you suspect?'

'It's just that in these last dockets, sir, the writing on the dockets seems similar.' Cowper explained.

'And do you think that is something which should concern me?'

'Only if you wish to be concerned, sir', Freer replied.

Webster sighed with relief. So they didn't want him to report this to Dickenson after all.

'Then I am sure there is some satisfactory explanation.'

'Yes. I quite understand sir, that this isn't a matter of great concern to you,' Freer replied.

'Good.'

'But we still thought we should bring it to your attention.' Cowper didn't seem to want to let it go. Webster looked the man as squarely in the eye as he dared, and tried to smile. Corporal Cowper was known for being quietly persistent.

'Of course, you were absolutely right to bring it to my attention.'

He stood up, walked to the window and then turned to the two men. 'So we are settled.'

But even with such a clear signal that they were being dismissed, Cowper managed to have the last word. 'Then these are now ready to present to the Paymaster, sir?'

'Indeed they are.'

'But ... Private Sparrow's saddle, sir. I'm concerned that if we don't obtain a new one we may put the man's life in some danger.'

Webster swallowed hard. The money for a cavalry saddle would be hard to lay his hands on, but Cowper was right. Sparrow should not be put at any more risk. 'I will attend to that.'

'Understood, sir.'

Webster inclined his head. 'Well done. You have preserved the reputation of the company for sound organisation in a most thorough and diligent manner.'

'Thank you, sir,' Freer and Cowper chorused.

Freer turned, Cowper followed and both marched out of the room, their faces slightly pink, but their manner entirely respectful.

Webster felt both relieved and ashamed. It was Fallowfield who had first suggested using the genuine muddle of his accounts to cover some modest diversion of monies directly to themselves. Fallowfield had somehow discovered that Webster was sinking under his debts. Hythe had proved far too expensive a place for him to keep up his spirits and, as Fallowfield had also discovered, there were far too many opportunities for purchasing French *objets d'art* and all manner of contraband which the locals smuggled across from France. Not that he gambled or drank to excess like Fallowfield, but he now would have to find other ways of distracting himself from the deepening troughs of military life. His situation was not of his choosing, but as his father had said after purchasing his first cavalry commission for him, 'Choice? What choice?'

Webster walked over to the window and looked at the distant expanse of the English Channel before him. He remembered the brief months of peace in 1802, and his first visit to Paris; its gravelled gardens, criss-crossed with limes and chestnuts; the marble Italian sculptures he had sketched in the salons of the Louvre; the shattered remnants of figured stonework on the great façade of Notre Dame.

Webster sighed, for when the Regiment moved back to Hounslow he would be faced with a London life to fund, not that he would ever be persuaded to do such a thing again. But he imagined now he would always have Fallowfield at his back, reminding him of his obligations, threatening him in that oblique way of his. But perhaps, perhaps he might persuade Dickenson to transfer Fallowfield out of C troop to A troop before the newly commissioned captain of A troop finally arrived?

Webster bent his head quickly in prayer. Having the Serjeant transferred would be a devious enough act; but as for the other transgressions, what was to be done? Would God forgive him? Not if he failed to find the means to purchase Private Sparrow a new saddle, he reminded himself as the memory of Cowper's disapproving tone once again pricked his conscience.

~

'Fallowfield's bloody well got to him too.'

Freer stamped down to the shore, his limp more apparent than usual, though Thomas could hardly keep up with him. It was dark and cold and not the best evening to be off to The Hope.

Freer was in a foul mood. His immediate disappointment with Lieutenant Webster was sharpened by the discovery that Thomas had just received a letter from Louise Young. Freer had noticed her flowing hand on the envelope Thomas tried to hide from him.

'It's for a very good reason that Louise has written to me alone. Please trust me, Will.' He tried to reassure Freer yet again.

Freer grunted disbelievingly.

Thomas repeated, 'She has sworn me to secrecy.'

Freer wheeled round. 'What about?' You must be able to tell me something.'

'Just wait and see.'

Thomas tried to keep a straight face. Surely Freer must suspect what the secret was by now, though Thomas had said only that it would be the best of surprises.

And so it was, for as they made their way into the low rooms of The Hope Tavern, there, as arranged, sitting in the best room in a corner by the fire, was Louise. Thomas took one look at their faces. It confirmed what he'd been telling Freer ever since they'd left Romford over eighteen months ago; that whilst Miss Louise Young might value the friendship of both of them, it was Freer she had the greater affection for; and here she was to prove it, having contrived to visit her aunt, who lived in the very next village. As Louise had already instructed, Thomas was to do his best to distract the aunt in conversation, so Louise could talk to Freer unimpeded.

Thomas looked away to hide the tears welling up in his eyes, fearful he might lose both his friends to each other. As for the ill-doings of Fallowfield and his obvious sway over Webster, what could any of them do about that?

~

If only that had been the end of it. If only Fallowfield hadn't decided that this was a good moment to take to Captain Dickenson his Nottingham's informant's reports about Freer and his seditious remarks made in one of the town's most notorious taverns. 'Soldiers in their cups say all kinds of foolish things,' Dickenson had calmly remarked as he instructed Webster to dock a week's pay for drunken behaviour … a minor blemish on Freer's record. Thomas shuddered to imagine Fallowfield's reaction.

Still, for the time being, Freer was at least assured of Dickenson's renewed confidence in his bootmaker's loyalty. Freer raised his tankard and whispered to Thomas, 'Next time I'm as drunk as I was that night in Nottingham, knock me out first, will you?'

Thomas smiled and clapped Freer on the back. If only he had his friend's unending optimism that he would be able to keep on getting the better of Fallowfield. Thomas judged Fallowfield to be a man not given to accepting defeat. So Thomas was mightily relieved to see Dickenson allocate Fallowfield to more recruiting party duties back in the Midlands.

30

Royal Escort Duty

Summer 1808, Hampton Court

Thomas stared at the running-damp walls of their Hampton Court barracks and wished himself back in Hythe.

It was the arrival of Private Harry Byrne that had also helped make that summer of two years ago one to remember. Byrne had originally been a paid substitute in the militia before enlisting in the Regular Army. Agricultural labourer, it said on his enlistment papers, but his true trade was cricketer, playing for his master against other gentlemen's estate teams. As he never tired of pointing out, his cricketing skills could mean the difference between his master winning or losing a wager of hundreds of guineas; and so, ever since he'd joined the Regiment he'd been threatening to set up a cricket team, or rather two cricket teams, so that they could play each other – once he could find a decent-sized bit of ground. A game of Gentlemen versus Players or Other Ranks playing Officers was his ultimate aim, for Byrne was a man determined to give his betters a run for their money. So to hell with it; Byrne was going to teach them how to play cricket according to Essex rules and Byrne's own ideas of fair play – which he did.

Sparrow at last had a new saddle; Lieutenant Webster had taken up sketching local churches; and Dickenson and Fallowfield were away recruiting.

But most important of all, Grace was now writing regularly to Thomas as though she might just have forgiven him. Freer agreed too that it was the happiest of times. With Louise's extended visit to her aunt in Shorncliffe, he and Louise had been able to advance their courtship under less watchful eyes than her father's.

It couldn't last and it didn't. The Regiment was moved back to Hounslow before being shifted to Hampton to undertake royal escort duties. But their present quarters at Hampton Court, although pleasing to the eye, suffered greatly from cold and damp. Freer, only half in jest, claimed that the waters of the great Thames itself must have been fed by the streams of moisture which ran down their barrack-room walls. Freer, though, seemed to thrive on their closer involvement in national events, however fleetingly.

Today, they were to accompany King George to St James's Palace to receive foreign ambassadors. Freer, as well informed as ever, had found out from Lieutenant Webster that Britain had acquired some new allies who were in the mood to fight Boney: the Spanish and Portuguese governments in exile.

Freer was in a high state of excitement. 'What did the Tyrant think the Spanish people would do when he marched in and put his own brother on the throne? And as for his claim on Portugal ... '

Thomas too was looking forward to their week's stay in London, but for quite another reason. Grace was in town with Squire Rearsby's household. She had, at first, thought the family might be visiting London earlier in the year, though she also reported there was talk of Mistress Rearsby taking the waters at Scarborough Spa on account of her recent stomach troubles. Thomas had written back immediately, urging Grace to get her mistress to try one of his grandmother's remedies to be found in the Reverend Crabbe's book rather than travel to Scarborough. Besides, there were always Burton's own medicinal waters. Had she not tried them?

Thomas by now had convinced himself that Grace's coming to London would be perfect. He would make amends for everything, ask her to marry him, and somehow they would work out what to do about getting permission from the Regiment. Freer had already devised a plan to convince Captain Dickenson to grant him permission to marry Louise as soon as they returned to Romford. But Freer's engagement to Louise had to remain secret until the day came when he could reassure her father that he could support her. Truth be told, Freer suspected that Landlord Young would be the main obstacle to their happiness.

~

The Rearsby family were staying somewhere close to St James's Park. Grace suggested meeting there one afternoon if Thomas was on duty at the Palace. Thomas knew the Park well as it was close to Horse Guards, in whose huge white buildings decisions about all matters cavalry were made. They'd arranged to meet by the canal, midway along, under the right-hand avenue of trees facing towards the Queen's House. It was as precise a location as Grace could suggest.

Arriving slightly after the agreed time, Thomas thought Grace must have decided not to wait for him. But then he noticed an elegantly dressed lady some hundred yards away. Surely that couldn't be Grace? He moved slowly towards the distant woman, half hoping it was, half hoping it wasn't. In the three years since he'd last seen her she might well have changed.

~

It was her. Thomas took a deep breath and moved forward, calling her name, smiling, holding out his hand to her. Grace turned and smiled back. Thomas wiped his hand again on his breeches. Grace was more than ever like her name. She had grown at least three inches, her auburn hair now curling neatly under a straw bonnet. Wearing shoes and clothes probably once fashionable enough for her mistress to have worn, she even held herself like a gentlewoman. What could he say to her? He thought of her happy letters and saw she'd blossomed in a way he doubted he had. He felt a tiredness in his jaw and weariness in his eyes; and they'd not even had a chance to fight Boney yet.

Thomas blurted out, 'You look more beautiful than ever, Grace.' He blushed.

Grace smiled and pushed a curl back under her bonnet. 'I must say, Thomas Cowper, you cut a fine figure in your uniform.'

Thomas offered her his arm, as he had seen many a gentleman do. It was hardly the way they would have greeted each other in Burton, but Grace seemed happy to accept the civility.

Thomas smiled. 'I couldn't bring my horse. You'd like my horse, Grace.'

Grace nodded. 'Fearless? Yes. She sounds like another good friend to you, like Ramillies and Blenheim.'

Thomas turned to kiss Grace quickly on the cheek. 'How lovely it is to see you again.'

Grace blushed and whispered back, 'Remember now, Thomas, if we see anyone of my acquaintance, you are my cousin from Leicester. I am ruled by the fiercest of housekeepers, who forbids sweethearts.'

Thomas nodded but couldn't have felt more despondent. Clearly the last thing Grace wanted to do was jeopardise her steady rise through the Rearsby household's hierarchy of servants. What had he to offer? He almost wished them back in Burton, where nobody worried when they snatched a kiss on May Day or after Harvest Supper, or at any other time for that matter.

Thomas's face reddened again. 'I don't suppose you see very much of my father and sisters now you live at the Hall.'

Grace paused and looked at her feet. 'Just at church but not really to speak to.'

Thomas straightened his jacket. 'And your family?'

'My mother is in good spirits and Sarah's much the same as ever.'

Thomas nodded. 'Still causing mischief?'

Grace said, without looking at Thomas, 'I know you must think it was all Sarah's fault and, in truth, I'm glad to be away from home and the dairy. I'm sure Bailiff Strutt finds her trying too.'

Thomas stared straight ahead at the path, not daring to turn and look at her.

But then Grace stopped, disentangled her arm from Thomas's and turned to face him.

'I'm truly sorry about your mother. She was always very kind to me. It was difficult for everyone when she lost her wits.'

Thomas pressed her. 'There wasn't anything more she said or you've been able to remember since... about Michael?'

Grace shook her head. 'She talked a great deal about you both, but then sometimes she seemed not to know the difference between you. None of it made much sense.'

Thomas sighed. 'I only wish I hadn't lost my temper ...'

Grace touched his hand. 'Even if she wasn't in her right mind, it was a very provoking thing to say about you and Michael. I hadn't realised exactly what she'd said till you wrote and told me.'

But what if it was true? He wanted to shout out. What if I did kill Michael on account of him being the favourite, on account of him trying to steal you away from me? Suppose my mother was right?

He must have looked as absent as he felt, for Grace tugged at his sleeve. 'Thomas? Breathe in deep now. Breathe slowly. Remember what your grandmother told you.'

He finally gathered his wits. 'I was just thinking.'

Grace started to apologise. 'You looked so far away I thought you were having one of your turns.'

He tried again to reassure her. 'I don't have so many of those nowadays.'

Grace smiled. 'That's good, then.'

Thomas cleared his throat. 'So, Hannah and the little ones? Are they well?'

Grace seemed doubtful. 'Hannah is much grown now and has carried the world's troubles on her shoulders ever since Michael died. She has a good deal of responsibility looking after the little ones and your father, who's no better in temper.'

'He doesn't beat the girls though? He doesn't hurt them, does he?'

Grace touched his hand again. 'I've never heard tell of that. It was only you he used to beat; everyone in the village knew that.'

Thomas flinched at the thought of the whole village regarding him as an object of their pity, as mad as his mother, and therefore, unsurprisingly, horsewhipped by an exasperated father.

As they walked on, Grace began to explain why they were in London even though it was the end of the season. 'Squire Rearsby has just purchased a cornet's commission for Master Andrew, and they are here to see him leave for active duty.'

Thomas blinked. 'I thought Master Andrew more interested in his books than the War.'

Grace nodded. 'But he's left the University now and with Master Welby helping to run the estate, I suppose Master Andrew feels he must do his duty like everyone else and fight Boney.' Grace squeezed his arm.

Thomas smiled back at her. 'So, which regiment has he joined?'

Grace shook her head. 'I'm not sure, but it's one of those going to Spain. Master Andrew has high hopes of General Moore bringing the War to an end.'

Thomas squeezed her arm back. It was what they all hoped for when they'd heard the news of a fresh expedition to the Peninsula. Grace continued, 'But I fear that may be too much to expect of one man.'

Thomas smiled. 'You're right. It's a good deal to ask of anyone. But if anyone can do it, he can. He's not only a good soldier, he's of good character too, I hear.'

Grace placed her hand over his. 'So are you, Thomas. And so are you.' She pulled a face. 'Most of the time.'

Hearing her words of praise, he finally understood that he couldn't ask her to marry him that day. Not until such time as he could provide for her properly, and what was even more important, not until such time as he too could truly believe himself to be of good character.

31

Disaster

June 1809, Goodwin Sands, Deal

Thomas couldn't be entirely sure, but it was probably Landlord Charlie Filmer who'd first suggested the match that evening back in January when Sparrow had burst into The Three Kings looking as if Napoleon himself had landed on the foreshore.

'Moore's men are back into Portsmouth, half dead, with everything they possessed left behind.'

'Slow down, Sparrow. It'll be another one of those bloody rumours.' Tranter took a sip of ale and went back to his game of goose.

'No, it's true I'm telling you. Nine thousand, they reckon they've lost. General Moore and all.' Sparrow was now quite pink. 'All dead.'

Sparrow's sweetheart Jeannie lived in Shorncliffe and the village kept up with all the news on General Moore. So the chances were, Sparrow was right.

Suddenly everybody was listening and Sparrow was the centre of attention.

Byrne banged his fist on the table. 'We'll be losing all our best generals before they're even sent out to bat.'

Freer responded with a grim smile. 'Moore was supposed to be bowling the French out, not defending the damn wicket. That's supposed to be our job, isn't it?'

Everybody laughed; there was little use in crying. But victory seemed further away than ever to Thomas. Was this war never going to end? How were they going to defeat Boney now they were back on the south coast again, dodging the smugglers and the raids of the preventive men, while still on the look-out for Boney's invading forces?

Sparrow's news prompted Landlord Filmer to ask how Moore's body had been transported back but Sparrow interrupted him mid-flow. 'He was buried in Spain at …' Sparrow sniffed and wrinkled up his nose. '… a place called Corunna.'

Tranter spat out some phlegm. 'Can't have thought him worth the bother of fetching home …'

'There'd have been an outcry if they hadn't brought Nelson back,' Landlord Filmer pronounced, warming to his theme as he reminisced: not only how Nelson himself once graced those very rooms, but how the hero's body had been transported home along this very same coast.

'It might have been preserved in a barrel of French brandy, but they didn't reckon on having to shelter in the Downs for an extra three days, did they? You should have seen the flags in the Navy Yard and the Customs House flying at half-mast, while our little boats lowered their pennants. It was a sight to behold. Made you proud, it did. Three days it took them before they could get up the Thames. Mind, with a storm like they had, they were lucky not to get blown onto the Goodwins. That would have done for them, to a man.'

Although Thomas had heard the story many times before, he found that this account of Nelson's last sea journey still had the power to move him.

Thomas had a soft spot too for Charlie Filmer, whose delight in re-telling his stock of stories was almost as great as his skill at secreting the supplies of contraband that flowed through his cellar. Those who knew about the rich pickings to be made on these shores spoke of The Three Kings' landlord with some awe.

Thomas stared out through the front window, ignoring the banter and speculation about what else could be done about the War. He listened instead to the steady flow of icy waves tugging at the steep shingle bank where the Deal men stacked their luggers, mile after lonely mile.

It was as they slurred into their fifth round of toasts to the life and death of General Moore, that the equally tipsy landlord suggested they might crown their wake with a drop of fine French brandy he just happened to have by; but only on condition Byrne let him organise the betting on one of his much-talked-about regimental cricket matches; the ones Filmer had heard so much about but had never witnessed.

'As long as you can find me a decent pitch not overrun with fortifications ... or farmers for that matter. You'd think we were Boney himself the way they scowl at us. No wonder Dickenson's always moaning there's nowhere to drill without their damn hedges and ditches getting in our way.'

So Filmer's idea was to organise a match on the great expanse of the Goodwin Sands, the great ship-swallowers, which revealed themselves at low tides. He assured them that expeditions were regularly arranged to explore these perilous banks; and the match was no sooner proposed than organised ... for that summer. Filmer would pay for expert boatmen to take them out and Byrne would assemble a couple of smaller teams from their main regimental team. The landlord would provide an umpire, several barrels of ale and a few hand-picked spectators to cheer them on.

~

It had all seemed so simple, which was why they now found themselves clambering in the June heat across a vast becalmed sandscape, lugging their casks of ale and cricketing paraphernalia around its many pools and ridges and deep gullies full of water. They eventually found a pitch dry and flat enough to begin the game, cheerfully marking out its boundaries with their casks of ale.

Thomas scrutinised them with a renewed interest as laughing and joking they set about their allotted tasks. Who would he have picked to play against Napoleon?

Murphy, rough rider and drummer, only just tall enough to be a cavalryman? Tranter, with no front teeth and a crooked nose, but with far more vanity about his charms than his looks deserved? Sparrow, as tall as they came, and so bashful, with his chin tucked in but his stomach pushed out like a bewildered dancing bear that's had its claws pulled?

~

It was Sparrow's turn to bat. He defended his wicket with such tenacity that all the bowlers, but especially Josh Tranter, began to curse; then, growing in confidence, he hit the balls so hard they disappeared into the gullies and other distant dips in the sand. Tranter was the Regiment's best bowler, but he usually played on the same team as Sparrow and hadn't come across such stubborn resistance before. Thomas began to fret that the more Tranter was humiliated by Sparrow's increasing score of runs, the more of Charlie Filmer's ale he would consume. Someone would have to take him off soon, before he got too drunk to bowl. Looking around him, Thomas wondered if maybe all of them were getting too drunk to play.

Gradually the sky began to darken as a wind got up from the sea. The weather was changing. But Charlie's friend, the umpire, no doubt mindful of the bets placed upon the outcome, insisted they played on as agreed until the approach of sunset, and so Thomas tried to turn his mind once again to the game. Soon he could hardly stand up for the force of the wind. The boatmen started to shout. But Sparrow refused to move and it was only when Tranter finally bowled him out that they comprehended what the boatmen had been shouting. Byrne hurriedly picked up the remaining balls and bats and Thomas yelled,

'Get back to the boats.'

But Tranter suddenly remembered he'd left a cask of ale behind.

'I'm not leaving a whole bloody barrel.' He turned back and was gone.

The wind began to blow even more violently and the party quickly sobered up as they realised the danger. They all shouted for Tranter, telling him to hurry up, but Thomas, realising Tranter could be some time, urged Freer and those who were ready to take the luggers whilst he waited in the smallest boat for Tranter to return. Sparrow too decided to wait, hunched in the bow as if still guarding his wicket. Thomas had never been more relieved than when he saw Tranter reappear, but the man was in such haste that he fell heavily into the boat just as a flurry of waves hit, tipping all three of them into the water.

As the nearest boatman tried to turn his boat back towards them, Thomas immediately realised his difficulty. He knew neither Sparrow nor Tranter could swim, and Sparrow already looked set to drown, his head bobbing for a few moments above the waves before dipping below them once more. Thomas could only help one of them. He looked around for Tranter, who was still clutching his cask of ale; he would likely stay afloat until the boatman reached him. Thomas swam closer to Sparrow and shoved a cricket bat under the man's chin, somehow keeping his head above the water as he pushed, pulled and dragged him to the lugger. Freer and the others leant over to haul them both to safety, all the time shouting to Tranter, bobbing in the water some distance away, that he must keep kicking his legs. Hindered by the now heavy rain, the boatmen were finally able to row towards him, but suddenly he was nowhere to be seen. They shouted louder. They cried, they yelled, they cursed; but Tranter was gone. They couldn't believe it. Tranter was strong. He would find a way to clamber back onto the Sands. He'd be back on the Goodwins somewhere safe. Thomas scanned the Sands now rapidly disappearing from view as the waters lapped and ate into their banks, but there was no sign of him.

The ship-swallowers had had their way, after all. Tranter had paid all their dues. Thomas looked at Sparrow, Sparrow at him. He'd made his choice, the best he could at the time. Tranter had had something to hold onto and Sparrow was already disappearing under the waves. And Tranter was the strongest man he knew. But it hadn't been enough to save him from the waters. The boatman insisted they move away. They couldn't risk lingering in the coming storm. As Thomas scoured the horizon, all of them were shouting and cursing again and again, but it was useless. Josh Tranter was lost. And it was Thomas's fault. His mother, though, might have called it Divine Providence.

32

Last Chance

October 1810, Deal

For nearly two years now the disgrace of Moore and the loss of so many men at Corunna had continued to haunt them. Few soldiers were left unscathed by this death of all their hopes, and even Grace wrote to tell of how Cornet Andrew Rearsby had returned to recuperate at the Hall, a broken man.

As for the loss of Tranter, Byrne seemed almost as deeply affected by his death as Thomas, muttering that he should never have accepted Filmer's challenge to go out to the Goodwins. Even Charlie Filmer was subdued.

Sixteen months on and it had taken that long for the Company's spirits to revive. But now they were marching back to his adopted homeland of Essex, Byrne began to talk once more about reviving the regimental teams, whilst Freer was almost delirious at the prospect of seeing Louise. Even Thomas felt returning to Romford was almost a homecoming, but Freer was sure they wouldn't be there for long, as the new Spanish campaign under Wellington would require their services sooner or later. Failing that, they might well be posted to Ireland, the Americas or India, for the general opinion was that the Tyrant had lost interest in launching an immediate invasion.

This prospect seemed to make Freer more rather than less determined to obtain regimental permission to marry, though he'd had little success so far. Thomas had already heard Freer telling Webster that as Louise was of such good character, she couldn't be expected to enter into the usual common-law arrangement; though, of course, Louise would not be above undertaking whatever regimental duties were allocated to her.

On hearing Freer rehearse his prepared speech designed to persuade Lieutenant Webster to petition Captain Dickenson yet again, Thomas couldn't imagine Louise being satisfied with mending and washing the men's clothes, or any of the tasks the Army deemed suitable for wives on the strength, but said nothing. Freer knew full well that what officers considered suitable for the wives of other ranks wouldn't suit Louise. In any case, getting permission looked increasingly unlikely. A corporal's rank wouldn't carry any weight, though occasionally serjeants, and more usually troop serjeant-majorss, had permission granted on the basis of their rank alone.

Thomas also couldn't imagine how Louise's father would ever give his blessing to the marriage, even though she was now of full age. So, as well as worrying about the conduct of the war, Freer also began to fret about the unpredictability of the human heart and the many obstacles that lay in the way of Happiness. It was not a thing a Rational man could easily talk about, but Thomas understood and accepted his swings of mood and impatience over those many months before their return to Romford was confirmed.

But, at last, after three days of travelling they were on their way back, Freer worrying that Louise would change her mind and go back on their understanding, or her father would find them out. As they passed the desolate

Thames marshes, only good for wildfowlers and cannonry practice, the maze of creeks and rivulets reminded Thomas of those desolate gullies on the Goodwins and he fell into a melancholy mood. But as the Regiment approached Romford in their full dress uniforms, parading past the great grounds of Gidea Hall, over Waterman Bridge, past the tollhouse, the charity school, the sheep pens, and the familiar gabled roofs of The Cock and Bell, Thomas's spirits began to rise. Freer signalled Thomas to look upwards, and there she was, leaning out of the top window; Louise Young waving and blowing Freer a kiss.

33

Last Orders

May 16th, 1811. Romford Barracks

Dear Grace,

We have just received orders for six of our troops to be sent to the aid of Viscount Wellington in the Peninsula. The men are talking of nothing else. It is hard to keep them sober as they whirl round the town saying their goodbyes. Freer and I have had to spend these last two evenings dragging our troop's men back to the barracks out of the reach of any ignorant townspeople who might call their courage into question, for I swear it is not fear that drowns these men's senses in good Essex ale. We have been waiting these last seven years to give Boney a good thrashing. Now it is time to take this war to the enemy, avenge the retreat of Corunna, and prove that a British cavalryman can fight as well as any British sailor. But try not to fear unduly. We have good provisions, well-trained horses and a newLieutenant-Colonel called Pennington, who joins us in Portsmouth. His family have estates in Leicestershire as well as in Ireland and he comes highly recommended by Captain Dickenson.

Yours, Thomas

PS. I will try to write from Portsmouth but do not know whether we will have time to do other than supervise the loading of our horses. The men too must be embarked sober or we shall lose them to the harbour waters, and of course, the same goes for those womenfolk permitted to accompany us. This will not be an easy undertaking.

Thomas put the letter down. He'd utterly failed to say how much he would miss her letters; maybe he should explain how hard it was to be a soldier's wife and tell her of the privations the women went through; how it was a lottery as to which six of them would be allowed to join their husbands abroad. Maybe he should give her permission to look for another.

The last he quickly dismissed, for it was said the war was now turning and Wellington would be running the Tyrant back to France any day now. Thomas looked again at his letter and wondered if he should take advice from Freer as to their chances of military success, but discarded the thought. Webster had just informed Freer that their retiringLieutenant-Colonel would not put Grace on the strength or agree to their marriage; it seemed that Freer would have to attain the rank of serjeant and possibly even troop serjeant-major before his request would even be considered again.

Freer was furious. 'What with only six troop serjeant-major posts in the entire bloody Regiment. Chance would be a fine thing!'

Thomas had tried to console him. 'You wouldn't really want Louise to do the kind of jobs rank-and-file wives have to do, would you, never mind you both having to share a barracks room with the rest of us? Would you?' But Freer had been out of sorts for the last week now.

It was unclear too what would be the mailing arrangements from overseas. He imagined that the officers would have priority and, after that, the final letters from the dead men to their families. Maybe he should add that postal arrangements would be difficult but delays would not mean he wasn't thinking of her.

Thomas picked up his pen again. It was almost time for Freer and him to begin their nightly patrol to retrieve their men.

So what should it be? What could he add that would make sense to Grace? He read the letter twice more, finally adding the words, *I am not sure yet of the postal arrangements when serving overseas. There may be some delay in getting letters to you but I will let you know where to write to me. Please do not think that any failure to receive letters from me means that I am not writing them or that I am not thinking of you. Any difficulties that you may have I will regard in the same way. Trusting that we shall see each other again soon in more peaceful times.*

It was mealy-mouthed. Thomas knew it even as he twisted himself into this knot of non-committal sentiments. He sighed and told himself that his thoughts must lie with the tasks ahead, the trial of his courage he had yet to face. He feinted instead and added to the letter. *Truly it is a hard life being a soldier's wife. Tomorrow the officers will draw lots to permit just six of them to embark with their men. I hope it is not a scene you will ever have to witness or be part of. A soldier's wife has very little to look forward to, whilst a soldier, at least, has the excitement of the campaign ahead of him.*

Thomas folded and sealed his letter, ready to leave it at The Cock and Bottle early tomorrow morning. It would be some time before Grace read his news. He had, as yet, no forwarding address and besides there would be no opportunity for her to reply before he left Portsmouth.

But he still imagined her running her long fingers over his bold black script, and in that moment he felt as though her hand was touching his. That would have to suffice for the moment. For both of them.

34

Sally Port

30 May 1811, Portsmouth

Thomas and Freer were making their way to the docks, some distance from their camp at Hilsea. Thomas had seen nothing like it before. It was as if the whole town's enterprise was being devoted to the defeat of Napoleon; everywhere a man could look there were redoubts, bastions and walls and, in the dockyards, all manner of industry.

'What I don't understand,' said Freer, 'is how Bonnie Murphy gets to go with Murphy on every bloody campaign.'

'Who else can half-kill a new recruit doing his hair? She's the official regimental hairdresser, remember?'

'But none of us have worn queues and powdered our damned hair for three years or more.'

'But she'll still be on the muster roll, I expect.'

Fearless was not living up to her name. Getting the right quality of cavalry horse in the Peninsula was well-nigh impossible, so their mounts were to be shipped with them whether they liked it or not. No wonder they were protesting at being put into slings. Thomas noticed Fearless standing some distance away, bucking the sling off every time the men tried to fix it in place: teeth bared, ears back, ready to protest with either back or front legs. He turned to Freer.

'I'll go and try to calm Fearless down.' However, almost as soon as Thomas had spoken Freer pointed at the beach. They saw a couple of the new recruits standing chest-deep in the shallows with the horses, one looping the sling under the horse's belly and swimming it closer to the boat, whilst the other guided the rope attached to the winch until the horse could be hauled up by the sailors at a safe angle.

Freer muttered, 'Clever man. That's exactly how to do it though he's still risking a kicking.'

Thomas smiled and pointed to the taller one swimming with the horses. 'That's Littlethorpe, the recruit with too much to say for himself I told you about.'

Freer grinned. 'Like me, Thomas? Still, good to have another man on board who can look after himself in the water, eh?'

Thomas nodded and dismissed any lingering thoughts about Tranter. There would be plenty more dead men where they were going. He remembered their last night in Romford: he'd felt a shiver of recognition run down his back when Freer, the great rationalist, wondered about premonitions of death and whether Nelson himself might have felt them the night he left Portsmouth for the last time.

It was only then that Thomas glimpsed some more dragoons approaching further along the quay.

Thomas touched Freer on the arm and gestured in their direction.

Freer screwed up his eyes against the sun. 'Who the hell are they?'

Thomas focused his own gaze on a tall man riding bolt upright on the outside of the column of men. Thomas clenched his jaw, waiting a moment longer to be quite sure before he said anything. 'It's Fallowfield with Troop A.'

Freer gasped. 'I thought they were one of the depot companies.'

Thomas sighed. 'Well, they're not coming to wave us off, are they?'

Freer spat. 'That's the last thing we need – bloody Fallowfield on our backs as well as the French.'

35

Belem

25 June 1811, Lisbon

Freer stared over the side. 'Maybe we'll all be turning round and going back home again dying of the fever like those poor bastards at Walcheren.'

Thomas grunted. The previous seven days, bobbing aimlessly and becalmed off Vigo had been particularly hard on the horses.

Freer shook his head. 'Still, returning with our tail between our legs is not likely with Wellington in charge. Much more likely to end up dying in a proper battle.' Freer slapped Thomas rather too heartily on the back, and Thomas cuffed his head lightly in reply. Freer walked over to speak to Lieutenant Webster, who'd just appeared on deck.

But by then Thomas's mind was elsewhere. As the convoy sailed up the river mid-channel, he couldn't take his eyes off the layer upon layer of gleaming white buildings climbing the hillsides, lodged between spires and huge palaces fronting the crowded quays.

Freer, back from speaking with Lieutenant Webster, was struck less by its beauty than by its fabled resurrection.

'Hard to imagine most of this was in ruins only fifty or so years ago.'

Whilst on board, Lieutenant Webster had enthralled Freer and Thomas with stories of the great Lisbon earthquake; how the river had then risen high above the land to sweep away everything in its path; how the city's miraculous reconstruction so quickly afterwards had been the talk of Europe.

'Which just goes to show that what God metes out with his right hand, he occasionally deigns to correct with the left,' Freer whispered to Thomas. It was not a sentiment that Freer would have dared utter louder within Lieutenant Webster's hearing, for it was clear to them both that Webster had recently become the most devout of men. Freer turned to the deeply forested opposite banks of the wide river.

'That's where we should be … away from this damn sun.'

Thomas put his hand to his eyes. Even when cooled by the breezes rising off the river, the early morning heat was already beating down on them and Freer, with his ginger colouring, suffered more than most of them in the sun.

'Look at that.' Thomas had caught sight of a great tower standing proud in the river, partly ruined but linked by a causeway to the bank; its topmost battlements, but not its base, were ragged and blackened.

'I'd wager that yonder ruination was done by the French, not any earthquake.'

Freer turned to eye up the tower.

'You'd have thought the crapauds could have done a better job of cannonading than that.'

Thomas nodded.

'Aye, you'd have thought so.'

Suddenly the boat lurched and turned closer to the shore, making for the shallows, gliding nearer to the crowded quays.

The horses were mostly to be disembarked in slings directly into the water. This time, much to Thomas's relief, Fearless lived up to her name and accepted her transfer over the water with greater fortitude; glad perhaps, like the men, to escape the cramped quarters below deck. But by the time all the horses had been disembarked onto the quayside, landing ashore either from boats anchored in the mid-channel or directly from the shallows, the sun had almost set.

So Thomas and Freer found themselves supervising the last of the straggling columns of men and horses by lamplight, as they made their way to the Royal Stables. Thomas could hardly believe their good fortune and, as he paused under one of the multitude of stubby parkland trees, letting the evening breezes freshen his face, he took the deepest of breaths, inhaling such exquisite scents that he could have imagined himself to be in Paradise.

36

Slops

June 1811, Lisbon

'Shite!' Freer flung himself back against the wall of the nearest building, trying to wipe off the contents of a piss pot that had landed on his head.

'It's bloody Nottingham all over again.'

Thomas took refuge next to him, squinting up at the many narrow balconies stacked high above them. He pressed hard against the wall as he saw the woman return again, but this time to fling kitchen slops down into the street.

'I don't think she's aiming at us. Look, it's everywhere. Can't you smell it?' Thomas pointed to the stone paving they'd slithered on as they'd turned into the alley.

Freer grunted. 'Lieutenant Webster can go and buy his own bloody mule, if this is what we have to put up with.'

Freer hadn't taken kindly to landing up in a place where he could neither understand the language nor read the newspapers. But Thomas was still entranced by all the sights and smells, fair or foul. He hadn't expected to be, for, although the alleyways stank and Freer had been in an ill temper all morning, he felt happy. At long last they were going to be doing something. They were going to take the fight to Napoleon, not cower behind coastal defences, constantly scanning the horizon.

Thomas conceded, 'You'd never guess this was the same place we could see from the ship.'

Freer pointed upwards. 'Just look at this stuff peeling off the wall, the rubbish, and the bloody dogs.' Freer aimed several well-placed kicks at a couple of mangy creatures trying to nip their ankles. 'What's wrong with this place? As for the women …'

Thomas knew why Freer was so irritable. He could hear the homesickness in his voice. Freer was missing not only his Louise, but all the other landlords' daughters he could have been joking and flirting with, instantly making himself at home in whatever English town they found themselves in. The reality of being hundreds of miles away from home had finally registered.

Thomas put his hand on Freer's shoulder. 'None of them are ever going to be a patch on your Louise, eh?'

Freer shook his head, quickly wiping his hand across his face. 'It might help if we could speak the damn language.'

Thomas looked up once more at the narrow iron balcony they were sheltering beneath.

'They don't seem to shout a warning beforehand.'

Freer by now had shifted most of the muck off his uniform, but before they could once again set off in search of mules, they heard the most tremendous commotion round the corner further up the alley, a commotion conducted almost entirely in English. Thomas and Freer rushed forward, turned the corner and saw Littlethorpe and a couple of other new recruits trying to fend off a gang of Portuguese youths armed with sturdy sticks. Two of the recruits were managing to hold them off whilst Littlethorpe tried to scoop up a tangled, bloody heap of fur from the ground.

By the time Thomas and Freer reached them, Littlethorpe was already taking off, with what turned out to be small dog tucked under his arm; but the gang seemed so intent on finishing the job they were now in pursuit of both Littlethorpe and the dog.

37

Sanctuary

Whatever had possessed him? Private Richard Littlethorpe thought he'd surely gone weak in the head with too much sun. But, for whatever reason, he'd seen red when they'd come across the Portuguese lads intent on beating this whimpering creature to a certain death.

Hearing the gang shouting behind him, Littlethorpe kept asking himself this, as he ran this way and that, not knowing where he was going. Littlethorpe racked his brains for any better ideas. About the only thing he remembered from the talks Lieutenant Webster felt impelled to give the company was how religious the Portuguese were and how, although very different from their own places of worship, their churches were not only much more decorated but even more greatly revered. And no soldier, upon pain of the severest punishment, the Lieutenant had emphasised, was to desecrate one of their churches in any fashion whatsoever.

Yes, he would have to look for a church. That would do it. So as soon as Littlethorpe spotted the heavy oak doors that might offer the sanctuary he needed, he flung himself into the cool darkness of a large interior chamber lit only by the occasional candle. He perched on one of the low stools in front of a large statue of a woman draped in blue and holding a baby.

Feeling confident he would be safe there, he began to inspect the dog's wounds. There was already a small puddle of blood gathering under the stool, almost as much blood as such a small animal could hold. But looking more closely, Littlethorpe was pleased to see that it didn't seem to be losing any blood through its mouth or backside. Good signs. Maybe he'd rescued the creature before serious damage had been done. Hard to say, but he was hopeful. Casting about for some way to staunch the bleeding, Littlethorpe eyed the lace and linen cloths lying across the altars. It wasn't as though he believed so much in the wrath of God, but if those lads were anything to go by he didn't wish to provoke the anger of any more Portuguese citizens. He quickly took off his jacket and shirt and wrapped the dog as tightly as he could in his shirt, applying pressure to the most grievous of the cuts. He knew that he should keep the wounds under pressure for as long as was needed to stem the flow of blood, and so he sat in almost complete darkness, the coolness of the previous evening still lingering. Nursing the little dog, he remembered what it was like to be a creature pursued, someone who'd once taken so much for granted until his world started falling apart just four months ago.

He let his mind wander back to the time when he first toyed with the notion of becoming a soldier, before that day when he realised he had no choice in the matter, when he could either become a fugitive fit only for the gallows or a new recruit who'd be marched off sharpish, well out of the way of any magistrates in possession of his description.

Yes, he knew what it was like to be hunted down, called a Luddite, with posters hung on every other gatepost in Nottingham County offering a fifty-guinea reward; and he hadn't even taken the oath. All he'd ever done was help out with a bit of frame-breaking to show the damned factory owners they couldn't keep beating down honest men's wages. His family had had enough of that already, driven off their own patches of land for the sake of bloody improving landlords.

Littlethorpe was roused from his thoughts by the gentle whimpering of the dog tightly swaddled in his shirt. It was trying to wag its tail. He stroked its nose and muzzle.

'Well, Dog, that's twice now I've gone daft in the head.'

38

This Sunny Land

Lisbon, July 3rd, 1811

Dearest Grace,

Tomorrow we leave Lisbon. I shall write to you again as soon as I can but we will be moving further inland, into the Centro as they call it. But even though I am now overseas, it will still be possible for you to send me a letter (not weighing more than a quarter of an ounce) for just one penny, and I can do likewise, so long as my commanding officer signs his approval on the envelope. So do not be surprised to see our new Lieutenant-Colonel's signature across the back of my envelope. Lieutenant-Colonel Pennington has already made himself agreeable to us all by the cheerful and fair way he conducts the affairs of the Regiment.

I am told that there is a weekly packet service from Falmouth to the British Post Office here, where the agent will pass any letters on to the army postmasters. I have already been asked by a couple of new recruits in my troop to help them by sending some news to their loved ones through their local clergymen. If only our own parson were so obliging with his parishioners.

Lisbon with its blue sky and bright sun looks like a fine place from a distance but on closer inspection turns out to be a crowded and mean city, though there are one or two grand squares, even larger than Horse Guards Parade in London. I shall be more sad though to leave its gardens, full of flowers and trees I have never seen before, most of which smell so strongly they float above the most tremendous stink. I have pressed a few of these flowers between the sheets of this letter in the hope that they will still bear the scent of this sunny land when you come to open it.

Sometimes I remind myself of home by opening and smelling the many packets of herbs and medicines I brought from England. I spent some months last year writing out Grandma Cowper's remedies before deciding which to bring with me. As you will remember, they are even more pungent than those I send to you.

We are fortunate to be billeted much closer to Belem, where the horses are kept in the royal palace's stables, but do not imagine that we rough soldiers disturb the king! The royal family left for the safety of their Brazilian colonies some years ago. Freer and I have been staying with an old widow in humble circumstances near to the harbour, so the horses have a grander home than we do.

Freer is missing Louise a good deal, but it is no life for a woman to follow the drum. Only last week there was a pitiful display down by the quays. A number of soldiers' wives and sweethearts, who had somehow got to Lisbon, were barred from going any further and had to content themselves with waiting for news of their men-folk down by the shore, making what living they could in the meantime. Our former Serjeant Fallowfield, was exceedingly uncharitable towards them. I am glad to say he is now in a different troop from ourselves, for he is an unforgiving man. Still, we have high hopes that Wellington will have us chasing Boney's troops back to France as quickly as they came, and before long I trust that I will be with you again, though I fear, perhaps not in Burton itself.

Yours us ever, Thomas

39

Whereon the Wild Thyme Blows

Grace had made it a rule never to open one of Thomas's letters until she was well away from Melton's Receiving House.

She smiled at the postmistress's usual quizzical expression and escaped as quickly and decently as she could. It was only when she'd walked the three miles home and gained the safety of her own tiny room that she broke the seal with enough force to shoot flower petals of numerous hues all over the floor. She quickly gathered them up and pressed them to her nose. There was scarcely any perfume left within their papery skins.

Grace hadn't been sure she wanted to meet Thomas face to face again in London. It was easier to write. She could chat about her life, and he about his – cricket matches, horses, and friends, and it was enough; so to see him again and discover she loved him as much as she'd always done was not what she had wanted.

She placed some of the faded pink flowers carefully on the coverlet and pushed the white sweeter-smelling flowerets next to her pillow. Thomas always used to pick her flowers from the hedgerows, a habit he'd got from his grandmother. But those, picked mainly for his grandmother's remedies, to be cut up or ground down and put into twists of paper, usually stank.

Grace threw herself onto her bed. It was only then that she unfolded Thomas's letter properly and read every word. She enjoyed Thomas's letters. But then he'd always been good with words. It was one of the things she'd liked about him. He picked up turns of phrase from his betters as easily as he calmed his horses with sweet nothings. She missed that. Grace liked words too.

Grace got up again and walked to the skylight and, standing on her pine box, put her head out of the window, calculating just how far she had already travelled from East Farm's cow byres. She then stepped down from her box, opened it quickly and pulled out the calfskin gold-lettered volume of plays that Master Andrew had lent her to read just before he returned to his regiment. She flung herself back on the bed, kissed Thomas's letter before placing it as a bookmark in *A Midsummer Night's Dream,* which she had been reading the whole of that week. She had been acting all the parts, from the King of the Fairies to the naughty Puck, even the rude mechanicals, striding up and down her room savouring every word; and not until the play finally ran its course, then, and only then, would she sit down to reply to Thomas.

She sniffed again at the petals he'd sent and turned to one of her favourite passages, wondered whether she should copy it out and send it to Thomas.

I know a bank whereon the wild thyme blows,
Where oxlips and the nodding violet grows,
Quite over-canopied with luscious woodbine,
With sweet musk-roses, and with eglantine.

40

Winter Quarters

January 1812, Celerico da Beira, Portugal

Thomas woke up stiff as a corpse. He would not have believed how the heat of the sun could disappear so quickly overnight; how their winter quarters had turned into a death camp where horses died by the day and men were shipped out, like so many bundles of blankets, to live or die in the hospital beyond the mountains. He stood up, shook his head as though to deny death itself a hearing, and pulled on his overalls. He had no intention of being buried in this God-forsaken place, men pick-axed into graves so shallow the mountain cats came hunting most nights.

He took off the small bag of soil from around his neck and raised it to his nose. He smelt summer-dry ash-lined lanes and winter-deep waterlogged tracks dipping over the horizon across the high fields of the township of Burton Lazarus. Home.

Freer suddenly appeared. 'Thomas, we're off.'

'Where?'

'To one of the Spanish frontier forts.'

'In the middle of winter!'

'Aye, that's the clever thing – when the crapauds are least expecting it.'

Freer had just returned from Lieutenant Webster's quarters down by the river. The officers were billeted all over the town whilst the men were placed mostly further out, together with their horses. The church was already full of the less seriously ill, the great castle half ruined, and the locals not convinced that an occupying army of British soldiers was better than the French, in spite of the commissariat's best efforts to buy supplies rather than just help themselves. But then, there was hardly enough food to go round, either for the townspeople or the men, never mind the mules, horses and camp followers. No wonder they were all half-dead on their feet.

The horses had particularly hated the Indian corn until the men hit upon the idea of soaking it first; the beginning of many more privations they were forced to find ways round. There was never enough litter for them to lie on, and spirited horses like Fearless hated sleeping tethered to the picket line under the stars. Like the men, they preferred four walls and a good roof over their heads. It was a constant battle to keep them well and prevent them from developing sores; their saddles often stayed in place for twenty-four hours or more at a stretch and they were forced to eat with their bits hanging loose, ready at a moment's notice to resume active service. But at least Fearless's coat was still glossy. She'd lost weight, though little of her energy or spirit.

But to hear the excitement in Freer's voice gave Thomas fresh hope that they would face the enemy at last, rather than just marching up and down across the hills and valleys, second-guessing where the French would strike next. Lisbon was now behind them, inside the Torres Vedras Lines, whose towers and redoubts were cut into the hills and valleys to its rear. The first line protecting the outer perimeter was already finished, but there were yet more to be built. This was Wellington's secret weapon, defence being the best form of attack at this stage in the Peninsula campaign, Webster had explained; he seemed a good deal sorrier than the men to have left Lisbon, for the Lieutenant had been completely mesmerised by Lisbon's churches, their shrines and their statues of bleeding Christs, painted saints in gruesome death throes and Virgin Marys in every shape and form. He'd said as much to Freer and Thomas, when explaining how he'd come across Private Richard Littlethorpe in one of the smaller, gloomier churches, nursing Dog, as everyone now called the little mongrel. Dog had survived against all the odds and had consequently attached himself to Littlethorpe and the whole company of troopers, even following them on their slow march into the interior.

Last summer and autumn had been harder on the nerves than scanning the English Channel for an invasion fleet; not that a light cavalryman could ever be idle. There was always work to be done when posted as forward outposts, roaming about on reconnaissance duties, or on watch as picquets and videttes. There was never a moment when the men could relax their vigilance as every village, every hedge or ditch might conceal the enemy. Their drills at home had scarcely prepared them for this kind of warfare on the move, but they told themselves that now Wellington was taking the fight into Spain itself, it would be the French who would have to look out.

Thomas thought it a great pity they'd now been brigaded with the First Royal Dragoons under the command of Major General John Slade. Not for nothing was he known as Black Jack Slade; not for nothing was he known as one of the most incompetent officers ever to be put in charge of a brigade of cavalry. Even so, none of them expected their first active engagement to be against their own troops.

41

Securing the Frontier

April 1812, Extremadura, Spain

For three weeks now they had been camped in a valley some miles away from the great frontier fortress of Badajoz in order to block any potential escape routes, should the French defenders succeed in breaking out of the besieged town. For three weeks they'd listened to the sound of Wellington's howitzers and heavy guns pound against the thick walls, wondering which army might prevail; and for several days now they'd sensed the great battle was coming to its end, as surely neither attackers nor defenders could keep up such ferocity for much longer. Then the big guns gradually fell silent and they waited for news.

~

Freer and Thomas were reading letters from home, which had finally arrived; one of the benefits the arrival of Wellington's new siege train brought. Grace had sent him some verse she had copied out for him.

I know a bank whereon the wild thyme blows,
Where oxlips and the nodding violet grows,
Quite over-canopied with luscious woodbine,
With sweet musk- roses, and with eglantine:

Suddenly they heard a great commotion. Murphy was back. He'd been acting as one of the messengers between the Regiment and Wellington's headquarters and looked like Death itself, so grim were his features. He could not contain himself.

'A great victory,' he stuttered, 'but at a terrible cost.'

By now Webster and Dickenson had arrived and Murphy quickly saluted and presented his dispatches to Dickenson. 'ForLieutenant-Colonel Pennington, sir.'

~

Thomas saw that Murphy was close to tears. 'It's not a sight I'd ever want to see again. Never again, on this earth ...' He began to stammer, hardly able to get his words out. 'Hundreds ... Thousands of our men dead ... where they fell ... and those not dead attacking and killing hundreds of women and children, old men ... bodies everywhere ... on the streets ... blood running in the gutters. Doing the Devil's work.'

Thomas looked at Freer. Freer shook his head. But Murphy was quite clear:

their own soldiers, fuelled by drink, were taking their revenge in whatever way they could, not just on the city's French defenders but on its Spanish inhabitants. Murphy had heard it said already that even the bloody siege of Ciudad Rodrigo was nothing compared with what they'd all seen that day.

Not even Black Jack Slade could be blamed for this.

Thomas signalled Murphy to sit down and passed him some beef stew, which he began to pick at until Ashby, one of the new recruits and a recent convert to Methodism, reached over and put his hand on Murphy's shoulder.

'God knows we are all sinners, but He will call those responsible to account.' Thomas saw Freer bite his lip at the mention of God, and the company again fell into a silence finally broken by Littlethorpe, who ran to tell them Fallowfield had just arrived back in camp.

~

Fallowfield, spitting with rage, banged his fist on the table. He blamed the dead.

'Damn me if Wellington didn't know they would resist to the death. As for the damned Spanish, they knew they'd be our targets too. Bloody fools should have persuaded the French to surrender earlier. All the French had to do was surrender on terms.'

Thomas was perplexed. Fallowfield was such a disciplinarian; how could he accept that British troops were running wild, ignoring all their orders, doing exactly as they liked? Thomas began to think that perhaps Fallowfield too, under the cover of the righteous anger the besieging forces claimed, had taken advantage of the misrule to do exactly as he liked. After all, he'd returned to camp laden with goods he declared to be fair booty.

Thomas dreaded to think what it might be like if the French were to ever set foot in an English fortress town. How might they treat the citizens of Portsmouth, if they ever managed to break through the sally ports and had to slash their way across the many bridges and moats that defended the harbour from seaward invaders?

He folded the letter from Grace back into his pocket book for safekeeping as though to protect Grace herself from this bloody contagion of war.

~

Dickenson and Webster returned almost immediately after speaking to Pennington. Three companies of dragoons were to be dispatched immediately to restore order by any means within their powers. Thomas and Freer looked at each other. Pennington had clearly judged his three commanders and their companies both willing and able to do just that.

~

It was the nearest thing to a vision of hell Thomas had ever seen. Heads blown off, bodies tumbling over ramparts. Not only the Forlorn Hope but company after company of men piled up against the curtain wall fallen into the breach, defenders cheek by jowl with attackers. Great mounds of the dead left where they'd fallen, with not a burial party in sight. Spanish women, skulls smashed against the stone pavers, skirts thrown over their heads with bloody thighs, babies clinging to their breasts, women older than his grandmother stamped almost flat into the ground, old men, intestines bulging, kicked to death.

As they entered the city it wasn't long before they could hear British soldiers now fighting another war between the men and their officers, the drunk and the sober, the profane and the pious, the strong and the weak. Even the erection of gallows in the town square seemed to have had no effect.

But, using the sheer muscle power of their horses and the flats of their sabres, the 36th succeeded in fashioning a narrow swathe through allowing them to enter further into the city, dragoons and horses holding their nerve as sticks, stones and curses hailed down.

Thomas and Fearless picked their way as best they could through the scattered bodies lying before them. He told himself he had to look, he couldn't count himself a soldier if he didn't face up to the slaughter, but this was a kind of killing he'd never imagined. With British troops still rampaging, it definitely wasn't safe to stop, but then Thomas heard a child crying. Throwing his reins to Freer, he dismounted and made his way cautiously towards the noise – and found a small boy, his head resting in a pool of blood. The child was cowering between his dead mother's legs and peeping out from beneath her skirts. The boy began to scream when he saw Thomas's uniform. Thomas was well used to looking after his small sisters and in his most gentle voice tried to reassure the boy as he bent to pick him up; but the boy held tightly to his mother's skirts, biting and kicking, doing his best to protect himself. Thomas held the boy as firmly as he could; the small teeth made little impression through his uniform, though he occasionally felt a bite on his hand. Thomas wondered if he was mad to try to rescue him. What would he do with him? Who would look after him? Should he not leave him with his own people? But, hearing in the distance the jeering and swelling waves of rage from the rioting soldiers, Thomas dismissed the thought almost immediately. It was clear that even children were not being spared. He pressed the now exhausted boy to his chest and made his way back to Fearless. Freer shook his head but quickly passed a spare horse blanket over to Thomas.

'Best swaddle him close to you.' So with the boy firmly bound to Thomas, he and Freer hurried to catch up with the rest of their troop.

It had been Lieutenant Webster's idea to commandeer one of the larger churches as their headquarters with the strict proviso that any religious items must be left well alone; any of those still left, that is, for the church was almost bare except for some wall statues too high up to steal or smash easily. Reaching the church at last, Freer helped Thomas lift the boy and lay him down, but still swaddled so he couldn't run away.

'Try some grog.' Freer offered the lad a drink from his canteen. The boy seemed to like the sweet taste and opened his mouth wide for more. Thomas then found some biscuits he had in his sabretache and offered them to the boy as they carefully unwrapped his arms. By now they'd been joined by Littlethorpe and Dog. The boy's eyes followed Dog and he began to relax his vigilance a little.

'What's to be done?' Freer whispered to Thomas. Thomas blinked as he remembered the stink of the mother's intestines looped outside her body, her blood soaking her skirts, her child sticky with her congealed blood. 'What the hell can we do … except look after him?'

Littlethorpe, taking one look, had marched off towards the vestry and was now coming back bearing a ewer of water … 'Holy water, I expect.' Freer smiled wryly, and between them they gently unwrapped the boy, bathing each part of his body as they released him from his confinement. Thomas next wondered how they would keep him warm and clothed, for the air was frosty. The boy's own clothes would need to be soaked for many hours to allow his mother's blood to leach away. Littlethorpe disappeared once again to the vestry and returned bearing some spare altar cloths and wrapped the naked child in cloth after cloth. When Thomas's stables jacket and his spare woollen socks were added the little lad stopped whimpering and finally let himself be tucked into an old box covered with a horse blanket. Thomas ran his fingers through the boy's dark hair, and felt a sudden yearning to be home again with his small sisters, looking after them with Hannah. Then he remembered: Hannah shivering in the apple loft while Michael lay dying, and then himself, just moments before, lifting his hand to Michael at the top of the ladder.

~

Leaving Freer and Thomas and some privates to defend their newly acquired citadel, Webster ordered the rest of the company to patrol their allocated third of the city, producing a sketch map he'd drawn hastily from memory of their journey so far. He quickly ran through their orders to remove all alcohol, weapons and ammunition, to detain all ringleaders they could safely confine and protect what civilians they could, women and children being their first priority.

Thomas heard Littlethorpe exhale a quiet 'Bloody Hell. That's not asking for miracles, is it?'

Webster looked grim. 'You must remember that these are men who in their present state will give you no quarter, and if either your life or the life of an innocent bystander is threatened you must give them none either.' And with that the others left.

Thomas and Freer next lugged three semi-comatose infantrymen they'd discovered at the back of the altar into one of the cellars, slammed the door shut and turned the key, and after checking that the boy was sleeping, Freer sat down heavily on the altar steps and put his head in his hands.

'How they could they bloody do this? How could anyone bloody think they're entitled to kill old men, women and children, anyone who just happens to be in their path? Our own men acting like animals ... worse than animals.'

Thomas, who had come to expect the worst of both men and women, and whose dreams were mainly nightmares, found what he'd seen today more dreadful than the bitterest vision of humanity he'd ever imagined; but Freer looked like a man utterly destroyed by the scenes they'd just witnessed.

Freer looked up at Thomas. 'You've always understood that, haven't you, that we're no better than animals?'

Freer, the great believer in progress, in the ultimate rationality of man, the pursuit of happiness and the perfectibility of human moral behaviour had come smack up against their home-grown version of the rampaging mob with not a government informer or Tyrant in sight, whose impulse to kill, rape and maim seemed to come from within themselves. Thomas felt strangely the stronger for understanding that what he'd seen today underlined his mother's worst fears; that men and women couldn't be trusted to act better than the beasts in the fields and perhaps they were all in need of a Chosen One to redeem mankind from its sins. Although Thomas preferred his grandmother's notion of religion, its practical healing works, its indignation about life's injustices and its resistance to the supposed mysteries of human existence, he suddenly felt he began to understand something about his mother's superstitious ways; her sense of the horrors of existence. Her anguished visions told him she had seen into the darkness of people's souls. He didn't know if and from where forgiveness might ever come, but maybe if he faced up to the darkness in his own soul then maybe he too might be forgiven one day. He looked again at Freer, who seemed to have shrunk inside his thin frame as though no longer able to support the necessary weight of optimism about the human race.

Freer was digging his fingers hard into his palms. 'How could they do this?'

'Perhaps we have to face up to the darkness within us before we can hope to behave better,' Thomas ventured.

Freer nodded. 'Huh. You mean scratch the surface and what you'll get is a mob, an out-of-control mob.'

Thomas remembered the surge of anger when he'd pushed his mother into Michael's grave. He reached across and put his hand on Freer's shoulder.

'They've been sorely provoked, and they've lost so many of their friends and comrades. It's no excuse, but anger's a terrible thing to tame.'

Freer looked at Thomas, white-faced. 'But what good does it do? What in whichever God's name does all this accomplish – this great blood-letting, this revenge? All it does is provoke others to take their own revenge, and so on and on … our own men just like Herod's soldiers massacring the innocents. Go on like this and there'll never be an end to it.'

Thomas had never seen Freer look so distraught and realised that it was now his turn to watch over his friend and to offer comfort. Thomas patted his shoulder.

'But, like you've always said, we still have to try, because if we don't treat our fellow men in the best possible way, even if we fail, then all is lost.'

Thomas recalled his response to his mother's distress, remembered both his own and his father's rage and thought none of them much better than those rampaging through the streets of Badajoz. The human condition, he'd heard Webster call it once when discussions on the nature of God had turned to the sinfulness of Man.

Thomas blushed. 'Webster says it's the human condition for us to have to constantly struggle against our sins, our vanity and rage. He says we have to acknowledge our baser instincts but still have to believe we can behave better than that. Some people talk about God helping them to behave better. Others think we must manage to find our own way without bringing God into it.'

Thomas remembered sitting quietly with Freer in the Great Meeting chapel in Leicester, and Freer asking him what he believed in; and he hadn't been able to answer. Had it taken seven years and the sight of such carnage in

Badajoz for him to be able to say this was it, this was what he believed in?

Suddenly Thomas heard one of the pre-arranged signals they'd agreed on hammered on the front doors and immediately they lifted up the great bar which held the doors shut. Littlethorpe, followed by Dog, burst in carrying a young woman semi-conscious and bleeding.

Littlethorpe grinned. 'Gave the bastard who did this a right headache.'

Thomas was glad that Littlethorpe, if not always on the side of the angels, seemed to have few problems administering justice, however rough and ready.

42

Parole

July 1812, Spain

It was the news Thomas had been dreading. The thinning ranks of Troop A and C companies were to be amalgamated. He and Freer would be directly under the command of Serjeant Fallowfield. The two companies had been ordered to strengthen the rear of the Regiment, which in practice, as they were retreating, meant the rear of the entire British army. Freer was of the opinion thatLieutenant-Colonel Pennington had decided that Dickenson's experience, but, even more importantly, his cheerfully combative approach was what was needed in these desperate times; but Fallowfield, once again designated Dickenson's cover serjeant, would be their immediate superior.

So now they were fighting the French skirmishers hand-to-hand, sabre-to-sabre, holding onto every broken rock, not giving an inch, whilst the rest of the troops tried to gain ground away from the implacable and well-rested French columns. They'd had a few successes here and there, and they already had in tow one French officer caught outside his patrol area by a detachment led by Webster. Dickenson had accepted the officer's parole he would not escape and intended to hand him over for more vigorous questioning once they had time to do more than keep one step ahead of his compatriots.

~

Thomas found picquet duties at night were the worst – staring into the darkness, straining to hear twigs snapping, or stones skittering down the barren slopes of the valley sides. That night they were patrolling the copses scattered across the lower valley floor. Fallowfield had just joined Sparrow, Freer and Thomas, and in his usual way immediately disturbed the precarious equanimity they had established.

Moving slowly across the open plain they'd just reached the perimeter of another copse when Fallowfield suddenly dived to the left of them, bringing down a man off his horse, a rider who'd clearly had been as unaware of their presence as they had been of his. Quickly following Fallowfield, Thomas could see the fallen soldier was French, probably an exploring officer. Fallowfield already had him pinned to the ground as the three of them arrived to assist. The officer looked younger than his countryman already in custody, and was as ragged and as dusty as themselves. He shouted, 'Parole, parole, my word, my word, my word; no escape.' Fallowfield leant back and smiled.

'I'll give you your parole, crapaud,' and with that he stood up and drew his sabre, then sliced it so deeply across the officer's neck that it would only be a matter of moments before the man expired.

Sparrow froze but Freer was furious. He choked back 'You bastard.'

Fallowfield laughed and bent down to rifle through the officer's papers and belongings. 'The man resisted; wouldn't hand over his orders, would he now?'

Thomas could see it was too late to help the dying officer and pulled Freer and Sparrow back to the picquet line, where he ordered the rest of the guard to be on high alert. 'Best assume the crapaud wasn't alone.'

Thomas went about his duties like a sleepwalker, neither he nor Freer saying a word in front of the rest of the men. The rules of command demanded that; but just before dawn, out of immediate earshot of the others, Freer was scathing. 'It wasn't like it was in the heat of battle, life for life. He had the man on the ground offering him his parole. Why do it? The man was terrified and I wager he could have given us more useful information than would have been kept in his pocket book.'

Thomas agreed but urged Freer to say nothing until they were out of Fallowfield's reach. He knew that Fallowfield liked nothing better than to provoke his own men, to test their loyalty to the limit and then break them to his will.

Freer agreed it wouldn't be wise to tell Webster because of Fallowfield's apparent hold over him, but maybe they should report it to Dickenson. In view of Fallowfield's rank, Thomas thought that pointless, but Freer persisted: 'Fallowfield won't trust us to keep quiet over such a flagrant breach of etiquette between officers, will he now?'

Thomas knew he would have to insist. Freer never could walk away from injustice. 'But it's not the right bloody time to try and bring Fallowfield to book; not while we're fighting just to survive.'

'Aye, you're right,' Freer grunted. 'Still, Fallowfield's not back yet. Let's hope some French serjeant returned the compliment.' And with that they returned to the rest of the men on watch.

As for Sparrow, although Thomas cautioned him to say nothing, it came too late, as his tale had already snaked through the ranks of his fellow guards, and all too soon Thomas realised Sparrow's indiscretion might cost all of them their lives.

~

Shortly after they returned to camp the next morning Fallowfield arrived back, claiming to have obtained vital intelligence after being forced to fight a French picquet single-handed. Thomas would certainly have believed him had he and Freer not seen for themselves what had actually happened. This is war, he tried to tell himself. Maybe Fallowfield would prove to be a good man to have at his side if ever the day came when a full-scale battle took the place of all this feinting and retreating, only just holding the French advance parties back as they snapped at their tails. But he'd never want Fallowfield at his back.

Fallowfield was so full of his triumph that Webster agreed to his next plan: the same watch party of men, led by himself, would move up the hill towards the monastery to lie in wait for the small French party Fallowfield expected shortly.

But at the foot of the hill Fallowfield suddenly turned to head back towards the camp. 'I must speak to Lieutenant Webster urgently. Proceed to the top and wait there.' Thomas and Freer looked at each other.

It smelt bad.

Thomas made himself as tall as he could. 'Serjeant, I have nothing to say about last night, but this proposed manoeuvre risks unnecessary loss of life.'

Fallowfield tightened his jaw. 'Corporals Freer and Cowper, if you don't join your men and take them to the top of that bloody hill, I shall have you before a firing squad for disobeying orders.'

Thomas knew Fallowfield to be a man of his word in such matters, but he also knew Captain Dickenson didn't squander his troops and had been hard-pressed to sacrifice even the notorious bounty collector Quilley. He felt sure that he and Freer stood a reasonable chance of not being shot, even if they risked demotion, and the more that he saw Fallowfield was determined to order them up the hill into enemy territory the more Thomas was determined not to go.

Freer muttered, 'We're dead men either way.'

Thomas shook his head. 'Not yet we aren't,' he whispered. 'I'm going to call his bluff.'

He looked steadily at Fallowfield. 'Then we'll await your return with Lieutenant Webster's orders.'

Fallowfield spat on the palms of his hands, took the reins and turned to bellow at Sparrow. 'You men take yourselves to the top of that hill immediately,' then rode away, shouting at Thomas, 'You've not heard the bloody last of this.'

As soon as Fallowfield was out of earshot, Thomas galloped after Sparrow, yelling, 'For God's sake, stop, Sparrow! Stop, all of you! If any man is to be disciplined it will be me, not you.'

Sparrow slowed his mount, turned momentarily and shouted back. 'He'll have us all shot first.'

Catching up, Thomas begged, 'Sparrow, none of this makes any sense. None of us know what's lying in wait over that bloody hill, except Fallowfield.'

Sparrow shook his head and whipped his horse to catch up the others.

Freer looked at Thomas. 'Fallowfield's playing at something, ain't he?'

Thomas nodded. 'But we can't just leave them, can we?'

By the time Thomas and Freer had decided they had little choice but to rejoin their men and began cantering after them, they heard a sharp volley of musketry on the hilltop, and saw shot blast into their small troop as it topped the crest of the hill. Horses scattered downhill, riders hanging on, covered in blood. Thomas and Freer rushed cursing towards them, scooping up riders and horses and guiding them back towards camp, though by the time Freer and Thomas got to their own lines, it was apparent that they were all desperately wounded.

Thomas at first refused to believe Sparrow's chest wound could be mortal, denying the evidence of his own eyes, even though the lead balls had forced the fragments of dirty cloth so deep into its cavity that there was little hope of extracting them without causing further damage. But unless they were removed, his blood would be poisoned beyond all possibility of help. Thomas set about cleaning as much of the wound as he could, though he knew deep wounds required a surgeon's intervention. But what could a surgeon do here? A bad leg wound and the surgeon would have said amputation. But you can't amputate a man's chest. Sparrow was just about conscious and seemed equally aware of the seriousness of his plight. Thomas feared all the men were doomed.

Then Thomas overheard Fallowfield explaining to Captain Dickenson that he had only just turned back to check his exact orders with Lieutenant Webster when the unfortunate incident occurred. As for the tardy attendance of Corporals Freer and Cowper, they had deliberately defied him and delayed following orders. But then, quite unexpectedly, Thomas heard Webster's voice rise to a high pitch of indignation. He turned away from Sparrow to look at the three mounted men.

'Serjeant Fallowfield knew exactly what was to be done as he had devised the plan himself and therefore required no further instruction from me.'

Lieutenant Webster flipped his reins across his horse's neck as though to emphasise his point, flushed with what Thomas could only read as rage, whilst Captain Dickenson was now looking increasingly puzzled.

Webster continued, 'As for Corporals Freer and Cowper, we should be thankful they were spared to fight another day.'

~

George Dickenson realised that there must be more to this than was being said, but could not believe that any serjeant of his would recklessly endanger his own troops' lives; besides, he was far too busy to think about it further. He would make it clear to Serjeant Fallowfield he didn't like the sound of it, didn't like it at all and Fallowfield would have to offer a better explanation in the fullness of time, as soon as they'd got the crapauds off their backs once and for all. Damn it! The loss of five lives, all useful well-trained men, now seemed inevitable.

~

With another patrol on guard as they lifted the survivors into the few carts they had left, they worked in hope. Thomas, searching through all his remedies, instructed Littlethorpe, Byrne and Ashby how they might minister, to the three still alive, remedies for fever and pain, though not for mortal injury. But, when Sparrow was the last one alive, he just held him in his arms and talked: that he was sorry he'd not called the men back sooner, that Sparrow was a good honest friend; that he was the Regiment's best batsman ever.

Thomas mourned. If only he'd been killed instead. Maybe then, all his own sins would have been finally washed away and Sparrow would have been able to go home to his sweetheart in Shorncliffe. But Thomas soon chided himself for this thought. He still had work to do, men to lead.

Sparrow, with a tremendous effort, choking on his own blood and spit, muttered something.

Thomas bent closer to hear. 'Tell her. Tell her ...'

'I'll tell her, Sparrow. Don't worry. I'll tell Jeannie you love her,' Thomas whispered. 'And she loves you, I'm sure of that.'

Thomas remembered her frightened tear-stained face on the dockside at Portsmouth as she waved, with all the other women unsuccessful in the ballot, to the soldiers and horses finally departing.

Sparrow squeezed his hand just once and it was over.

~

Bonnie wiped away an uncharacteristic tear. She must be getting mardy in her old age. Getting killed is what happens to soldiers. They die and you marry the next one. It's the way of the world. And Sparrow's sweetheart, stuck back in Shorncliffe with the barracks so close, would be able to have her pick. But Bonnie shed another tear. Really, she'd have to stop this. She glanced at the burial party all set to leave, Fallowfield with his purple arse-face leading the way. Dermot reckons he's in real trouble with Webster and Dickenson this time for getting his men into that ambush. Everyone agreed it had to be an ambush the way the guns fired all together. Dermot's never seen Webster look so cross. He practically called Fallowfield a liar in front of his own men and Dickenson was furious too. Losing five good men like that. There he goes, Lieutenant Webster with God have mercy upon him and a tear in his eye as well, and Cowper looking like he might throw himself at Fallowfield and slit his throat. As for Freer, I've never seen him look so miserable. Pity the enemy was running them so close. Another full evening in their cups might have done the trick, like after the Quilley business. Now that was a proper wake.

Well, at least she had something else to occupy her mind. She bent down and wiped some muck off Boy's face. Everyone called him Boy now just as they called Dog, Dog. He seemed to like that, not that he'd ever said. Boy didn't speak. He could hear all right and his understanding of English was getting better all the time. So Bonnie just accepted it and told the other women that if they were him, they wouldn't want to talk about what happened in Badajoz either. And that was that. He was Bonnie's now to look after, in spite of arse-face, who'd said, 'Next convent we come to, in he goes. That's an order.' Of course, she'd said nothing but she'd no intention of taking orders from anyone other than Wellington himself. So she'd point-blank refused to hand him over to some over-eager Spanish nuns who seemed to think they had first call on his soul; and Dickenson, who didn't seem to care for nuns, had backed her up.

It was hard to say how old Boy might be but those who had children reckoned he might be about five or six. Bonnie sniffed. Of course that's why she was so soft in the head nowadays. It was looking after Boy, worrying about dead mothers and dead children.

Dermot's way with Boy was to teach him the pipe and tabour and declare him destined to be a regimental drummer boy. Bonnie shook her head. Sometimes Dermot couldn't see the wood for the trees. Boy clearly detested the whole business of war. Why, it was only a month or so ago, when arse-faced Fallowfield was putting his men through a few drills when they'd had some time on their hands that the lad had run and hid his head in her skirts until they'd finished. Anyway, Bonnie didn't even want to think about losing another mother's son to this bloody war.

~

Thomas hung back until the trumpeter called them to silence and Lieutenant Webster stepped forward to say a prayer over each of the five mounds of stones before them. The ground had been too hard for their shovels to make more than the shallowest indentation.

'Our father, which art in heaven,
Hallowed be thy name...'

Webster was full of dignity and feeling for all five men, and Thomas would have sworn he was fighting back tears. Freer was right. Damn him. He usually was. Lieutenant Webster might make a better parson than officer.

At first Thomas had blamed himself for not stopping the men in time; and he'd clearly made the wrong choice that day on the Goodwins too, for it must have been Sparrow's, not Tranter's turn to die then. But almost immediately he'd managed to shake himself out of the descending gloom and told himself not to be stupid. It was Fallowfield, courtesy of an advance French skirmish group he must have known about from the exploring officer's pocket book, who'd really killed Sparrow. It wasn't Thomas, or God for that matter. It would have suited Fallowfield if the entire night watch had died, taking their knowledge of his gross misconduct to their graves. But he and Freer were still alive ... till the next time. Thomas snorted his indignation and defiance. Just let him bloody try that again.

Thomas looked over at Fallowfield, who was staring intently into the distant hills. He looked down his carbine's sights, placed his cheek against the raised cheek piece and wondered how far a bullet might fly.

~

Time to go now, but Thomas started to walk back towards the graves. He bent down to scrape a little bit of the stony Arapiles soil into his hand, before securing it in an even smaller cloth bag than the one he kept round his neck.

'Well, Sparrow, my friend. This is for Jeannie.'

Thomas stood up, put the cloth bag safely away in his sabretache. He could still feel Sparrow's hand grasping his own in a last farewell and see his face as he tried to raise his head to speak.

It would be Webster's or Dickenson's job to notify the Paymaster about the back pay Sparrow was owed. It would be his and Freer's to auction Sparrow's effects and make sure the money was sent to Jeannie.

43

Not a Quiet Day

21 July 1812, Salamanca, Spain

Confounded dust. Lieutenant Charles Webster pulled his neck cloth to cover his mouth and nostrils as best he could. The infantry were disappearing ahead of them like weevils wriggling through a sack of flour, their uniforms tracing a faint red trail in the morning heat. He glanced at the sun rising in the sky and feared the day was going to be most uncommonly hot.

He turned to look at his own troop and decided to ride down the file of horses to check that the army's own rearguard weren't themselves becoming stragglers. In their faded overalls, practically in rags, their helmets broken or lost, the men were scarcely recognisable as the same soldiers who had landed in Lisbon only a year before. The horses looked in no better condition. All of them were hungry. With no pay since April, it was now every man and officer for himself; the officers' last doubloons had already been sewn into their jackets. With fewer and fewer of the commissariat rations getting up the supply lines, and with the land here providing little prospect of game, it was no wonder Wellington was marching them back to Lisbon ... if he could.

It had been all too brief a taste of Spain. At least he had seen Salamanca and had not been disappointed. He had even taken time from their reconnoitring mission to the Alba de Tormes bridge to inspect the tomb of St Theresa. He had been astounded, transfixed even, by the bodily relicts preserved in silver and gold within. Although by now accustomed to the crowded altars of gold and silver he had marvelled at in Lisbon, this was different. He saw a rage and a pain in this faith he had not understood before. It seemed to presage all the battles he might fight in, the bleeding wounds and the amputated limbs like amulets. Perhaps he would have made a better clergyman than his brother after all. Dismissing yet again such speculations, he repositioned himself at the front of his men.

'Morning, Lieutenant Webster.'

Captain Dickenson greeted Webster with the excessive conviviality of a fellow gambler arriving late at the gaming table.

'I'm looking for a couple of sound men to make up my reconnoitring party.'

'Not many sound men left, I'm afraid.' Webster shook his head.

'Quite.' Dickenson sighed. 'All this damned endless marching straight back to where we've come from. Could have done without running a damned exploring party this morning, I can tell you. Wellington never takes any notice of us unless he can see it for himself anyway. No use our saying, Marmont's fellows are marching faster than ours. They always do. They have more cannon than us. What can I tell him he doesn't already know? No. What I need are men who can read Marmont's mind. But, failing that, I need some fellows who are good navigators and know about river crossings.'

'Corporal Thomas Cowper has a decent grasp of topography and Private Littlethorpe seems to know something about rivers. '

'Excellent, Webster. I promise to return them safe and sound as soon as I can.'

Webster tried to look gratified at Dickenson's optimism, sustained in spite of last week's losses. Yet still the French marched as quiet as thieves, in parallel to the British columns, looking for any opportunity to pounce. Today was definitely not going to be a quiet day. If anything, this wretched country between the two rivers advantaged the French; and the British seemed to be marching straight into the trap the French were devising.

44

Crossing the Tormes

July 1812

They'd been scuttling like crabs across a stony beach for nearly a week now, endlessly targeted by cannonades and sharpshooters, the crapauds' skirmishing parties trying to finish off what the others had missed.

It was warm work keeping alive. Sweat drenched Thomas's entire body, though so far the sheepskin over his saddle had kept him from chafing. He leant forward to run his fingers under his mare's saddle cloth. Her skin was damp rather than saturated, the cloth absorbing her sweat, preventing more serious sores developing on her back and withers. Such was the speed of this retreat, there'd been little opportunity to attend fully to the horses, and now, with the main supplies of forage being sent ahead with the rest of the baggage and the women, it didn't bode well for their survival.

Thomas patted the mare between her ears. 'They say we'll soon be dining like kings, back in Portugal. Aye, when pigs might fly,' he muttered.

Thomas tried not to think about food. They were already on half rations, and the rumour was that it would be quarter rations the day after next. And, should they come across women and children, old men, villagers trying to hide their own meagre provisions … he tried not to think about it.

~

'Corporal Cowper, Private Littlethorpe.'

Thomas rapidly fell into position behind Dickenson, reining his horse in and looked across at Littlethorpe, signalling him to move over towards them. Littlethorpe still retained a passable Tarleton helmet and his overalls and boots had not yet been frayed into oblivion. He took a pride in his appearance that deceived some officers into thinking he took a pride in being a private. Thomas was not deceived. Nevertheless he liked the fellow. Littlethorpe lifted the men's spirits with his jokes and songs and he could certainly hold a tune, his current favourite being: *Oh, the Grand Old Earl of Wellington had fifty thousand men, and he marched them up to the top of Spain and he marched them down again.* Thomas would rather have a sharp-witted songster any day than a dull croaker in their midst.

Littlethorpe promptly swallowed down the last chorus of *The Grand Old Earl of Wellington,* mid-hill, and joined Thomas and Dickenson. Thomas wondered how keen Captain Dickenson's hearing was, but Dickenson kept a steady countenance as Littlethorpe rode up.

'Lieutenant Webster tells me you're a useful man when it comes to rivers.'

'Lived by the Trent near Newark all my life, sir. Know those currents and mud banks like the back of my own hand, sir.'

'It's this ruddy Tormes we need to know about, Littlethorpe. Think you can find a sizeable ford on our present line of retreat?'

'Wherever it loops; I expect it'll be shallow there.'

'So. On this map. Show me.'

Littlethorpe rode closer as Dickenson uncurled his battered campaign map.

Littlethorpe squinted at the river's course and pointed to the map.

'There, sir. That place.'

'You're quite sure?'

'Aye, sir.'

Dickenson rolled up his map and waved Littlethorpe away, back to Thomas.

Littlethorpe whispered, 'Captain Dickenson thinks I don't know my rivers from my canals.'

'Wait till he sees you in action, Littlethorpe.'

Littlethorpe nodded. 'Bet he's never seen the Aegir ride like a wild creature up the Trent, against the flow all the way up to Newark.'

When he was a lad, Littlethorpe had been taken to see this freak of nature and the more his audience plied him with ale, the more this adventure was embroidered with heroic deeds. 'Like one of those sea women with long hair rising out from the deep, swimming the wrong way to escape from the devil himself. We took our life in our hands just standing there.'

Thomas had heard this story several times, told under the stars, when a man could believe anything. But he knew Littlethorpe understood rivers, much as he himself understood horses. A man doesn't grow up cheek by jowl with such awesome beings of nature and not learn something of their ways.

~

Captain Dickenson congratulated himself on having kept faith in young Littlethorpe. The river Tormes was split into sandbanks and shoals of stones laid down in the rainy season, making what looked like a series of easy crossings even for that number of men. But before Dickenson had time to plunge his horse through the thickets of trees and shrubs protecting the shallow banks, Littlethorpe had got ahead of him and signalled him to halt.

'Bound to be quicksands in that mud, sir. Best let me take a look first.'

Littlethorpe dismounted and Cowper reached over to take his horse.

'I'll need a couple of long branches.'

Littlethorpe raked through some storm debris and found two suitably sturdy branches.

Dickenson had just had time to set his look-outs when Littlethorpe waded into the shallow waters. Leaving his first pole standing proud on the river bank, he eyed the two nearest sandbanks, choosing the one to his left to test first. He placed his second pole firmly ahead of him and then waited for a moment or two, until he was sure the ground would not liquefy under it. He repeated this methodically, up and down and across the river, before declaring it suitable for four columns of men and two of horse to cross, so long as they kept to a hundred feet either side of the pole.

~

Dickenson was pleased. Mission completed. Well, at least the first part of it. Now it was just a question of keeping out of the bloody crapauds' way.

'Let's save the rest of the paddling for later, shall we?'

He turned his horse sharply away, signalling Cowper and Littlethorpe to follow. The other men could stay as lookouts whilst he traced his way back to the line. The hounds had scented their quarry and were not going to give up without a fight.

A fighting retreat indeed. Dickenson wondered whether the men realised they were now the fox and the crapauds the hounds. Did they really think they could outwit their pursuers? Well, he'd known a few damned cunning foxes in his time. He cheered up immediately at the thought of the fine chase they'd give Marmont.

~

Thomas looked up at the sky. It was a day much like any other that summer, but there was a heaviness and opacity to the sky that made him fear rain.

'Think it'll still be fordable by tonight?'

Littlethorpe followed his gaze.

'That's the last bloody thing we need. That river'll be a killer with a bit more water in it. And then they'll have us.'

Littlethorpe knew about drowning. He and the Fiskerton boatman used to fish corpses out of the Trent regularly, come autumn or spring, when the weather could change in an hour and people got careless. Bodies bloated like monsters; village girls screaming at the stink. All this talk of beating Boney and here they were, cornered like rats in a trap.

Thomas shook his head. 'Wellington's not going to let that happen, not to his best troops.'

Littlethorpe slapped his reins across his horse's neck. 'Well, I can tell you I'm bloody sick of all this covering our arses. When we took Salamanca, I thought that's it; we've got them on the run and we'll all be home before the year's out.'

Thomas felt exactly the same way but decided it would be prudent to change the subject. 'So where's home?'

'Stoke; East Stoke, south of Newark.'

'Vale of Belvoir way?'

Littlethorpe looked surprised. 'Nearly. A bit further over. By the Trent.'

'My parents were born in the Vale, at Stathern.'

Littlethorpe laughed. 'On the Duke of Rutland's estate? My mother was born within spitting distance of the Castle.' He slapped Thomas on the back. 'We could be kissing cousins.'

~

Charles Webster was agitated by the news that the French were still marching like men possessed. Still, all attention now was focused on getting the men and horses across the river before dark.

Webster knew it would be slow work. Keeping to the channels marked out by Private Littlethorpe required care and discipline. Men and horses were sunburnt, parched and reluctant to leave the waters of the Tormes behind before they had quenched their thirst from the deeper channels, and the heaviness of the afternoon air did not bode well as the officers endeavoured to hurry columns and horses over the shallow banks and rivulets.

~

The last of the horses was scarcely across before the storm exploded across the sky. The lightning forked and skewered down into the sparse groves of cork trees further over the valley, as though directed by some malevolent being who was on the enemy's side. Thomas pushed these superstitious thoughts to the back of his mind and focused his attention instead on the horses, which were pulling and protesting at this thunderous onslaught as if they'd never experienced noises as loud as cannon fire before.

~

As the rain fell in a steady torrent, Thomas pulled his cloak over him and tried to rest, but his uniform was soon as sodden as if he'd fallen into the swollen Tormes itself. Those few men who still had tents battled to put them up and protect themselves against any further beating from the weather. With the baggage train gone ahead, for most of them it was a matter of curling up under their cloaks and taking what shelter they could under the dripping trees and unforgiving sky. Thomas decided to investigate the lee side of a cork tree.

~

Although it was almost impossible to hear the neighing of the frightened horses and the muffled curses of the men above the cannonade of thunder and rain drumming down on them, Thomas was one of first to hear some horses break loose, spreading panic up and down the lines. He ran towards them, shouting for his troopers to catch the loose mounts.

~

'Wouldn't think you'd been under cannon fire for the last three years, would you now?' Thomas soothed, holding the stray horse firmly against his body. Then he leant his chest against her neck, his hands slipping a halter back over her ears, and the mare began to calm down. He ran his fingers down the white blaze on her nose – the most distinctive he'd ever seen; rather like forked lightning.

'Not the same, eh?' he conceded. 'Without a rider, eh? You need us as much as we need you,' he whispered, and remembered all the horses and men so recently ridden to their deaths. His body suddenly tensed and the mare pulled away from him. Another Ramillies. He turned his mind to soothing her terror rather than remembering his own, and once she'd quietened again, he inspected the branded initials on her rump. He should have known. She was one of their own: a King's German Legion horse, by the look of it.

'Best be taking you back where you belong, eh?'

~

Captain George Dickenson was restless. Without a tent, and the rain clearly set in for the duration, and the temperature dropping like a stone, he was reluctant to settle down for the night. He walked the two hundred yards or so back towards the river. The rain released by the heat of the day had turned Private Littlethorpe's crossing places into a seething torrent of white water that was churning the mud of the river bottom into a dark brew sweeping along rocks and branches in its onward rush. There was no turning back now.

45

Salamanca

22 July 1812, Los Arapiles, Salamanca, Spain

Captain George Dickenson was not pleased to see Lieutenant Webster return without fresh orders.

'You told them the bloody crapauds are catching up?'

Webster twitched his reins. 'Wellington knows that already, sir.'

'And he still thinks we should just run for it?' Dickenson could hardly believe it. Webster couldn't have been emphatic enough in conveying the urgency.

Webster shifted in the saddle. 'Keep our heads, but march like madmen, they said he said.'

Dickenson hated all this going through the staff officers nonsense.

Time was when he would have been able to say what he thought to more important people than them. 'We might as well be in Bedlam, for all the good we're doing.'

Webster had been back and forth between Lieutenant-Colonel Pennington, Wellington's staff officers and Dickenson himself since before dawn and now Dickenson was losing patience with the lot of them. And he'd thought Wellington to be a man of the hunt.

'If Wellington thinks he can bamboozle Marmont by skulking behind this ridge all morning ... You did tell them, didn't you? It's gone far too quiet back here. I mean, why aren't they biting the arse off us like every other damned day?'

'I told them you thought Marmont was up to something, sir.'

But had Webster said it with proper conviction? Dickenson wasn't sure Webster was capable of conviction.

'So, what did they say to that?'

'Nothing exactly, sir. But Wellington is clearly troubled; why else would he send the baggage wagons ahead of us in such a hurry?'

Dickenson detected in Webster's remark a certain favouring of Wellington's point of view. He knew his superiors saw him simply as a man of the shires; but he'd fought more than his fair share of battles, so he would not tolerate his lieutenant's questioning of his judgement, though he knew Wellington's staff officers did.

Dickenson gestured towards the great clouds of dust from the great convoy of wagons, spiralling up from the heat of the plain like smoke plumes into the scorching morning sky.

'And if that's not announcing we're running away with our tail between our legs, I don't what is.'

'Well, sir, at least, if we can connect with our supply lines again ...'

'We can die well fed?'

Dickenson was pleased to see Webster look suitably crestfallen.

'Do you think they are going to try to cut us off, sir?'

'What do you think, Lieutenant?'

'They can certainly march faster than our men.'

'And?'

Webster paused. 'Sir, do you think Marmont is planning to outrun us?'

Dickenson sighed. 'Think of our position from the French point of view.'

At times, Dickenson found his clever, but far too cerebral lieutenant irritating beyond words. As for the bloody heat ... He wiped his face vigorously with his kerchief.

'Come on, Lieutenant. Speak out. One of these fine days, if you ever get to be a captain, you'll be obliged to have an opinion.'

'Well, sir, there is a risk that Marmont might try and force the issue.'

'Tell me what the risk is. Come on. Explain.'

Dickenson hated to contemplate such a desperately unpleasant prospect, after their triumphant entry into Salamanca only a few weeks before. But it had to be faced.

Webster ventured, 'The fact that he is not skirmishing with our rearguard as vigorously as before might suggest that he is no longer content to merely harass us.'

Dickenson sighed again. Would Webster ever succeed in putting all his learning into plain English and to some military use?

'And so?'

'Well, sir, he might think it worth his while to head us off before we ever reach the Ciudad road.'

'At last. My point, exactly.' Dickenson jabbed his finger into the air.

'But are we not equally matched?' Webster suggested.

Dickenson leant forward. 'Remind me, Webster, how many reinforcements we're expecting? None. They're still recruiting our Johnny Newcomes, never mind teaching them not to fall off their damned horses. And how many is Marmont expecting? A whole army from the south. All he's got to do is cut us off, starve us for a week or two and wait for his parlez-vous friends to turn up!'

Webster nodded in apparent agreement, but persisted in Wellington's defence.

'I dare say, sir, that Wellington thinks we haven't the men to spare to give battle just for the sake of it.'

Dickenson suspected this was as much Webster's reading of the situation as Wellington's.

'Hmm.' Dickenson understood the implications of their shortage of men only too well. They'd just buried five of their own.

Webster continued in staff-officer mode. 'But, if we can secure our hold on that higher ground, we shall be better able to ascertain his intentions, sir.'

The lieutenant gestured towards the gunfire and smoke of combat rising from an old chapel across the valley.

Dickenson grunted. 'And if we do win the higher ground, then what? Stop for lunch? It's about time we gave that jumped-up Marmont a bloody nose.'

Dickenson pressed his spurs rather too sharply into his horse's sides and made off towards his cornet, who seemed to be having some difficulty in controlling his section of the column. Horses and men were getting out of kilter and distinctly ragged in their step.

~

Webster watched Dickenson reprimand the exhausted officer and move further down the column to check for more backsliding. He had to admire Dickenson's newly found bellicosity in this so-called fighting retreat, since they'd begun battling for their lives rather than for victory.

Webster looked again at the smoke from the chapel across the valley. He recalled all the smashed Madonnas, broken

Christs, and fractured crucifixes he'd seen already on this long journey from Lisbon. He flinched. There had been too many churches and Houses of God sacrificed already; so he tried to convince himself, what did one more matter?

Still, Dickenson was right. They could not afford to dawdle. The crapauds were indeed catching up, which was why Wellington's staff officers had ordered Webster to report back to them every hour to give news of their rear. Dickenson, already anticipating that the authority of a fully commissioned officer might be required instead, had made it quite clear that a simple orderly would not be adequate for this role today; for today, perhaps, would be the day of reckoning when Marmont would at last catch up with them.

~

It was early afternoon when Charles Webster was due to make his report relaying the news that Dickenson's men had increased the pace of their horses' stride, but without developing any significant gaps in their columns.

Webster arrived to find Wellington and his staff in a quite different frame of mind. They had just been informed that three of Marmont's divisions had been diverted from his main body in what appeared to be an attempt to outflank them and cut them off from reaching the Ciudad Rodrigo road, something they had all feared. Wellington had thereby deduced that Marmont was assuming that his enemy's main army was ahead of him. Wellington had clearly kept his troops well hidden in the lee of the lesser of the two hills to good purpose. But the exciting intelligence was that Marmont's leading first division was marching so fast that the entire column of three divisions was slipping and spinning across the landscape like a piece of weakened thread; and Wellington had, at that moment, decided it was ready for the snipping.

Webster galloped back to Dickenson with his battle orders. Wellington had seen how he might use the parallel hills skirting this open plain to their advantage. When the time came, and it could be soon, they were to support the heavy cavalry who were to attack Marmont's centre. Dickenson appeared delighted, and the men, too, undertook their preparations with some enthusiasm. Whether it was the prospect of extra rum or giving the crapauds a decent thrashing for all the trouble they had caused them, Webster wouldn't have liked to say. Whatever the case, after the storms of last night, they could all do with the extra rum.

Webster surveyed his troops as the men filed into their places, ranked behind in their squadrons, ready to form into line on Dickenson's trumpeter's signal. This would be their first truly offensive set piece battle since arriving in Lisbon a year ago.

Dickenson was emphatic. 'This is how wars should be fought, not this sniping and endless skirmishing with no one really sure who's won.'

Webster nodded. Not that Dickenson cared what he thought.

~

Soon there was little else to be seen or heard but gunfire explosions and smoke. But still they waited. Webster was beginning to think that the waiting might prove to be the hardest part of the whole day. He could see that the men and horses were restless, beginning to lose faith that their officers would give them their chance to kill the enemy, who had been picking off comrades like sandflies all last week. It was when he turned round to indicate to his men they must keep battle-ready that he saw the birds.

They were approaching from the west, wheeling high in the sky. Of course, it was to be expected; wherever there was kill, vultures would hover and wait their turn. It was their sheer number that was disconcerting.

~

It was Freer who saw them first. He turned to his neighbours. 'Bloody hell, they haven't wasted much time getting here.'

As more vultures arrived to circle on the early afternoon thermals, soon all the men were looking at the great creatures skimming the sky with wing-tips as black as congealed blood. Like troops, they jockeyed and skirmished for position, ready to rip open the dead as though there might not be enough to satisfy all their appetites.

'You can kiss my arse, and all!' Freer swore at them.

Thomas told himself that vultures were just like larger and uglier carrion crows, their behaviour natural and signifying nothing sinister. But not so the men. He watched them pointing to the sky and drawing their fingers across their throats as they looked at their neighbours, as if picking out cattle at market for slaughter. The men might have grinned as they did this, but something was unnerving their horses. Thomas realised this, for the more he suppressed his own feelings, the more Fearless pawed at the ground and shifted her hindquarters backwards. It took him all his skill to calm her down. But other horses were succeeding in shuffling their riders out of place. The columns were in danger of collapsing.

Thomas whispered to Freer, who nodded and turned towards Littlethorpe and gestured for him to sing one of his campfire songs, for the Private's unwavering tenor could almost miraculously turn a man's mind to the comradeship of battle.

~

Littlethorpe understood immediately. Better than church, this. He could make his own music, sing his favourite tunes any time he wanted.

Hark now the drums beat up again,
For all true soldiers gentlemen,
Then let us 'list and march, I say,
Over the hills and far away.

It wasn't as though a man could hear much at all except for his own voice, but like an underground stream Littlethorpe's song flowed through the ranks. Gradually each man shared the tune with his neighbour like an ant signalling the finding of food.

~

Webster was close enough to feel the groundswell of the song running and worming its way through the ranks. He watched the horses move slowly back into line and settle into their positions. He thanked God for his men's good humour and tried to ignore the vultures sweeping across the sky. But then he felt the hand of St Theresa resting on his shoulder, its shrivelled flesh and bone tapping lightly its reminder of his own mortality.

Our 'prentice Tom may now refuse
To wipe his scoundrel Master's shoes,
For now he's free to sing and play
Over the hills and far away.

~

Thomas studied the crumbling red earth tumbled into a low ridge and pressed the small cloth bag of Burton Lazarus soil close against his chest and told himself this was not where he intended to end his days. He slapped his reins across the side of Fearless's neck.

'Eh lass. We'll show 'em.'

He swallowed hard as he heard Littlethorpe's next verse roll towards them, and instinctively turned to where Freer was standing by his column of men. He joined in as lustily as he could.

Courage, boys, 'tis one to ten,
But we return all gentlemen
All gentlemen as well as they,
Over the hills and far away

~

Littlethorpe sipped his extra ration of rum between verses. He wanted to hold the buzz as long as possible, beyond its natural life. Then he'd be ready. Ready to feel his sabre slashing through flesh. Ready to cut down the enemy as easily as he could stick pigs. He, who could strike down the angry sow who'd pinned his father against the sty wall, knew how to give as good as he got. More than that. He knew how to do the bastards down before they did for you. He wasn't afraid of the crapauds. He'd seen their pale skinny bodies bathing in the Douro. Naked, they were as pink and defenceless as any pig.

~

As staff officers rode up and down the line with news no one could make sense of, the day began to darken. Webster thought the moment would never come. At last the order came to advance. Le Marchant's heavy cavalry, flanked by two of their own squadrons, were to attack the French centre. Webster swallowed the last of his grog and could have sworn he'd tasted the blood of Christ and felt His forgiveness for all his sins. He felt truly alive, truly in touch with all the saints and martyrs that had walked this earth before him. Whatever happened, he would face death in sure and certain hope of the Resurrection to eternal life.

~

Thomas checked his sword knot and touched his sabre's hilt. He pledged every cut for Sparrow, every parry for Grace and, as for himself, only God would know about that and if … Well, his grandmother's God was no tyrant. There would be a reason for it. Some good would come out of it. Grace would marry someone else, have another man's children. So long as that damned Boney doesn't win this bloody war. He took his last sip of grog, the one he'd saved for this moment.

~

Littlethorpe gripped the hilt of his sabre. Pig-sticking was what he was good at, what he did best, what he was known for back in Stoke. It was only what his mother would expect of him. Treat the crapauds like pigs; cure their hams for the long winter ahead.

~

Dickenson raised his helmet aloft on his sabre point and the trumpeters gave the signal to move forward. Dickenson was excited. At last the chase; the chase which back home shaped his days and weeks; the flushing of the fox out of the coverts; the hounds scenting their quarry; the sheer joy and noise of the kill. The preparatory order being given, he rode his horse now at a moderate pace. They were soon atop the hill, and ready to support Le Marchant in his first strike. Le

Marchant's men, the heavier hounds, would be in first to cut the French down with their great blades; Dickenson's Light Dragoons were there to support him and to deal with the rest. It was a role Dickenson understood to perfection. He placed his hand on his hilt, ready to draw. Not too soon though, or they would frighten the fox away from the hounds still closing in.

He recalled crisp autumn days, hills cool green, hedges jumped, streams waded, the fox's brush carried high on their shoulders for blooding the youngest child. Now another day for some fine hunting. Feet firm against the stirrups, spurs held off for an inch or two longer, he signalled the squadron to a hand gallop. Three hundred or so yards to go through the smoke that obliterated all else. Le Marchant ahead. The crapauds' columns broken. Ready to strike, spurs in, sabres horizontal. Charge. Now. Strike.

~

Webster could see Le Marchant sweeping down on the French like a fox into a coop, first two French battalions, then a third, fourth and fifth, cut down. It was time for them to mop up the rest, one by one, each soldier a broken link in a broken chain, thrown down on the blood-red earth.

~

It was Thomas who saw Dickenson go down. He dismounted to establish the severity of Dickenson's wounds and protect him from further injury. A musket ball had torn into his left breast. Thomas tried to staunch the wound with his neck cloth but feared the task was hopeless. He pulled out Dickenson's sabre and looped Fearless's reins around it. He remembered seven years previously, the first time he'd set eyes on Dickenson riding tall though Leicester on a dark hunter, blue uniform and crimson sash, white braids looping across his chest, Tarleton helmet; plump and plumed. Like some god he'd seemed then to Thomas. What an evening they'd had of it at The Blue Boar with Murphy's tales of glory. And now, this half-god seemed very like to die in his arms. Freer rode up and mounted guard to the rear.

'Where the hell's Fallowfield?'

Thomas, thankful to have Freer with him, shook his head. 'Don't know. Maybe he's down too?'

Freer stood in his stirrups. 'Can't see him, but then again, who can bloody see anything? You were lucky I saw Fearless; for a minute there I thought you'd fallen.'

With Freer watching over him, Thomas tried once again to stem Dickenson's loss of blood by pressing hard against the wound.

They were soon joined by Littlethorpe, who took up guard opposite Freer and to the front of Dickenson. Littlethorpe yelled, 'Tell him we've seen the buggers off and Private Littlethorpe is the best river man Salamanca side of the Tormes.'

Thomas rather hoped Dickenson hadn't heard Littlethorpe's last remark, but pressed his mouth to Dickenson's left ear and whispered.

'We have the crapauds on the run, sir. They're well and truly done for.'

Who knew whether Dickenson could hear, but Thomas felt it his duty to tell him of their victory before he expired. But as soon as it was clear that no further comfort could be offered, Thomas left Littlethorpe to guard the body whilst Freer tried to find Webster. He remounted his mare and rejoined the battle. The French were truly on the run. Too busy running to even think about looting a dead officer.

~

Bloody good riddance. It was worth the self-inflicted flesh wound he'd gone to the rear with, though some might question his loyalty. Still, Jack Fallowfield's plan to abandon his role as Dickenson's cover serjeant had paid off. Without Fallowfield guarding his back, Dickenson was an easy target for any crapaud who knew the meaning of extra lace and gold bloody trimmings.

Though Webster didn't have any more backbone than Dickenson in disciplinary matters, at least he and Webster had some understanding of each other. But he hadn't been able to turn Webster again recently. The Lieutenant was back to living within his means, renouncing all luxuries except for his bloody painting – which was how Fallowfield might just be able to catch him out again; though nowadays Webster seemed more bothered about protecting the local churches from being chopped up for firewood than sketching them. Not that Webster had any better ideas as to how they were going to cook their meat rations. And as for bloody Dickenson accusing him of this and that over one miserable dead French officer who was supposed to have given his parole to behave himself, but who obviously couldn't be trusted … In his experience officers always stuck together, even if one of them was French. As for the men, you could tell by their bloody disrespectful looks, he'd never have been able to keep them under his control again if Dickenson had had his way. But Dickenson was no more and Fallowfield was almost a free man … except for bloody Freer and Cowper. But he'd already made sure Webster would never take their side against him, and so far they'd had the good sense to keep quiet about the French officer. He could be patient. Their time would come.

~

With Dickenson dead, Webster took his place at the head of the men, and raised himself in his stirrups, lifting his sabre to indicate to them and to the enemy that he was now in charge. Like the vultures of this morning, his men might be late at the feast, but they were cleaning up as effectively as any carrion birds. At last he signalled the men to withdraw and regroup to await further orders. With the French dead or surrendering, their job in the centre was nearly done.

The fighting on the flanks too was routing the last of the French divisions, who had tried but failed to regroup. The entire brigade of cavalry had been ordered to stay put and not pursue the disorderly retreat any further; a Spanish brigade was guarding the only bridge at Alma and would deal with the rest of the French.

Night was now falling. The sky darkened quickly and the scorched grass ignited by gunpowder and shot was incinerating the wounded and the dead, the sweet smell of burning flesh making men and horses alike gag for breath.

~

Thomas and Littlethorpe found themselves riding together, away from the immediate battlefield.

Thomas leant across to Littlethorpe. 'That was a fine song.'

Littlethorpe looked up. 'Calmed the horses down, anyways.'

Thomas wondered what else could possibly be said at such a time. He tightened his hold on the reins. 'So, Dickenson is dead.'

'Aye, well, he's not the only one.'

Thomas guessed that Littlethorpe had lost a couple of pals too. He hadn't tried to do a head count yet.

'Best see to the horses, eh?' With every cut of his sabre, he'd taken his revenge for the killing of Sparrow and the rest of the night picquet, but revenge couldn't bring back Sparrow or any other of his friends. Now his wounds and gashes merely mocked his own survival.

Littlethorpe reached into his sabretache and pulled out a fine-looking hip flask. 'Here, have some of this first. Poor bugger don't need it no more, where he's going. Time to look after the living, eh?'

After Thomas and Littlethorpe had emptied the flask, they dismounted somewhat unsteadily, wiped the animals down as best they could, then brushed and combed their coats back into life, checking for wounds as they fed them forage from their saddle sacks. But as they cleaned their weapons, wiping the blood from their sabres, the soldiers felt the wind suddenly return, and the temperature begin to drop.

'Here, they'll give us a bit of shelter.'

Littlethorpe had spotted some dead French infantrymen already looted and no use to man or beast, until now. They'd make some kind of windbreak if two or three were piled on top of each other.

Thomas wanted to protest but really Littlethorpe was right. It was time to look after the living. He was glad these stinking flames were warming the night air. They'd have to bury the rest of their dead tomorrow.

~

Webster had ordered Dickenson's body to be fetched off the battlefield before the other casualties. Now, cloaks draped over swords made a serviceable mortuary to protect the body from the scrutiny of the men whilst Webster went through the Captain's personal necessaries and wondered what he should write to Dickenson's parents. As a second son, Dickenson's loss would not entail rearrangement of estates and property and Webster had been given to understand that Dickenson and his father were not close, but he was very fond of his mother. Dickenson clearly favoured her a great deal. Webster was not sure what he hoped for; that Dickenson's mother would be thrown into deepest mourning, or that she would cheerfully console herself with her other sons. He imagined Dickenson as a plump, good-natured child tugging at his mother's skirts; and suddenly knew she would miss him terribly. He laid out Dickenson's few possessions on the rough ground: a crumpled kerchief, a memorandum book with its attached pencil, five doubloons retrieved from the safety of his jacket hem, together with his brown leather wallet, its wrap-around strap still guarding its contents. Webster noticed that Dickenson's silver hip flask appeared to be missing. Webster took out his notebook and precious pencil stub from his own pocket. He should draft a letter to Dickenson's parents for Pennington to write in the morning. With Dickenson dead and Webster next in order of seniority, this promotion would cost him nothing. Webster would, in truth, profit substantially by Dickenson's death. He tried to shake off any thought of his being unworthy.

~

Littlethorpe awoke at dawn and wandered to the blackened edge of the battlefield. So this was what East Stoke must have looked like all those years ago, bodies heaped upon bodies, waiting for the living to roll them into pits, their loosened knuckle bones found and fashioned into jacks by young boys like him, three hundred years or more later. Cousins fighting cousins for the crown of England, they said.

~

As the morning brought a little more heat, Thomas awoke, still sore and exhausted. He was glad to see the trail of women with bandages and lotions making their way up from the villages. The bandsmen, too, were busy rolling the wounded into blankets, settling them into groups to await the return of more wagons. But where was Freer? Surely Freer hadn't been lost too? Thomas had seen him talking to Webster only a short while before the French finally left the field. So where the hell was he?

~

Webster woke early. Wellington had ordered the rest of Bock and Anson's cavalry to investigate the lack of news about the expected capture of the retreating French at Alma. Wellington suspected the worst; that the Spanish had abandoned their allotted task: to guard the bridge. What else could explain the lack of information? Bock's King's German Legion was to lead the hunt, with their lighter cavalry units in support. So Webster gathered up his men and set off at some speed towards Alba, where the French had clearly succeeded in crossing the bridge unscathed and were undoubtedly making for their heartlands marching back towards Madrid.

By now, Bock's officers had quickened the pace to a fast but steady trot, and just before the village of Garcia Hernandez they all caught up with the French rearguard. These were fresh troops, Marmont's reserve, eight battalions in all, in position in the gap and up the hillside. Webster thought the French position strong. But then the most extraordinary thing happened. The French cavalry, on sighting them, melted away at a gallop, leaving their infantry to fend for themselves. Perhaps the cavalry fled, fearing the King's German Legion's formidable reputation, or perhaps they ran, because they could, whilst the infantry had no choice other than to form into squares.

Webster saw that his opportunity to destroy the French rearguard was about to disappear; charging squares that had had time to form was not something cavalry undertook lightly unless supporting artillery had blasted gaps in the ranks first. Charging row upon row of fixed bayonets was like setting a cat on a hedgehog. Then again, the KGL excelled at such assaults, their yard-long sabres as formidable as any sword yet invented. Webster turned to check that his men were drawn up in an orderly fashion. His exhausted Cornet, dutiful as ever, had the men battle ready and awaiting his orders. To Webster's surprise, the KGL had obviously decided this was a challenge they could meet. The heavy cavalry moved forward, steadily increasing their speed until they were barely a blade's length away from the first square. At first the French appeared paralysed, their volleys of gunfire almost too late to hit the leading horsemen.

Webster kept his men on the flanks, heading for the corners of the square in support of the KGL. Then he saw one of the leading KGL horsemen fall heavily into the French front line. Like some apocalyptic vision, horse and dragoon plunged forward until the dragoon finally fell from the saddle. But the magnificent bay, a white blaze like forked lightning running the length of its nose, plunged still deeper into the square. Blood streaming from its chest, it reared and bucked, hooves slicing a path through to the centre. Here, it lashed out, felling soldier after soldier, like the blind Samson bringing down the temple of the Philistines. The KGL's second line poured through the gaps and all was lost, as square after square dissolved into chaos.

As they chased the stragglers to force a surrender, Webster felt the blood of Christ surge through his veins and

St Theresa clasp him to her bosom. Perhaps he would be forgiven for profiting from Dickenson's death after all?

~

Freer finally caught up with Thomas by the far hillside. Thomas could have embraced him from sheer relief. Freer had been made up to acting serjeant and then ordered by Webster to make sure none of their over-eager forces were tempted to pursue the fleeing reserves, as they would risk running into ambuscades.

Freer leant forward. 'Did you see that horse?'

Thomas hesitated. 'Found a horse rather like that one running wild, night before last. When we had that big storm. Took it back to the KGL lines.'

Freer whistled. 'The one and the same, eh? '

Thomas tried to be tentative. 'It was very like it.'

Now more sure than Thomas was, Freer leant back in his saddle. 'You couldn't mistake that set of markings.'

Thomas was relieved to hear Freer so definite. 'That's what I thought.'

Freer grinned. 'Pity the poor bugger on the horse though.'

Thomas closed his eyes and commended all the dead, even the Papists, to his Grandmother's God. Maybe both he and the horse had been chosen to survive the previous day's battle for a purpose. Perhaps he had more work to do yet, before his race was run.

'Bloody hell, they're back again sharp.'

Thomas opened his eyes and followed Freer's hand pointing upwards.

Vultures, wing tips black as dried blood, circling in the thermals, biding their time.

~

By that evening Will Freer could see Cowper was babbling nonsense about him being The Chosen One. Freer had at first thought that Cowper's wounds, like his own, were mostly superficial and clean enough to look at, but somewhere in his friend's body there burned a pain and a fever he couldn't fathom. He shouted for Byrne, Ashby and Littlethorpe to help him apply some of the remedies Cowper had used for Sparrow and the others wounded in the hilltop ambush.

'Can you remember what he used and how he mashed them up?'

Ashby nodded in that precise manner of his. 'For the fever? I've still got some of them made up. I labelled them. They seemed fresh enough the other day when I checked.'

So they lathered him, poulticed him and fed him every combination of medicine Ashby had prepared, whilst Cowper protested and vehemently denied any previous acquaintance with them.

It wasn't long before Webster appeared and sent for the surgeon, who declared the illness to be a mystery and advised that Thomas be taken back to Belem, to the general hospital there. The surgeon had men waiting who urgently required his skills with the knife, and no, he didn't have any wagons to spare.

It took four of them to lash Cowper onto his horse. Awake enough to keep in the saddle, but incapable of much else. It was going to be a long ride to Belem. Cowper's possessions were slung onto a following mule; Littlethorpe had felt his fingers itch as he loaded them up. No, it was enough to have carried off Dickenson's silver hip flask. After all, his family wouldn't miss it.

~

Thomas felt he was being pulled into position like Christ onto the cross, making his triumphant entry into Jerusalem on the donkey, palms spread in his path all the way, garlanded in the desert heat with leaves. His mind wavered with things that smelt of homecomings, dark earthy green. He heard his disciples cheer. But then he saw the black-robed friars, their bony hands grasping his fingers, tying him down, great bald-necked vultures dipping their heads into his open wounds, drinking his blood.

~

Will Freer could have burst into tears when he saw Cowper ready to leave, lashed upon Fearless, who at once seemed to understand the great responsibility she bore for Cowper's safe passage to Belem. Freer had begged Webster to be allowed to take him, but Webster had insisted that as a newly promoted serjeant he should stay and take some responsibility for getting their ragged forces back into action. The Lieutenant had already heard numerous accounts of Cowper's and Littlethorpe's outstanding behaviour on the battlefield, and he'd promised Freer that if Cowper recovered, he too would be promoted. If he recovered. Freer heard the words float in the dust like a death sentence as Cowper was led away by Littlethorpe and Ashby, who at least seemed to understand Cowper's potions and remedies whilst also offering up prayers for his deliverance. What could Freer do other than wait and hope?

46

The General Hospital

September 1812, Belem, Lisbon

Dearest Grace,

I am not sure of the precise date for I have been sick in the general hospital here in Belem. I recall little of the last few weeks since my journey here under the rough-and-ready care of Privates Ashby and Littlethorpe and the faithful Dog.

Freer and Littlethorpe apparently took it upon themselves to declare me a man on the brink of dying of fever, so Littlethorpe and Ashby dragged me here half- insensible, lashed upon the back of Fearless, administering my own grandmother's remedies to me.

Littlethorpe said I was raving, saying I was The Chosen One and not the son of Beelzebub. Of course he does not know about the rift between my mother and me, so I laugh it off but I fear the matter is not settled in my own mind and never will be, so long as I am unforgiven, and the dead cannot forgive, can they?

The doctor here tells me their care undoubtedly saved my life. But Littlethorpe is not one to accept gratitude, and has told me that he accompanied me merely to ensure that he and I both enjoyed a well-deserved rest on the cool shores of the Tagus. But it does not do to stay too long in Belem. Ashby has already returned. Those who have become sick in body can easily find themselves too sick at heart to return to the rigours of the campaign. So, soon we must make our way back to our Regiment, but at present we await orders for our disposition to winter quarters, for the summer campaigns now close. They say that we have lost yet more men on the retreat from a place in the north of Spain called Burgos and that this has been the hardest year since General Moore's forced march to Corunna. Yet so much seemed to be going well.

Littlethorpe is an attentive visitor. Dog is as joyful a creature as ever and has acquired an admirer, who seems to have attached herself to both Littlethorpe and Dog. Her name is Maria, one of the Convent servants working here in the hospital. She seems much taken by Littlethorpe. I suppose now he's as washed and tidy as the next man, he's a handsome enough fellow with a good set of teeth.

I must rest now but wanted to let you know that I have survived our great battle with the French at Salamanca. Littlethorpe says that the doctors here tell him that all Wellington's despatches are sent immediately to London by the fastest packet boat available, so I expect you and the Squire's household are already celebrating Wellington's great triumph.

I will write with more news when I feel a little stronger.

Yours as ever, Thomas

47

Theatricals

September 1812, Belem, Portugal,

Thomas slit open his letter from Grace with mixed feelings. He'd begun to resent her accounts of her new life as a lady's maid to Miss Susan, Mistress Rearsby's young niece, who'd recently come to live in the Squire's household. Grace thought that Mistress Rearsby was planning to marry her niece to Master Andrew. It was all so far away from any life he'd known that sometimes he felt she'd become a complete stranger to him.

Last week, as Mistress Rearsby was indisposed, I accompanied Miss Susan to one of the assemblies in the Rooms in Leicester until we could conveniently meet her appointed chaperon there. The rooms are extremely grand and all manner of dances and games of chance are regularly arranged for ladies and gentlemen of quality. Some of the ladies have adopted the more outlandish gauzy French fashions, which are to be seen throughout society here, in spite of the War.

And now she was prattling about the great theatricals held in the Hall and how Master Andrew had converted one of the stable blocks into a theatre for public performances no less, and how whenever he was back from Horse Guards to visit his parents – and Miss Susan, Grace added – he would put on a play for the entertainment of the entire household.

His mother was happy to indulge him in whatever way she could since his great illness after Corunna.

You see, Thomas, Master Andrew is a great believer in the magic as well as the healing powers of the dramatic art. The power of the illusion, he calls it and commends us to read the plays of a man called Shakespeare. You will remember I sent you some lines from his play Midsummer Night's Dream for you.

Thomas stopped reading for a moment and tried to imagine Grace, in her new life wearing the pretty dress and shoes she had worn in St James's Park. But he wasn't so sure about the positive powers of magic or illusions, though he did like the verse she'd sent him in the letter he received at Badajoz; the one he kept close by to try and remind him of home.

I know a bank whereon the wild thyme blows,
Where oxlips and the nodding violet grows,
Quite over-canopied with luscious woodbine,
With sweet musk-roses, and with eglantine:

He could almost smell the thyme and feel the tug of his grandmother's hand pulling him up steep stream banks, but however hard he tried these memories slithered from his grasp, leaving him alone with his mother's accusations and Michael's broken body.

48

Winter 1812

October 1812, Winter quarters, Oliveira de Conde

Dearest Grace,

I was glad to receive your letters in September whilst I was still in the hospital. Letters from England can cross with our own and can get very mixed up in their order on account of our supply ships taking anything from a fortnight to two months to arrive, depending on the weather. But now I have read your letter about Master Andrew's venture into theatricals at the Hall and I thank you also for the verse.

So, to let you know how we fare. We were joined on our march here by a new officer, Lieutenant Haywood. He has exchanged from the 45th Dragoons to the 36th and is replacing Lieutenant Webster, who has been promoted to Captain, in place of poor Dickenson, who was killed at Salamanca. Our own cornets were considered too inexperienced to be promoted by virtue of our lieutenant's vacancy. Haywood too had been delayed in Belem by an attack of ague and like myself has only recently recovered. So we all made our way together slowly up the country to our winter quarters, close to where we wintered last year, due west of Ciudad Rodrigo. Haywood, his servant and baggage mules led the way, myself riding Fearless as *feebly as any new recruit, Littlethorpe bringing up the rear with Maria and Dog. Lieutenant Haywood seemed a little surprised to find Maria and Dog in our party, but he is a kind and jovial fellow and declared himself happy for them to make themselves useful, Dog catching rats and Maria doing our laundry. He reminds me a little of Dickenson and, since our long journey together began, he and I have established an amiable relationship. Then, on my return I found myself promoted to be his cover serjeant instead of Evans, who died on the Burgos retreat. As Haywood says, both of us have stepped into dead men's boots, one way or another, which is just as well, for Haywood admits to being far too short of cash to have purchased a lieutenant's commission. I suppose it is likely that many officers will obtain their promotions in this way as the fighting becomes ever fiercer.*

Littlethorpe continues to be as cheerfully reckless as ever. Maria seems to be a most sweet-natured girl, even when at the beck and call of Bonnie Murphy and the other campaign-hardened women. She seems to take it all in good heart and, being quick to learn English, she has helped us become better friends with both our Portuguese comrades and the local villagers. So Littlethorpe is very happy. It does us good to see some happiness again in our midst for we may yet have a long road ahead of us before we come home.

Yours ever truly, Thomas

49

Victory

28 April 1814, Bayonne, France

Thomas wriggled in his saddle, the sunshine warming his back. The standards of England, Spain and Portugal and the Bourbons hung loose, ready to be raised upon the ramparts in this final ceremony to mark victory. Thomas and Fearless stood to attention, the men dressed in the best uniforms they could patch together, the horses better groomed than at any time since they'd left England. Thomas guessed he wasn't the only one hiding his tears.

Thomas looked around him to judge how his men were faring, but all he could see in his mind now were empty places; spaces where plump and cheerful Dickenson should have been at the head of the men; and further down the ranks, where Tranter and Sparrow had once stood alongside him and Freer. Thomas frowned; there were now more battle-scars in their ranks than there had been in prize-fighter Tranter's mouth. As for the loss of their best batsman, Sparrow; well, even Byrne hadn't felt able to mourn the absence of decent cricket pitches in the inhospitable Peninsula. Thomas shook himself free of regrets as best he could, concentrating his attention instead on those still alive: garrulous Murphy; 'let's beat the hell out of the Gentleman players' Byrne; displaced hand frame weaver turned

Methodist Ashby; reckless Littlethorpe; chatty Lieutenant Haywood; the ever-solemn Captain Webster; and a subdued Freer, standing further down the ranks with his section of the company. Not forgetting bloody Fallowfield, holding himself ramrod-straight but sporting the ruddy complexion and purple nose of a heavy drinker. Poised like a snake coiled on a rock ready to strike should its prey come close, Fallowfield had wheedled his way back into their company just before Bayonne. After Dickenson's death at Salamanca, Webster had persuaded another captain to take Fallowfield to fill a serjeant's vacancy in his company. Webster seemed to have thought that would be the end of it, but damn it, Fallowfield was back again only a few columns' distance away from them. At least now he and Freer were serjeants too. But would that be enough to stop him from taking his revenge?

~

Will Freer just hoped it had all been for the best. After nearly twenty years of soldiers just like themselves killing each other, he couldn't quite believe this was the end of it. Mind, it had been a hard time coming, nearly two more years of fighting after Salamanca, rock by rock through the mountains till they reached France.

More's the pity they hadn't come face to face with Boney himself, who'd been too busy fighting a rearguard action in the north to support his Peninsula troops. Still, without their defeat of Marshal Soult, who knows how long Boney might have held out?

As for their own conduct in the war, he'd seen men at their best and men at their worst, but at least there'd been no repeat of the excesses of Badajoz.

~

Captain Charles Webster tried to feel happy, knew he should be grateful. At least some basic etiquette was honoured in France and, as the local population was inclined to support the return of the Bourbons, both peasants and gentlemen were considerably more hospitable. But they had all paid a heavy price, Dickenson and countless men left behind them in graves hastily scraped out of an unforgiving landscape. Not that they had had anything in common, but he missed Dickenson and his straightforward approach to life, so unlike himself. He was pleased, though, to find that Wellington's decision last spring to surprise the French from across the Esla concurred with his own thoughts, as he had always held that Wellington should aim to drive the French out the same way they had come in; through the Pyrenees.

~

Will Freer shifted his bad leg in the stirrup. He only had to think about their march up the Ebro after crossing the Douro at Oporto and it twinged. It was the worst kind of terrain, the kind cavalrymen dreaded, constantly hauling themselves up and down the steepest and narrowest of paths, higher and higher, with the mountains breathing down on them like ill-tempered ghosts. Many a time they'd had to get off and walk, leading their horses rather than risk their legs on that rough ground.

~

Thomas just wished they hadn't thrown away their great triumph at Vittoria that summer before, allowing the entire French army to escape, for the sole sake of gathering plunder. Not that the 36th had had much to do with it, as they'd been delayed by heavy artillery fire on the far bank of the Zadorra. Thomas shook his head. If only they hadn't been so damn distracted and had kept on chasing the French back there and then, they might have saved another winter of lost lives.

~

Captain Charles Webster wondered whether he could manage on half pay if he left the army. He wouldn't want to have to endure another winter like the last one, billeted in mountain villages twenty miles or so to the rear of San Sebastian in order to keep the army's communication lines open, constantly on the move to wherever the enemy showed an inclination to attack …

~

Thomas rubbed Fearless's neck. 'That winter was the worst, eh? Living on whins till we arranged with the damned crapauds to take turns getting in our forage without us feeling obliged to shoot each other. Never properly unsaddled; night patrols every hour; and then having to swim across the Adour! You were not happy. Never were keen on water, eh Fearless?'

~

Will Freer looked across at the troops and lamented. They were so tired they'd hardly found the strength to celebrate, except in the customary way of drinking Wellington's health and in the process entirely neglecting their own. Even Ashby and the other Methodists, usually so disapproving of drink, joined them when they heard the Tyrant had abdicated. Even Cowper was three sheets to the wind. Getting so drunk nobody cared anymore about anything.

~

Charles Webster turned to look across the courtyard, to where the Governor of Bayonne now sat unsmiling and tight-jawed. Hard to think that even after Toulouse, Marshal Soult and the Governor didn't believe Boney had abdicated, refusing to surrender until they'd all lost yet more men.

~

Richard Littlethorpe cursed the lot of them, starting with Boney, abdicating two months before Maria's baby was due, then Wellington for sending all the Portuguese home, and then Freer and Cowper for dragging him back to dry land when he'd have been happier dead. He'd thought he could swim over to one of the little boats before they got onto the ships, but he hadn't reckoned on Fallowfield and the infantry marksmen keeping watch and his bloody kissing cousin Cowper working out what he was going to do, Dog yapping like an idiot, not knowing if he should follow Maria or stay with him. He'd done his best … given Maria all his booty. He'd told her not to let Dickenson's hip flask go too cheap, and to ask the nuns to take her in again – and to remember him always. But it wasn't enough. It could never be enough. He just wished the war could have gone on forever.

~

Thomas could now see the standards of England, Spain and Portugal and the Bourbons flying upon the ramparts. Fearless flinched as a signal gun was fired from one of the batteries. The Tricolor was gradually lowered, whilst guns in every part of the city fired a salute, and a small white standard of the Bourbons, grubby and torn, was run up in its place.

50

Going Home

Dearest Grace,

You probably heard the news before it reached us. To our great joy Napoleon has abdicated, leaving the way clear for us to march home as soon as everything can be agreed and arranged, for there are many things to make sure of before we set off through this countryside so recently hostile to us. It has been decided that the cavalry are to march in two great separate columns through France until we reach the Channel. We do not know whether this is to save the horses, who are happier marching than being on the water, or whether the transport requirements of such a large army from this distance away are too taxing. We begin our march tomorrow and there is great excitement at the thought of home. We expect to be in England by the summer and, although it is not certain where our depot will be, we should have news by then as to our future. But there is much talk of the army being reduced, with even long-serving officers going on half pay, and it may be that our Regiment will be disbanded or halved in size, in which case I may be with you sooner than I had expected. In the meantime I send you my dearest wishes. Thomas

51

The Proposals

Summer and winter 1814, Weymouth and Dorchester

Lieutenant Haywood counselled caution when Thomas wondered if it would be better to volunteer to leave rather than await compulsory discharges.

'Our countrymen will still have need of our services.'

'Aye,' Freer whispered afterwards to Cowper, 'We cavalry are a bit too useful for keeping down the poor sods returning home with no other means of making an honest living.'

It was the risk of unemployment more than anything else that finally persuaded Thomas against writing to Grace with the proposal of marriage he'd been planning during the long march home through France. The summer soon enough turned into winter, and it was still not clear what the future of the Regiment would be. It unsettled him for weeks, leaving him unable to do more than write the most cursory letters to Grace. *Write as an honest man,* Louise had said the very first time he'd met her, and now he felt he was acting like a thief.

Making sense of the peace was proving to be more difficult than making sense of the war. Matters came to a head when Old Bones, otherwise known as Troop Serjeant-Major Beckwith, came visiting him and Freer in the New

Year. Old Bones had been complaining about his arthritic joints since he was thirty-five, but now, at forty-five his hands were so gnarled he could scarcely grasp his horse's reins. He appeared to have an entirely detached attitude towards the men under his command, so Thomas was much surprised when he sought them both out to tell them his application to the pension board had been granted and his position would need to be filled before the month was out.

Old Bones, in an uncharacteristic fit of loose talk, spoke quietly.

'I did say to Captain Webster I thought the next troop serjeant-major should be one of the younger serjeants, who then might get to marry his sweetheart.'

With that parting shot, Old Bones creaked slowly away.

Freer pulled a face. 'As if Fallowfield would let a chance like this slip through his fingers.'

Thomas wasn't sure. 'Perhaps Old Bones just wanted us to know what he's said to Webster.'

Freer shook his head. 'As if that would make any bloody difference. I'm telling you that man would see off any officer by fair means or foul.'

Thomas and Freer had concluded a long time ago that Fallowfield had deliberately abandoned Dickenson to his death at Salamanca and didn't expect anything better of him if any other officer dared to stand in his way.

With only a quietly drunken gathering at The King's Arms to mark nineteen years of fighting the Tyrant, Old Bones slipped away a few days later into his new life, whilst his wife Molly bade a stoical farewell to the flock of wives as if she'd personally schooled them in the ways of war but now felt unsure how to advise them with the country at peace.

Old Bones's vacancy hung over the Regiment for another week before Fallowfield fired his first salvo.

~

It was when Thomas saw Freer being marched over toLieutenant-Colonel Pennington's office, escorted by two other sergeants, that he realised Fallowfield had resumed hostilities. Freer was obviously in some kind of trouble. Thomas remembered the right of an accused to have a friend with him and ran after them. As they approached Pennington's office, Freer spoke over his shoulder to Thomas.

'Best keep out of his way, Cowper.'.

But Thomas took no notice, and by the time they reached Pennington's office they were almost side-by-side.

Lieutenant Colonel Pennington looked up with an expression Thomas had never seen on his face before. Whilst he and Freer were not on close terms with Pennington, all three had seen a great deal of each other during the Peninsular campaign.

Pennington, scarcely half a dozen years older than Thomas, had probably seen more active service than either of his serjeants. Handsome enough to turn the head of any soldier's wife, he conducted regimental affairs with an open countenance and an attention to detail. But today… Today Thomas couldn't read his expression at all.

Fallowfield was standing near the door. Webster was on Pennington's right. Thomas stated he was there as Freer's official friend.

Pennington looked at Freer to see if he was in agreement, nodded and cleared his throat, riffling through the papers in front of him.

'Serjeant Freer, I have before me a sworn affidavit from a recognised government informant that on July 6th in the year 1805, in a public place in Nottingham, you were heard to bring the Regiment's reputation into disrepute. I am aware that this charge was brought before Captain Dickenson some time later, but Captain Dickenson understood there to be mitigating circumstances which led to this drunken outburst. Accordingly a week's pay was docked.'

Pennington paused and looked Freer in the eye. 'Given the circumstances, I see no reason to overrule Captain Dickenson's decision in respect of your conduct on that occasion.'

Another pause, before Pennington shuffled through his papers and spoke again. Thomas could hear the distaste in Pennington's voice.

'However, Sergeant Fallowfield has brought to my attention some outstanding matters not formerly adjudicated upon by Captain Dickenson. I have here a written statement from the clergyman who was officiating at a solemn service, which testifies to Serjeant Freer's references to and advocacy of Thomas Paine's writings in his church on an occasion when the rank and file were clearly mutinous and indeed had turned upon their own officers. I am referring, of course, to the funeral at East Blatchington of a certain Private Wintergreen in March 1806. This reverend gentlemen alleges that Sergeant Freer, then Private Freer, not only committed sacrilege by standing on the altar but also referred to the banned and seditious works of Thomas Paine in an approving manner in front of these mutinous troops.'

Thomas could see that Captain Webster hadn't heard these accusations officially presented before. As for Fallowfield, as he hadn't been at Wintergreen's funeral he must have garnered this information on his return, but then had decided to hold the clergyman's statement in reserve until it would be useful to him.

Captain Webster whispered something to Pennington, who nodded. Then Webster spoke up, his face gradually reddening.

'As the senior officer who was present on that occasion, sir, I should like to review this account, in order to help you draw your own conclusions regarding the exact nature of Sergeant Freer's actions.'

Webster, his own reputation clearly at risk, swallowed hard before managing to speak again.

'The men were indeed restive, sir, with some cause, I might add, as they were exceedingly ill-fed and poorly housed in a very harsh winter. The death of Private Wintergreen, which was a result of such deprivations, was the cause of much sorrow; and indeed there were some hot-heads who were prepared to act upon their grievances. If Private Freer, as the Serjeant then was, had not intervened, the day might have ended badly for all of us. But Serjeant Freer's actions – yes, including his standing on the altar to secure the men's attention and pointing out the dire consequences if they were to proceed – were both timely and necessary, allowing us to restore order.'

Thomas was relieved. Webster's account was near enough the truth to exonerate Freer whilst sparing Webster a few more blushes.

Fallowfield protested, 'Sir, this is the sworn testimony of a gentleman of the cloth.'

Webster's voice trembled slightly. 'As an officer, and as a gentleman, I declare this to be a true account of what happened which I am also prepared to swear to. I might also add, I observed at the time that the officiating clergyman's careless and unfeeling manner further enflamed the men's feelings.'

Fallowfield clenched his fists and bowed slightly. 'It's a pity I wasn't there or none of it would have happened in the first place, but as you were there, sir, your account of events must prevail.'

Pennington stood up. Thomas had never seen him look so angry. Fallowfield's scarcely veiled taunt at Webster's failure to control his men had not gone unnoticed.

'Case dismissed.'

But it was not quite the end of the matter for Webster,

~

Jack Fallowfield was seething. To be overlooked for the first troop serjeant-major vacancy in years in favour of Freer was an outrage, and by Webster too, after all he'd threatened him with; but Webster had stood his ground. Well, he'd get his own back, one way or another. Webster would regret this decision for the rest of his days.

~

Captain Charles Webster could see that Fallowfield was not going to let it rest. By refusing to back down in the face of Fallowfield's threats, he would be obliged to face up to the consequences of his own youthful indiscretions. He thought again of Samson, eyeless in Gaza, but who had been given not only the physical strength to pull the temple down upon the Philistines but also the strength of spirit to sacrifice himself together with his enemies. He owed it to the Regiment not to appoint Fallowfield to such a position of trust as troop serjeant-major. More than that, he also owed it to himself to confront the man, experience the worst he could do to him, rather than this constant looking over his shoulder, being in thrall to wickedness. He understood now that suffering was part of God's plan. He welcomed the penance he would have to suffer, as he would welcome the redemption he would perhaps one day be granted. Let Fallowfield do as he threatened. He, not his enemy, would ultimately be redeemed.

~

Thomas was sorry to see Captain Webster bundled away like a common criminal, although that was what he was now, landing up in a debtors' prison; with yet a further charge of being party to smuggling contraband spirits and French works of art. But Webster seemed positively cheerful when he'd spoken to Thomas only an hour or two before the bailiffs arrived.

'At least Sparrow got his new saddle, did he not?'

'He did, sir, and Private Littlethorpe has it now and a very good saddle it is. Indeed it's in a far better state than many.'

'I am pleased to hear that, Serjeant.' Webster cleared his throat. 'We have had many enlightening conversations, over the years, have we not?'

Thomas smiled. 'Freer and I have always enjoyed our discussions with you, sir.'

Webster brushed the back of his hand lightly across his eyes. 'Indeed! Well, I'll speak to Serjeant Freer next. I need to confirm something with him rather urgently.'

Webster pulled himself up even straighter, then looked down and fiddled with papers on his desk.

'I asked Freer not to tell you yet, but I have recommended that he be promoted to troop serjeant-major, and I wanted to let you know that had there been two vacancies then I would have had no hesitation in recommending you also.

But I have been aware, for a number of years now, of Serjeant Freer's engagement to Miss Louise Young; and I would not want the Army, or myself, for that matter, to stand in their way any longer.'

Thomas smiled. 'That's excellent news, sir.'

Webster nodded. He looked tired. 'Thank you for your understanding … in so many things, Cowper.'

Thomas thought it an odd thing for Webster to say but smiled again. 'He's my best friend sir. I wouldn't begrudge him promotion or the chance of happiness.'

Webster brightened. 'My sentiments exactly. Your turn will come, I'm sure of it, though I may not be able to have a hand in it directly.'

~

In the end, Thomas noted with satisfaction it was Troop Serjeant-Major Freer's winning of Louise with the approval of the Regiment, and of Landlord Young, that brought some joyfulness back into their lives.

Freer and Louise were married on a frosty February morning in Fordington Church, and after a day and night of dancing and drinking toasts to every man and woman that ever walked on earth, excepting the Tyrant, Thomas felt he might, at last, be worthy enough to propose to Grace.

~

Fordington, Dorchester, February 3rd, 1815

Dearest Grace,

Today we have celebrated the marriage of my dear friend Freer, who has at last wed his sweetheart, Louise. This happy event has made me think even more about the promise I made to you so long ago, before I left Burton.

I know your father may still have objections to our union, but now that you are of full age and I have won promotion, I feel able to ask you if you will consent to be my wife. In previous correspondence, I have often commented upon the hardships that army wives have to bear but now I am a serjeant, matters are far more promising and we are certain to be allocated a room of our own. Serjeants' wives too are not required to undertake such onerous duties within the Regiment in order to be put on the strength. Also, Freer tells me that they are now establishing regimental schools, and wives of good character and education may be appointed as schoolmistresses for the girls. His wife Louise is very clever, and good with her numbers and her letters, so Freer has high hopes that she will find work within one of these new schools. If he had not just been promoted to troop serjeant-major, I fancy he himself would have applied for a position as a schoolmaster serjeant. So it would be a great honour if you would become my wife, Grace.

On pausing to re-read his letter Thomas wasn't at all sure that he'd managed to convey how much he truly cared about her; he wondered how best to do this without seeming false in his manner. He simply had to find a way of telling her that he did love her, even after all this time.

I am sure that you know, Grace, I have always, always held you in the highest esteem and cared for you above any other, but I also know I have not always been good at telling you so. Forgive me, Grace, for sometimes I have been so full of what I have done and what I am thinking, perhaps you tired of hearing about my adventures. But I love you truly, Grace, and always have done and always will do. I look forward to your reply and hope that soon we will be making arrangements for our own wedding.

Ever your loving Thomas.

PS. You can use my bounty money to travel down in whatever manner you choose and to pay for suitable lodgings and anything else you need.

He sealed the letter, kissed it and stood it upright, ready to take to the morning post, and felt content. But that night the nightmares came back: his mother falling into Michael's grave mouthing 'murderer''; Michael leading a ragged procession of Black Friars; Grace pointing her finger at him, accusing him of killing Michael. It was not a good omen. So when they were ordered to march to Reading scarcely a month later, Thomas's letter to Grace was still in his sabretache.

~

Their regiment was considered lucky. They had neither been disbanded nor sent to the Indies, India or the Americas. They were on home duties. But once they'd returned to Dorchester there was remarkably little to do in Radipole barracks; not even watching out for the King and his family taking the waters on Weymouth beach now that His Majesty was confined to Windsor on account of, some whispered, his madness.

It had been just as quiet for the officers, Thomas concluded from his conversations with Haywood – hunting by day and playing cards by night. One winter of that and the officers were said to have cheered at the news the Regiment was to be sent to Reading to put down food riots and then on to Hounslow, as Londoners too were protesting against the new Corn Laws. This was not the kind of soldiering he nor Will Freer wanted to do – not that either of them approved of mob rule.

Freer had grumbled all the way to Reading. 'Haven't we just won the bloody War? What right do the landlords think they have to keep out foreign corn, to line their own pockets at the expense of ordinary people who can't even afford to eat the food they grow for their masters?'

But they'd no sooner arrived, at the tail end of Reading's food riots, than they heard the news of Napoleon's escape and his great march through France, gathering an army eager to follow him wherever he led.

Only Freer believed it could have been possible. 'Of course Napoleon was going to escape if you stuck him on a little island hardly any distance from his homeland, from both of his homelands, with nothing to do, no one to tyrannise, no one to make laws over, no one to conquer. What did they expect him to do? Of course he'd try to escape. Of course he'd call upon his old soldiers. What else can old soldiers do but fight?'

It was a thought that Thomas himself had hardly dared entertain, and Freer relished this chance to fight the Tyrant on his home ground. Thomas too took it as a sign and at last placed his letter with its marriage proposal into the care of Dover's biggest Receiving House: let God decide if I'm to live or die, and let Grace decide if I'm truly deserving of happiness.

~

Grace hadn't expected this. She'd thought of Bailiff Strutt's kindnesses as no more than that; but then to discover that ever since his wife died last autumn, he'd been imagining that she would become his wife and a mother to his children. Did he assume that with Thomas out of sight he was also out of mind?

Bailiff Strutt had been as courteous as always when he'd first discussed his feelings for her under the plum trees in the walled kitchen garden, but she had been so taken aback she'd prevaricated, saying she'd have to think seriously about it; which, perhaps, she should do. After all, the War was over and Thomas back in England, but Grace had still heard nothing definite. She'd have to bide her time before giving Bailiff Strutt her reply. Perhaps once they'd put the play on she would be able to turn her mind to it. She was far too busy at the moment, for now that Master Andrew had been released from his military duties for the time being, the Hall's great barn was echoing to Shakespeare. Master Andrew's mother ensured that more modern plays were kept from its door; she had no intention of letting any servant of hers be compromised by taking an unseemly part whilst under her roof; which is how Grace found herself playing Ophelia opposite Master Andrew's Hamlet. Apparently Mistress Rearsby had no objections to her niece's lady's maid portraying betrayal, madness and death.

52

Escape from Elba

16 June 1815, The Dender Valley, Flanders

Thomas could have thought himself back in Leicestershire. Hard to believe the Tyrant might be snapping at their heels at any minute. Their new cantonments in Vollezele looked southwards and westwards to the low hills fringing the fields wide open to the midsummer sun; and Vollezele itself, like Melton, was famous for its dray horses, light chestnut rather than the black Leicestershires, but just as magnificent.

Sometimes Thomas would walk across the fields to where they grazed, stroke their broad necks and tell them tales of his father's old plough horses, Ramillies and Blenheim. The soldiers too lived in greater comfort than they'd ever known on campaign, billeted in spacious farmhouses built like border fortresses with hay barns overflowing with forage, cellars stocked with enough provisions for whole armies, never mind the 36th Dragoons. That was probably why Thomas felt so much at home and probably also why he felt so uneasy about fighting a war in these lands.

He'd got used to warfare in a dusty foreign country, but this place seemed far too close to home. He had to admit that the rivers were a lot straighter, the loneliness of the landscape relieved only by trees as stiff as a serjeant's pike, but it was good cavalry country. Even after crossing the Dender

River, they could pick their way over vast open commons, unlike the hedged-in fields of England. Midsummer too was coming with its long days, ideal for the fighting of pitched battles. Yet still they and the Prussians waited for Boney to make his move. Would he or wouldn't he cross the border? Opinion at the picket lines was divided. Not one of the generals, including Wellington, had ever fought face to face with Boney in command. The new recruits were all excitement, half-wondering if Boney might really have two heads.

'But how will we recognise him? Truly?'

Old veterans were more cautious. 'This ain't Spain. Wellington don't know the territory, do he now? Napoleon's on his home ground.'

The Irish troopers reckoned themselves thirsty for battle and were ready to back their Wellington against Napoleon any day. 'Hah! The Corsican ogre.' The Irish dragoons preferred this particular insult. It seemed to allow their tongues to roll around the words with a fine flourish and contemptuous sneer. 'He'll be wishing himself back on Elba when we've finished with him.'

Officers tended to prefer the term the Usurper. Freer and Thomas stuck with Freer's heartfelt and simple phrase, the Tyrant.

But now Napoleon was back in France, who knew what might happen? Thomas glanced over his shoulder at the sun. It was only early evening and still light; all stable duties done for the day, but not late enough to be return to billets. He tried not to think of Grace and his belated proposal of marriage. He couldn't blame her for hesitating. He too wondered if they would ever finish this damned war. Even if he survived this campaign, would there still be another ten years of war ahead? Would they all have to soldier on like this until the Tyrant was finally defeated, perhaps dead? As he approached the glint of river reflecting the evening sky, Thomas heard the swifts screaming above, plundering the insects, diving and swirling, picking off their prey like a brigade of cavalry scattering an infantry line. This, Thomas mused, was exactly what the 36th Dragoons were good at. This was what their very capable Lieutenant-Colonel Pennington had his officers drill into their heads until they could have performed their duties in their sleep or even in their cups. After all, what else were soldiers good for?

53

The Camp Fire

As Thomas turned up the main road towards the distant brick church tower he heard the sound of a pipe and drum coming from the great courtyard of the furthest of the village farmhouses, now entirely occupied by dragoons. It was Freer who first saw him and beckoned him to join his companions round a small fire.

Freer returned to his fireside hay bale, and Louise emerged from the shadows, her belly now quite round with her first pregnancy. She leant back on Freer's knee, and he placed his arm around her thickening waist. Louise had some news to tell which Thomas had not yet heard.

She had just seenLieutenant-Colonel Pennington in his finest evening dress riding on his way to a ball in Brussels given by one of Britain's most eminent duchesses in honour of Wellington.

'I've never seen him so smart, in his white breeches as snug as his own skin,' she laughed.

As Thomas moved closer to the fire, Murphy retrieved his tabour from Bonnie whilst Boy smiled at Thomas and took up his pipe, ready to play at Murphy's signal. 'So, Serjeant, will you stay awhile with us?'

Murphy motioned Thomas to sit by him.

'We're in need of a deeper voice than the boy Littlethorpe here.'

Littlethorpe stepped forward into the glow of the fire. He was proud of having the finest light tenor voice in the Regiment but responded to Murphy's jest in the same spirit.

'As if anyone can hear anything over the great racket this man makes with his drum.'

Thomas was quickly ushered into the circle. A bale of hay was placed close, but not too close, to the flames, while the assembled company conducted its own ball 'attended by some of the finest men in the company', as Murphy put it.

Thomas had to agree. Byrne and Ashby were steady corporals who'd seen plenty of service in the Peninsula and in spite of everything kept faith with their abiding passions, Ashby his Methodism and Byrne his cricket. Byrne's occasional drunken lapses were nothing compared with the foolhardiness of their glorious tenor, Littlethorpe. Littlethorpe had already charmed a pretty golden-haired young woman from the village, who'd brought them some provisions; she agreed to stay when he offered her a seat next to him. Littlethorpe was no doubt hoping that she'd be joining him for the dancing that was soon to come. She in turn seemed to be fascinated by the soldiers, who even in their stable dress had a dashing air when compared with the local village men in their everyday working clothes.

Murphy coughed heartily. He was about to begin.

'The best tune to drink and dance to. The best tune that piper Dermot Murphy of Galway could welcome you with.'

Bonnie stood up to lead them. She could rouse even the shyest to get up and dance.

Whilst Bonnie Murphy led the dancing with Freer and his wife, Littlethorpe made free with the flagon of beer recently donated by their hosts. Thomas wondered when he and

Freer might have to intervene to stop the man's inevitably excessive consumption ending in a breach of discipline.

Murphy, having blown his own trumpet, passed the challenge to Byrne.

As I roved out thro' Dublin city
At the hour of twelve o'the night,
Who should I spy but a Spanish lady
Washing her feet by candlelight ...

Thomas could hardly contain his laughter. In Byrne's version the words of *The Spanish Lady* had been made quite inoffensive, most likely in deference to the sensibilities of Freer's Louise.

As they all joined in the chorus, Thomas took a hearty swig from the flagon too. What the hell.

He caught sight of Ashby's disapproving face. The Methodist immediately waved away the offer of the flagon, gesturing towards Littlethorpe: this only seemed to encourage Byrne to make the most dubious facial contortions and hand gestures.

... In all my life I ne'er did spy
A maid so blithe as the Spanish lady.

Thomas's clear baritone sang the chorus with such gusto that as they took the last line forcefully and *What for the too-ra loo-ra-lee* rang around the roof tiles, he knew it would be his turn to take the floor next.

He felt a great wave of sentiment wash over him. Boy, mute as long as he'd known him since he plucked him out from under his dead mother's skirts, was carefully cleaning the spittle from his pipe. Sometime Thomas just wished that he would talk, tell them what really happened that day; but as Bonnie Murphy kept reminding them, if they were him they wouldn't want to talk about what happened in Badajoz either. Thomas conferred with Murphy, took a deep breath, and told himself it was only a song.

... How sweet the hours I passed away,
With the girl I left behind me ...

He was into his stride, and the rolling rhythm of the tune seemed to echo what was to him the most pleasant of gaits, that of a cavalryman and his horse. His memories of Grace became one with the words of his song. When he'd left Burton, she'd been scarcely older than the yellow-haired village maid who'd sat so quietly by the fire with Littlethorpe before slipping into the night, back home again.

Byrne was now silent, probably because he only knew the more obscene version. Remembering the proper words, Ashby and Freer began the second verse lustily, Freer clutching his wife's swollen belly with such tenderness that Thomas almost lost his way as he sang the last verse:

... In constancy to her I love,
The girl I left behind me.

Freer seemed almost alight with love for Louise. He launched into *Hearts of Oak,* signalling Murphy to catch up as best he could.

Come cheer up, my lads! 'tis to glory we steer,
To add something more to this wonderful year;

Thomas remembered Josh Tranter singing that evening in Nottingham so long ago, before the army became all they knew. He grimaced at the memory of trying to stop Freer's tirade against those soldiers who'd put down the local food riots. After all, they'd nearly had to do the self-same thing in Reading. A bloody good job we're all drunk, eh, Freer.

By now, Littlethorpe and Byrne had finished the entire flagon of wine. Littlethorpe was singing the chorus and conducting in time to the martial tune with the aid of the paws of the ever-compliant Dog.

We always are ready; steady, boys, steady!
We'll fight and we'll conquer again and again.

They all stood to sing the chorus in a rousing and patriotic spirit. Littlethorpe was drunk enough to take up word-spinning with his two compatriots, and all returned to the dance floor, flinging their partners, male or female, round the yard as though they were in the best hall in the land, feet stamping and hands clapping to the pipe and drum.

Freer kissed his wife full on the lips and lifted her high in the air, and with the co-ordinated eye of a sabre-wielding soldier whirled her around and around until she cried out for him to stop, Dog leaping up to join in the fun.

Thomas found himself stepping out with Bonnie. She'd grabbed his arm and pulled him to his feet without ceremony.

'Let's see how well you dance, Serjeant.'

Littlethorpe had just started on the first verse again when Thomas and Freer heard the last post sounding though the village and came to themselves enough to remember their duties.

'Time, men. Time to go home.'

But Bonnie's merry evening was not to be closed down so abruptly without a proper farewell. She had sung this song on every one of their campaigns. It would be her talisman, her rabbit's foot of good luck, if she should sing of loss now rather than later.

My bonny light horseman, will I ne'er see him more?

~

Thomas felt a chill come over him. But Bonnie appeared much cheered, as though she had given them all her blessing.

As Byrne and Ashby propped him up between them on the road home, Littlethorpe replied to Bonnie's lament with a defiant rendering of *The Lincolnshire Farmer* in his soaring tenor, which eventually faded as they rolled gently into the short night.

54

To Quatre Bras

16 June 1815, The Dender Valley

'He's here. Wake up, Sergeant, wake up.'

Even half-awake, Thomas immediately understood the orderly's message. The Tyrant had crossed the border.

'Where is he?' Thomas pulled off his nightshirt.

The orderly grimaced. 'By the look on Lieutenant Haywood's face, close.'

Thomas yanked on his drawers. 'How close?'

'Who knows, Serjeant?' the orderly shook his head.

Thomas, half-buried in his shirt, muttered 'So where did he cross, then?'

The orderly continued to lean against the doorpost. 'Somewhere round Charleroi, they reckon, Serjeant.'

Thomas, wriggling into his overalls, looked up briefly in disbelief. 'Charleroi?

But what about the Prussians?'

'Fell back sharpish, by all accounts.'

Thomas's heart was jumping out of his chest. 'And now? Where is Bonaparte now?'

The orderly stopped leaning and stood up straight. 'I'm telling you, Serjeant. They've no idea. Not that they'd say as much to the likes of me, but you don't have to be Boney to know we ain't got the right men in the right place for this kind of lark.'

Thomas finished pulling on his overalls and his boots and straightened himself.

'So what are my orders?'

'To issue A troop with three days' rations and forage and get them into marching order. Immediately. Then you and Troop Serjeant-Major Freer are to report to Acting Captain Haywood for further instructions.'

'Understood. But before you go, what time is it?'

'Three o'clock, or thereabouts.'

So a couple of hours to sunrise. Not much time to get battle-ready. They'd got out of the habit since leaving Spain. The orderly left to give the other troops' serjeants their orders before the general reveille was sounded.

Thomas quickly finished his own preparations and went in search of Freer.

~

Thomas and Freer, having organised everything as best they could manage, quickly made their way to Haywood's quarters. In the absence of firm orders fromLieutenant-Colonel Pennington, who was taking a brief rest after his late-night dash back from Brussels, he was studying some maps.

Haywood jabbed at the map. 'Lie of the land. Very important.'

Thomas knew that Wellington had already instructed his officers to ensure they and their men had a full understanding of all possible routes which might take them either to or from Brussels or Ostend. Ever since the early campaigns in the Peninsula, Thomas hadn't needed his officers to urge him to develop a grasp of local topography.

In fact, Haywood now relied on him and Freer to undertake the initial reconnaissance of an area and the subsequent instruction of the men.

Freer interrupted, 'So where might the Usurper be heading for, sir?'

Haywood gestured at the sketch map resting on the table.

'Here or there. Who knows? Our evacuation route to Ostend, or maybe Brussels. The place is heaving with grand English visitors. All the more reason for Napoleon to attack, if only to rub our noses in it.'

Haywood liked to use the language employed in the training of puppies and other small beasts rather than regular military terms. Thomas put this down to his now being the owner of two magnificent red setters which accompanied him everywhere. They were as handsome as any dog Thomas had ever set eyes on, and towered both in breeding and stature over Dog, the Regiment's faithful ratting terrier.

'So you see,' Haywood went on, 'why Wellington has had to protect the west flank, why we're out this way rather than head-to-head with the French in Charleroi.'

'I thought the Prussians were guarding that part of the frontier, sir,' said Freer.

'Still are. Mark my words, we British and the Prussians are to take the brunt of it.'

Haywood stroked the side of his nose as if to emphasise his prediction.

'Pity more of our regular Peninsula veterans aren't with us.'

Haywood was not given to maintaining discretion in his discussions with Thomas and Freer and continued mournfully.

'It's not as though the locals can be relied upon either. Damn it, they were fighting for the French only a couple of years ago. Who knows where their loyalties lie? As for the Prince of Orange being second in command, everyone knows he's a f…'

Haywood trailed off as he realised what he was about to say.

One unanswerable question, almost followed by a major indiscretion. Haywood blushed scarlet. Thomas felt he'd better staunch the flow of embarrassment.

'You said you had further orders, sir.'

'Indeed. I meant to say that, in spite of certain elements of doubt we might harbour about out hosts, I want every man to understand that he is on no account to abuse or plunder or indeed cause any distress to anyone who has recently been a friend to France. We must win over our Lowlanders' hearts by sheer good manners, if we are to win this war.'

This, of course, was not what Acting Captain Haywood had intended to say. Besides, the two veterans had heard it all before and, to their credit, their men had mainly complied. Theirs was a regiment noted more for its officers' decent treatment of their men rather than for its floggings. But Thomas and Freer, like Haywood, knew what it was like to be starving on the road and to come across a field of crops, to come across an unprotected wine cellar; though the sacking of a town like Badajoz … That was quite another matter.

'Naturally, sir.'

'Well, back to the matter in hand. Lieutenant-Colonel Pennington has asked me to settle the matter of Captain Webster's new cover serjeant.'

Captain Webster? Thomas thought he'd misheard.

Haywood swallowed several times. 'I'm sure we are all pleased to welcome Captain Webster back and apprise him of the latest developments. On the ground as it were.'

Freer responded first. 'That's excellent news, Captain Haywood. When do we expect him?'

'Whenever he can catch up with us. As for his cover serjeant, Captain Webster has instructed me to appoint you, Freer, whilst Cowper here will act again as mine. Once Captain Webster arrives to take up his command I shall be reverting to my original post of lieutenant. Is that understood?'

'Perfectly, sir,' Freer and Thomas parroted.

'As for the damned French, we're to go south to Enghien. We concentrate our forces there.'

'And Bonaparte, sir? The Army of the North? Where are they right now?' asked Thomas.

'Wherever you care to look, from all accounts.'

~

It was almost dawn before the entire regiment was assembled, their senior officers, even as they were mounting their horses, still writing promissory notes for the villagers to present to the Commissariat. The 36th were to make their way as rapidly as possible towards Brussels, though not by the direct route but by sweeping south to the town of Enghien on the Paris road.

'Well, we're as ready as we'll ever be,' Thomas muttered to Freer as he joined the Regiment's squadrons, now in marching order, and looked across the ranks. Their new-blue and-gold uniforms flashed like kingfishers darting through early morning mists; their horses' coats gleamed from weeks of thorough grooming and good corn. Thomas settled into his position as an outrider on the left flank of his troop. To fight the Tyrant would be an honour, Freer always said, an honour to give him a bloody nose.

By the time they reached their assigned meeting place at Enghien the morning sun had broken through the mist to bathe the entire landscape in a sweat and once their horses were fed, the men were given permission to dismount and take it in turns to get some rest whilst they waited for the infantry to join them.

Thomas tried again to coax more information from Haywood, who eventually let slip the latest intelligence from Pennington.

'Well, Cowper, it seems pretty clear now it's not just a feint, not with the French still driving the Prussians towards Brussels. It's almost certain we'll be engaging with the enemy before the day is out.'

It was sobering news. Until yesterday, some officers had still been taking bets on there not being an invasion until possibly next year, or maybe never, now that all the frontier forts had been reinforced and troops stationed in their hinterlands. Yet Thomas detected an almost festive atmosphere. Some officers who'd arrived earlier even invited Haywood to join them for a hearty breakfast under the shade of the trees. With Haywood's two setters dashing around their feet, the meal was eaten in the best of humours, with occasional bursts of merriment, which Thomas could hear from where he kept watch. That was his job – being Haywood's cover serjeant even when off the battlefield.

So when Thomas noticed one of the locally hired servants kick Haywood's dogs out of the way before running his fingers over Haywood's valise, he didn't hesitate to challenge him. The servant feigned complete bewilderment at Thomas's broken French, but returned to grooming Haywood's charger. Light-fingered servants were the last thing they needed. There would be plundering enough during and after the battle they doubtless now faced. Thomas touched the small bag of soil he wore round his neck, Burton Lazarus's loamy clay. Precious to him but to nobody else, and round his neck he hoped it would stay should he, too, be in his grave by the end of this day.

~

At long last their orders came through and the horses eased forward, quickening their pace towards the Brussels road and its vital crossroads linking the Allied and Prussian armies. Eventually, but only as the light began to fade, Thomas began to make out the sounds of distant gunfire. But they were too late. By the time they arrived at Quatre Bras the day's fighting was over, though it did not seem clear to anyone as to which side might have advanced or gained the upper hand. So the 36th settled themselves down as best they could and as more cavalry regiments continued to ride in throughout the night, Thomas prepared himself for either another battle or an equally desperate retreat all the way back to Brussels. One way or another they could be in for a severe drubbing.

At dawn, Thomas scanned the desolate prospect in front of him. They were surrounded on three sides by dense woodland, with any crops in the fields flattened beyond recognition by the troop movements of the previous two days; but as daylight broke with no sign of a further French offensive, Wellington gave the order for his surviving infantry battalions to slip away north towards a ridge called Mont St Jean further north on the road to Brussels. The cavalry were to protect their rear.

Or as Littlethorpe quipped, 'Covering the infantry's arses again, eh?'

By one or two o'clock on that dreary afternoon, the Allied infantry finally managed what Haywood termed a perfect retreat, as prescribed in standing orders. Yet still the French made no move against them. What could they be planning? The French surely wouldn't permit so many Allied troops to escape without trying to inflict a mortal blow?

Haywood cheerfully speculated to Thomas.

'Ney, poor devil, must think he's still got all of Wellington's infantry in front of him.'

Soon they themselves, the last to leave, were ready to take to the road. Saddles adjusted and girths tightened, they stood waiting to take their turn, men and horses grateful for further rest after yesterday's frantic gallop from their distant cantonments. Meanwhile the sky continued to cloud over, grey and black, the atmosphere so close the air seemed suspended in water droplets. The horses clearly expected a storm and fidgeted unhappily. The men too.

It was Thomas who first noticed the great clouds of dust arising from each of the roads cutting though the great forest below them, the darkening plain almost flooded white. From the height of the clouds, it could only mean one thing: cavalry travelling at considerable speed. There must have been twenty thousand or more French: cuirassiers, lancers, and dragoons, their armour and helmets shining brassy gold, with fifty or so artillery guns in support.

They looked unbeatable. Outnumbered and without support, the Allied cavalry didn't stand a chance. They would have to run for it and find out if their horses were indeed second to none, galloping across a countryside cut about by forests, ditches and tree-lined roads.

Why aren't we running? Thomas felt an awful paralysis in his limbs. Was the entire cavalry command equally afflicted by such a stupor?

Yet still the French came on, their front line getting closer and closer until at last Thomas heard the order to retreat. It was official; and their squadron was to take the lead.

Thomas saw that Haywood, well experienced in leading a column of men, began as the manual instructed, in a measured way, first at a walk and then a trot, all calculated to maintain good order in the ranks. But still the French cavalry pressed forward, gaining ground with every step. At this point the skies burst open, lightning forking to the ground, thunderclaps louder than cannon fire, the rain hitting the ground like grapeshot. Soon every man and horse was drenched. It seemed to break the spell, urging them into action, but at the same time it seemed impossible to move any faster; the horses, even with spurs pressed hard into their flanks, found it difficult to head into the storm, straight into the wind and rain.

But still the French closed in, pursuing them down narrow lanes cross-country, the slippery clay surface deeply rutted and full of rainwater, and as the rear horses bumped and jostled the ones in front, men and their mounts slipped into the deep ditches at the side of the road; but they had been ordered not to stop. It was every man for himself. And every horse, thought Thomas, as Fearless proved her mettle yet again, her high spirits melded with such strength and capacity to endure that Thomas could have sworn she was enjoying the chase.

But gradually the French too began to flag …

Pennington stopped and turned to check with his spyglass. He was cock-a-hoop. 'We've done it!'

It had been a desperate chase but, at least for today, it had run its course. It wasn't a battle they could have won; it wasn't the battle Wellington planned to fight. Haywood reckoned he'd heard that Wellington and De Lancey had already chosen the Mont St Jean ridge as a possible location, and now they were all here…

They weren't to escape the rain though. The roads were already fetlock-deep in mud and water, and still it rained; but Thomas knew that if anyone could find fuel and sustenance it would be Richard Littlethorpe. Sure enough, a little further along the top road towards the nearby hamlet, he saw a faint fire struggling to keep alight. But fire it was and as he drew closer he came across Freer, Ashby, Byrne, Murphy and Boy huddled around a small blaze. Thomas sighed. What the hell was Murphy doing, bringing Boy with him? It was all very well and good training him to be a drummer boy, but he was far too bloody young for all this. Thomas suddenly stopped himself. Boy had already witnessed the carnage of Badajoz. Nothing could be worse than that.

Littlethorpe was boasting he'd sold some officers four chairs either for fuel or for sitting on for two francs each, earning it, he claimed, by risking a flogging and by carrying the chairs single-handed from the abandoned cottages. Littlethorpe felt no qualms about entering any of the dwellings left unoccupied, and had assembled not only the chairs he was selling, but even a wooden long-case clock he was holding in reserve to keep them warm through the night. Byrne and Murphy had also claimed a cuirassier's breast armour and helmet and had promptly turned them into a casserole pan and kettle, whilst Dog had been employed catching small creatures of the night. They'd been in desperate need of more meat and the creatures were soon chopped into the meagre stew of their remaining meat ration. The veterans knew the true value of food and warmth, rating them more even highly than the broken sleep into which the newer recruits had fallen.

Thomas took the proffered dish of stew, gulped it down, warmed his backside against the flames and then tried to take his leave, as did Freer, who had the rest of his men to see to. He was expecting Webster by dawn tomorrow.

'Horse picket lines,' Thomas explained. 'Overnight watch.'

Littlethorpe was currently taking bets on whether they faced a battle tomorrow and was canvassing opinions before he set his odds. 'What do you reckon to our chances of a fight with the crapauds tomorrow?'

Thomas wasn't sure he had an opinion.

'Well, it'll either rain so much no one will fight and Wellington and Boney'll decide we should all just go home and dry ourselves out. Or not.'

Littlethorpe threw another piece of chair on the fire. 'That's no bloody answer.'

Byrne decided to play the optimist. 'Na. It'll be a good day. We'll fight all right tomorrow. It'll be like Salamanca. Remember Salamanca, how it pissed down all night, and those KGL horses went wild?'

As if Thomas would ever forget Salamanca. It was true that night had been equally fierce, with rain and thunder and lightning, that night when he'd vowed to revenge Sparrow, when he'd saved the horse that broke the square at Garcia Hernandez. He and it had been chosen to survive. At least till the following day.

Swallowing down the last of his second helping of stew, he bade his comrades farewell and returned towards the horse lines. The men at the picket line were dismounted but had to keep the horses ready for immediate action, so they slept at their heads whilst the horses pawed the ground and tossed rain away from their manes. All was as well as it could be.

Thomas took himself to the highest ridges of earth he could find, only to feel yet more puddles forming under his feet. He tried to balance his body across two ridges. Maybe the water wouldn't rise much further. He tucked himself as best he could under his cape and fell asleep, remembering Salamanca.

55

Waterloo

Sunday 18 June 1815, Mont St Jean, The Low Countries

By sunrise Thomas was colder than ever; the rain had seeped up from the soil and penetrated everywhere, even through the cloak he'd so carefully wrapped himself in. He sat up, squelching further into the sodden earth, and looked around him at men wriggling out of their discarded chrysalises. He hugged his arms closer to his chest, fearing, as in his first winter in the Spanish mountains, he would never be warm again.

He moved across the open fields, behind the old farmhouse on the hill, closer to the horse picket lines, where some of the company had spent the night. He satisfied himself that their troop's horses were still tethered safe and sound. But as their farrier was nowhere to be seen, Thomas quickly checked the horses' feet. Some of the animals were snatching what they could of the clover still left in the field. The greedy ones perhaps risked colic, but so far they were all well; unlike the night before Salamanca, when horses had been lost from the picket lines in the terrors of the storm.

He quickly ran his hands down Fearless's fetlocks, checked her feet again, rubbed her back and belly and felt for saddle sores. She seemed none the worse for the last two days' hard riding.

'There, there, my beauty,' he whispered into her left ear as he began rubbing her down, getting rid of what mud he could.

He was soon joined by those of his troopers who knew, without his having to tell them, that when their Serjeant was attending to his horse, they were to attend to their own.

At about six, the rain finally stopped and he went in search of Byrne, Ashby, Murphy, and Littlethorpe. It looked as though they'd managed to keep their fire going overnight with their long-case clock. They'd all taken off their clothes, drying them as best they could over the embers, steam rising from their sodden uniforms.

Thomas shouted, 'Trying to scare Boney to death, eh!'

Once they were all back at the picket lines, it became clear that his friends' opinions were divided as to the day's outcome.

Byrne expected the worst. 'What's he waiting for? He could take us for the asking.'

Ashby wasn't convinced. 'Boney's got a bit more sense than to move this morning. No one's going to try to even shift themselves in this mud, never mind fight.'

But Littlethorpe disagreed. He favoured immediate action. 'Wellington wants to be quick off the mark and knock the stuffing out of the lot of 'em.'

Thomas, who'd earlier been listening intently to the officers' chat, suddenly found he'd arrived at a clear opinion of his own. 'Wellington will never attack. We don't have the men. His best option is to sit it out and defend this place to the last man until the Prussians get here.'

Murphy was scornful. 'The Prussians? I thought they'd been wiped out good and proper.'

Thomas leant over and lowered his voice, putting his finger to his lips. Spies amongst the camp followers were a constant hazard.

'Shh. Not all of 'em. They're up east, somewhere on our left flank, not a dozen miles away. They reckon they'll get here sometime about noon.'

Murphy shook his head and pointed to some Netherlanders making their way towards them. 'As long as they're steadier than some of the other Johnny Newcomes.'

Littlethorpe turned to inspect them. 'Just look at the state of 'em.'

Byrne shrugged his shoulders. 'Give Wellington a chance.'

Murphy pursed his lips and tapped his pipe out.

'Mebbe if he had time on his side to make real soldiers of them, but if you're saddled with men in front of you who don't want to fight, there's nothing much to be done – except shoot the lot of them and then they're no use to you anyway.'

Thomas knew there was no fooling these men. It was true they had too few veterans of the Peninsula and too many untried soldiers, either their own or, more worrying, those pressed into service from the Low Countries, former allies of Boney. But a serjeant's place was to instil hope, give a sense of purpose.

'So what if there is a shortage of experienced men? That's never stopped us before, eh?'

Littlethorpe nodded. 'Aye, but it'll still be up to us to cover 'em if they can't tell their arses from their elbows.'

Thomas grinned but shook his head. 'The Netherlanders'll have to hold their line in a fighting retreat or in battle just like the rest of us, with their elbows or their arses. Who cares, so long as they hold the line?'

'And if they don't?' Littlethorpe touched his sabre hilt.

Thomas tried to look his old friends straight in the eye but knew he wasn't ready to repeat the officers' speculation that they might be used to deter these raggle- taggle troops from deserting.

'Let's get ready, eh. Wellington's counting on us Peninsula men.'

~

His men's sabres sharpened, their weapons checked, and their horses ready, Thomas eventually felt in better heart. He breakfasted quickly on the last of his dry rations and urged his men to do likewise rather than hold out for the consignments of meat to arrive. He felt ready; and if he felt ready, he reasoned that the Tyrant would feel ready too.

Haywood agreed. A battle seemed inevitable. But when? First light had come and gone and, as they were practically at the longest day, it seemed careless of Boney not to make the most of the daylight hours, when an army might wear its enemy down before nightfall arrived. But there was still no sign of the French preparing for battle; yet they'd camped on the Brussels road the night before and would be no great distance away.

Thomas glanced around him. From previous experience, he didn't altogether trust Haywood's ability to connect a sketch map with its location; he'd feel better if he were allowed to work out the topography of the place for himself. He persuaded Haywood to lend him his set of sketch maps and took himself off to look out from the top of the ridge. At first glance it was a position well suited to Wellington's way of fighting, with a reverse slope ideal for concealing and protecting infantry behind a narrow front. This meant there would be a smaller area for the infantry to defend, which was just as well, as it was clear from Haywood's remarks that the shortage of experienced and loyal troops was of great concern to the Duke. It was one reason why such hardened Peninsula cavalry regiments like theirs had almost equal status with the more admired, but less experienced, heavy regiments.

But their own brigade under Vandeleur seemed to be standing fast on Wellington's far left flank, way off the centre, almost as if reserves. Thomas had overheard Haywood remark on it to Captain Webster, who'd joined them that morning. Freer was already in attendance on the Captain whilst also scouring the ranks for any obvious signs of unreadiness.

'… these are some of the most experienced troops on the field. What use will we be if we are placed this far out from the centre?'

But Webster maintained that they occupied a position of trust as part of a brigade deemed not in need of close supervision. 'Take Rowland Hill,' he said. 'He is one of Wellington's most trusted commanders; and yet, where has he been placed? With the reserves on the far right.'

So, so far as Thomas could tell, the 36th were likely to remain for the time being perched somewhat below and behind the highest ridge, which wound its way to a farm he identified on the map as part of the hamlet of Mont St Jean. Below them was sufficiently open country for cavalry squadrons to be able to manoeuvre down through the gently sloping fields. Their part of the ridge also overlooked the scattered houses of Papelotte village in the valley bottom, but they still had a reasonably clear run ahead of them. Hadn't that always been the problem in Spain? There had never been enough space for the cavalry to perform properly except at Salamanca. No wonder new troops and officers had become over-excited when given their head in a charge. It was a lesson they'd learnt the hard way.

Thomas noted the edge of the ridge. The immediate front was open to the rolling landscape, but a sunken lane just behind it, which cut across the length of the ridge, would serve either as a defensive ditch – or a trap, depending on which way the battle went. He counted the hasty gaps axed in the lane's hedges, fixing their locations as firmly as he could in his mind's eye.

Further to his right Thomas could see dense woodland, way to the rear of their centre behind a collection of smaller fields and small copses, and presenting even more of a barrier to enemy cavalry than their own position. So, not a bad place for infantry to retreat to, he judged.

Even further right, he could see the dip of the paved Charleroi road climbing out of the valley towards Brussels, and trees clumped, he presumed, around another sturdy farmhouse of the type they seemed to build in these parts. The two main roads to Brussels, from Nivelles and Charleroi, finally came together just before the old farmhouse at Mont St Jean, squeezing the valley between their separate arms like a wishbone.

Further down, in the centre of the valley, he picked out another stout farmhouse, La Haye Sainte, at the foot of the slope dipping down to the Charleroi road, where, Haywood had hinted, troops were already deployed to act as a redoubt. His eyes searched the valley bottom. It was scarcely two or three miles wide and long. Over on the far right, on the Nivelles road, he caught a glimpse of a rather grander building, mostly hidden by tall trees. It must be Hougoumont; also serving, he'd heard from Haywood, as one of Wellington's redoubts.

Listening intently, he began to detect sporadic commands, shouts and trumpet calls drifting from behind the opposite ridge. It seemed all too familiar, a pattern of silences and sounds he recognised immediately from their own last massive field review at Ninove two or so weeks ago. Boney was putting the troops through their paces, inspecting them, inspiring them. The battle was surely about to commence; though it had started to rain again.

Thomas cantered back to Haywood, who was scanning the terrain through his spyglass. Thomas handed back the sketch maps.

'You can hear them, sir, massing behind the ridge.'

'Indeed they are, Cowper. Indeed they are.'

Haywood handed Thomas his spyglass. The French artillery had, by now, topped the ridge on the slightly steeper side of the valley opposite and was getting into position. It wasn't long before the vast columns of French were assembling on the roads and the fields opposite their own lines; no doubt their officers would be scanning the British dispositions as eagerly as their officers would be now scanning the French ones.

It soon became clear that the 36th Dragoons would have an excellent viewing position above the battlefield. The French troops were now spread out wider than their own front, as well as to the left of their position. The woods at the rear of Mont St Jean, cut through by numerous paths – so they had been told – offered some cover for escape or retreat if required. But it was still wasn't obvious to Thomas whether this was to be a fighting retreat or a battle with some hope of success. When Freer had first seen the infantry's dispositions in the full light of day he'd seemed to be in no doubt that this encounter was going to end up, at best, as a fighting retreat. He trotted across to Haywood and Thomas.

'Wellington's strung all them Lowlander lads out and stuck them between the Peninsula infantry. I reckon he's hoping that'll make them hold the line.'

'And if they don't?' Thomas looked his old friend in the eye.

Freer shrugged. 'Then we'll all be bloody sunk. It'll be the infantry lads making for that wood over there and us cavalry jumping fences as though we were in one of them Leicestershire hunts Captain Dickenson used to talk about. Only pity is, we'll be the fox and them crapauds the hounds.'

'Best Wellington can do with the men's he got,' Thomas grunted.

But Freer was right. If the line broke, it wouldn't even be a fighting retreat; and their line wasn't looking good, whilst the French columns, at least from where they were standing, looked invincible, in spite of Freer's previous high hopes of thrashing the Tyrant in person.

This would be unlike Salamanca, where his anger had given him a peculiar strength. This was going to be different, a longer game, requiring the coolest of heads. Thomas knew he had to inhabit a different place for the next few hours, where steady thinking, rather than bravery alone, would be required. Thomas was a veteran, like most of the men standing behind him. That was what Wellington was relying on: their steadfastness under fire. Thomas knew that could make the difference between winning and losing. That and luck. He wasn't much given to dash any more. His strength was thinking ahead, anticipating the enemy's moves, thinking of ways to preserve his men. They'd been getting ready either to fight or to retreat since first light. Now there was only the waiting.

He looked behind him. Littlethorpe was still fired up and with a couple of tots of rum in him would become a giant-killer. Byrne also, though a little steadier and more cautious, was made from a similar mould. Ashby was a rock. Murphy too, talking to Boy before he sent him to the rear. As for Freer, he could, like Thomas, think ahead, know how his men might react under certain conditions and act on their behalf to preserve them from the enemy – and from themselves.

Thomas also had a great deal of faith in their commander. Lieutenant-Colonel Pennington was an energetic leader, but one who favoured conservation of his troops rather than reckless sacrifice. He was said to be thought well of, too, by their brigade commander, General Vandeleur. Thomas felt sure of Pennington; and Vandeleur's reputation was sound. Thomas shuddered at a sudden memory of Black Jack Slade.

Thomas and Freer quickly moved through the thickening reek of piss, sweat and shite of men and horses. They wound through the ranks and files, advising the younger ones to relieve themselves now rather than in the heat of battle; this was part of the pre-battle drill which Freer and Thomas had devised between them. Thomas realised that the drill was so unobtrusive that even the officers scarcely noticed it, but it was their way of keeping the men alert yet steady and unlikely to over-excite their imaginations. Anxiety would be soon enough upon them. Thomas and Freer next collected letters from the ranks to give to the orderlies, inspected again their men's weapons, horses, girths, saddles, bridles, striving to keep their men's minds half on the battlefield, half on their horses, and as little as possible on their own hopes and fears. Thomas noted again that the horses had mostly come through the terrors of the night calm, and now stood with coats brushed and manes teased out fit for battle. There were times when he pitied the poor infantry, who had nothing but each other and their weapons to concern themselves with.

Suddenly the French artillery started testing their gun ranges, and cannon shot flew overhead, falling close to their troop's position.

Pennington immediately gave orders. 'Dismount. Heads down. By your horses.'

They had been warned. The French artillerymen now turned their attention to decimating Wellington's infantry.

Thomas was puzzled. Hadn't anyone told the Tyrant that most of Wellington's battalions would be lying prone on the reverse slope and that cannonading them before they'd shown themselves would be a waste of ammunition? It wasn't as though they would achieve any measure of the distance or angle through the bounce of ricochets, not with the ground as soggy and unresponsive as it was. The horses were struggling with its heaviness, which made the enemy's cannon-balls useless. Still, maybe it was, as Freer had predicted, a way of intimidating the Johnny Newcomes and the Netherlanders, a way of breaking the line through sheer terror; and they'd find out if it worked soon enough.

Thomas turned his attention once more to the battlefield, or rather to as much of it as he could see. The sound of gunfire from the distant woods at Hougoumont was still carrying across the field, the sharper notes of the howitzers above the volleys of the heavy artillery, the lingering smoke rising above the horizon. Soon it would be hard to see anything at all; and yet still they waited.

~

By early afternoon the occasional showers of the morning had finally died out. Thomas, like the rest of his men, strained to see between the clouds of smoke released by the guns and at last began to make out several division-sized French columns massing in the centre of the field. It looked as though the Tyrant was planning a massive frontal assault on their centre that would surely test their line to its limit. Such an attack was something that would stir the blood of both attackers and defenders, though at this point there was very little evidence of the defenders taking action. Most were lying down on the reverse slope to protect themselves from the barrage of artillery that had been focused on them for the last couple of hours. Many lives must have been lost, Thomas was sure; but not perhaps as many as Napoleon expected.

But still the French columns marched on, doubtless hoping that a broken and demoralised line would allow them to sweep all before them. What the hell could Wellington do in the face of these thousands? Freer turned, looked at Thomas and mouthed 'fox and hounds.'

By now the troops had been ordered to remount in readiness, but for what? As the French columns pounded into the infantry line and the red and blue uniforms became one, lost in clouds of powder and dust, it became impossible to see who might be prevailing. They tried instead to listen for the trumpeters' calls.

Then they heard faint bugles, a cavalry rallying call. Uxbridge was sending in some of the heavy cavalry. Ponsonby's Scots Greys and Somerset's troops appeared from the rear, moving forward at a gallop from their positions, triumphantly scattering the front-line French columns; but then they kept on riding, riding straight on, towards the French guns.

Thomas cursed their useless bravery. Too far; much too far. Move back, retreat, regroup, reform, shouted Thomas silently into the air. The 36th knew only too well the dangers of running themselves to a dead stop in front of the enemy. The Greys would have to be rescued, the enemy distracted, attacked by fresher men on fresher horses. Was this now their chance to act?

Go. Go. Why aren't we going? mouthed Thomas. Don't wait about for orders. We can do it, but only if we go now. Now. He turned to see what Vandeleur's orders might be. Would he send in his light dragoons brigade to rescue the heavy cavalry from certain annihilation?

Vandeleur finally gave the signal. His orders rippled across to the officers. The order of battle was such that it was their company, in the 36th Dragoons' left squadron, who were to take the lead.

They were off.

Thomas followed Haywood, who directed him to squeeze their men through the narrow gaps in the lane hedge, hacked out earlier, onto the forward slopes. They set off at a steady hand gallop down towards the French guns across the valley. No point arriving with their own horses blown too, though there was little time to lose. But the horses had to navigate ditches and marshland at a pace that wouldn't exhaust them. They took a deep diagonal across the battlefield, heading to where they could best offer cover to the Scots Greys; Thomas in position behind Haywood, Freer behind Webster. Every man for himself so long as they could remember the basic drill of cavalry survival: charge, sabre to sabre, keep slashing or die, regroup, recover, make sure you can return to fight another day.

Pennington was in front.

'Right shoulders.'

'Charge!'

'Steady, Fearless, steady.'

Thomas could see that their charge was a desperate measure, providing cover to troops cut off deep in enemy lines, where enemy and friend were mixed up like a bag of beans; friends hard to find within the seething mass of Lancers and Curaissiers gathered for the kill; friends, when found, hard to rely on when no man could see clearly more than two horses' length across the battlefield. Thomas's job was to protect Haywood as well as to kill the enemy. Hard to maintain a safe distance from Haywood and yet provide cover. The riot of clashing sabres and swirling clouds of musket smoke made it almost impossible.

Suddenly Haywood was off his mount, his horse stumbling after the flat of a sabre had glanced off its right leg, spinning them both out of control. Haywood slowly began to pick himself up, his sabre hanging loose from the sword knot, as if time was standing still. Thomas knew he had to act at once. Haywood would be as dead as a fledgling flung from the nest if he didn't get there in time. As he sped to Haywood's side he noticed a young French officer also off his horse, sword raised, bearing down on Haywood. Thomas raised his own sabre. Wait till he gets within killing range. Wait. Wait. This manoeuvre was not in Le Marchant's drill.

Thomas saw the officer's wide eyes luminous with fear and with more force than he knew he possessed swung his sabre down cleaving through the officer's helmet and skull and into the brain. He shouted to Haywood, shouted at him to hang onto his stirrups and without ceremony pulled him away from the thick of the fighting towards another riderless horse, short-tailed, one of their own, one upon which Haywood might be able to remount. Thomas caught the horse in one swoop, covering Haywood with his sabre as he remounted, shoving and slashing to make space around him. Haywood was hardly able to acknowledge him before Thomas gestured to his right, where several men of the French heavy cavalry were cutting their way towards them. No time for further niceties. They rode away as a pair, both looking for the moment when they could call their men to order and return before they too were wiped out.

The light brigade had managed to contain the enemy but were becoming exhausted themselves when Thomas heard the call to reform and regroup. The 36th Dragoons had done their job of holding the French back to cover the Union Brigade's retreat. Some had been badly wounded, but many were now riding back to the safety of their own lines; and Thomas's troop, still in the thick of combat, now needed to retire too. Thomas and Haywood looked around and agreed with each other's hasty assessment. The 36th should leave in whatever order they could, as soon as they could; and the troop must get back into their position on the ridge before their own horses became too blown to retreat in good order. Thomas sensed that Fearless was still in reasonable condition, though probably cut about the legs, but they had yet to scramble back, up towards their own ridge; and going up that hill would seem much steeper to the horses now than when going down fresh and prepared for combat.

Thomas kept Haywood firmly in his sights as they struggled up the hill to their position, occasionally turning to shout encouragements to the men following. There seemed so few of them and so far back too. But onwards they rode to the sunken lane and the nearest gap hastily cut in its hedge that morning.

Soon they were scrambling down towards the lane. Almost back. Then Haywood's horse fell, flinging Haywood over its neck once more onto the ground. And closing in on him was a French Lancer, followed by more of his fellows. Thomas watched helplessly, too far away to intervene. Then, to his relief, men in a nearby infantry company, who'd also seen Haywood fall, brought down the first of the lancers with a burst of rapid musket fire. But neither of them was out of danger yet. Their only hope was to get themselves into the middle of the infantry's square without forcing open dangerous gaps in its defences.

~

Freer had lost sight of Webster very early on. He was everywhere and yet nowhere. At first Freer kept as close as he could but, in a moment of distraction as he slashed and hacked at the enemy, he lost sight of him completely. He turned his horse round to scan the uniforms through the drifting powder clouds. It was hopeless; not even a flash of Webster's epaulettes. He turned again and saw the Dragoons taking a drubbing but, at the same time, he could see the Scots Greys beginning to reform and make their escape, taking their precious horses and giants of men away from danger. Freer cut and slashed. That was his job. His life depended on it. But where was the hell was Webster? He glanced to his left. Only the French. To his right. Some of his own men but not the Captain. Webster must have moved closer to the guns.

~

Littlethorpe had made a bet with Byrne as to which of them would be the first to wound or kill a dozen crapauds, a wager dependent upon each man's accuracy of observation, veracity and survival. It had been a wager to boost bravado, take their minds off the unfavourable odds facing them on the battlefield. They would have to charge across fields heavy with mud, into the heart of the enemy, surrounded by guns. It wasn't the time for further calculation. Littlethorpe was as anxious as ever to get on with the job of sticking the pigs. It didn't take much for him to become angry with the enemy. All he had to do was to think first of those upstarts who'd stolen his grandfather's lands and reduced his father to a landless labourer, then of his dead comrades already killed by the crapauds, then of the so-called law of the land. Safer to fight the bloody crapauds than magistrates who go and put a reward on your head just for helping out some lads with a bit of machine breaking.

~

Murphy and Ashby rode side by side. They were used to it, and used to looking out for each other. Until, of course, they reached the thick of the fighting, where it was more or less every man for himself. Murphy was not a man to shirk realities. Was it not true the French had tried to conquer his own country and take their Godless creed into the very heart of Ireland? Better the devil you know than the one you don't was Murphy's philosophy. Murphy's blood was up at the first sign of the marching regiments. Once a trumpeter, always a trumpeter. He'd learnt to read the sound of battle, his ears able to scan the battlefield more accurately than a spyglass. He could tell by the trumpet calls the position of fire, where the enemy might be and, most important, where the enemy was planning to be. But this battle had a new tune, one he wasn't sure he recognized, one that was different from Salamanca, from Vittoria, the other great battles against French forces. He didn't like that. He didn't like this new tune at all.

~

Thomas had never been forced to take shelter within a square before. He'd had to leave Fearless to find her own way back and as he caught up with Haywood both were pulled to safety through the files of muskets. If they survived they would, of course, have to pay the price of being mocked by the infantry as only being as good as their horses. How many of their fellows would be so lucky as to land up next to an infantry square defending the ridge? Thomas silently gave thanks for the well-drilled ranks of infantrymen kneeling and standing with bayonets fixed, firing their muskets in turn. The small detachment of lancers eventually fell back. The musket fire had taken a heavy toll.

At last Haywood and Thomas were able to pass through the square. Fearless was waiting for Thomas about a hundred yards to the rear, snatching at some tufts of grass not yet churned into mud, and Haywood once again claimed a riderless horse grazing close by. They were to regroup by one of the copses behind the ridge. Men were getting themselves there as best they could to await further orders, and Thomas, glad of his earlier reconnaissance, led the way, with the cut and bruised Haywood slowly following on the winded horse. As he picked his way carefully past the front lines of waiting men, Thomas felt a strange emptiness in the wind, a great absence.

Once at the copse they fell into a well-rehearsed routine. Officers told off their men into their respective squadrons and companies, and serjeants took the muster roll of those present. Thomas silently counted. More than a third of the Regiment likely lost or wounded. Thomas scanned the survivors. He could see Littlethorpe, but no Murphy, Ashby or Byrne. And no Freer. He couldn't see Freer or Webster anywhere. He told himself not to think about Freer. He told himself he mustn't even contemplate Freer's death. In his head, Freer was alive and that was that. Freer was alive and he, Thomas Cowper, had the rest of his men to look after, to keep alive.

But some of the most experienced Peninsula veterans had disappeared in one short ride into the heart of the enemy;

and those who'd survived were now bent double over their lathered and blown horses. Lieutenant-Colonel Pennington was missing too. Thomas had never known such a dark day for the Regiment. He looked behind him to see if there were any stragglers still making their way back. His eyes strained in the hope he would see, at the very least, Freer riding back supporting Webster. He told himself to stop looking, to stop hoping. Freer was alive until proven otherwise.

Thomas looked around him. The gaps were only too clear as the men gradually reassembled in their ranks. Gap after gap. From three squadrons numbering fifty-four, fifty-three and forty-eight files each, all that could now be formed were two squadrons, one of twenty-four files, the other of twenty-three. Thomas looked across to Haywood, whose expression could not have been more serious. Gone was the half-smile, the dancing eyes, the jocular yet confiding manner. His face was without colour as he too cast his eye upon his depleted company and his downcast fellow officers.

'Perhaps, sir,' Thomas ventured, 'we should get the men to see to their horses.'

'Of course, Cowper, of course we must do that; it would be a good thing to restore discipline.'

'Troop Serjeant-Major Freer and I have found that if the horses are seen to first, men recover their spirits faster …'

His voice trailed off. Both of them knew that these men would not easily be restored.

Thomas moved slowly up and down his company of survivors as though to reassure them, and himself, that they were really present. He repeated Haywood's orders in turn, man to man. It was not a time to shout or bark out commands. It was a time only for quiet thoughts and low voices.

By the time he reached Littlethorpe there wasn't much more to be said. He had asked every dragoon, as he went, if they had seen their closest comrades in action and, in particular, aboutLieutenant-Colonel Pennington, Captain Webster or Troop Serjeant-Major Freer, Corporals Ashby, Murphy and Byrne.

'So can you recall where you last saw them?'

One or two men had followed the missing onto the field.

'... Troop Serjeant-Major Freer, he was sharp behind Captain Webster. As far as I could tell, he and the Captain were in the thick of it together. But then, you know, Serjeant, you can't see much more what with all the smoke.'

'No. None of us saw very much. I lost sight of Corporal Murphy straight away, ' the other dragoon added.

Thomas returned to Haywood. who'd also been busy.

'I've arranged for the men to be supplied with more rum.'

'And the Prussian troops?' queried Thomas. 'Have you heard when they are likely to get here?'

'Who knows with the going underfoot like it is. '

Thomas didn't ask further. Sometime then, or maybe never; even though Blücher had given his word.

And so they waited, Thomas fretting about Freer, wondering if he'd managed to get to the rear. Only one way to find out. Thomas asked Haywood if he might check the rear. Haywood readily agreed. He was worried about Pennington and Webster and agreed Thomas might be spared for a half hour or so.

~

Jack Fallowfield was suffering from a full-blown case of the ague but that wasn't going to stop him keeping an eye on the Netherlanders who'd only too recently been Boney's men. He wasn't going to have another Ireland on his hands.

He felt his neck hairs shiver at the memory of the so-called loyal forces plotting behind their backs; and as for the so-called innocents, the women and children begging for mercy, but as much the enemies of the state as any Whiteboy or Leveller ... Even Murphy could see the Protestant English were a better bet than supporting an invasion by the Godless French. Well, Jack Fallowfield wouldn't make that mistake again. He yanked at his jacket and pulled open his shirt collar to get his breath. The orderlies were dealing with the skulkers and malingerers. He'd have to deal with the deserters.

~

Thomas quickly searched the rear for any of their men, but especially for Freer. He couldn't even see Boy, who'd been sent to their rear earlier. He was about to return when he heard high-pitched shouts coming from behind some wagons drawn up in front of a copse. What the hell ...?

He urged Fearless onwards just in time to see Fallowfield, his carbine raised, half-cocked, aiming at Boy. Boy too held a carbine but his was clearly not ready to fire. Behind him a drummer-boy lay crumpled, blood from a leg wound pumping into the ground beside a dead Netherlander. In a heartbeat Thomas realised what must have happened. The two boys must have witnessed Fallowfield killing the Netherlander. And, although shooting a likely deserter might well be forgiven during today's battle, Fallowfield had obviously decided he would silence the boys as well – pure cold-blooded murder. But Boy had suddenly found his voice and was yelling all manner of defiance at Fallowfield.

'Don't you dare bloody touch him, arse-face. Don't you dare.'

Thomas, drawing on a steely resolve he scarcely realised he possessed, commanded Fallowfield, 'Lower your weapon, right now, or I'll shoot.'

Fallowfield stiffened, then laughed and slowly turned his head. Thomas felt the sweat run down his neck and wondered how accurate his aim might be. But Fallowfield merely glanced contemptuously at Thomas before turning round again to level his carbine at Boy. Thomas suddenly understood. Fallowfield was not going to drop his weapon or turn to face him. He was taunting Thomas: shoot me in the back and have me on your conscience or leave me alone. Thomas raised his carbine, Fallowfield's drills firmly lodged in his mind.

Bring the rifle to full cock.

Line up your sights.

Aim.

Fallowfield laughed again. The carbine was snug against his shoulder. His finger tightened on the trigger.

Fire.

~

Fallowfield dropped to the ground. Thomas rode forward, dismounted and lifted the wounded drummer-boy onto Fearless. He would take both lads to the nearest medical orderly. The drummer-boy might lose his leg but would probably live. As for Boy, covered in almost as much blood as when Thomas had found him cowering under his mother's skirts, he looked ready to take on Boney single-handed.

~

Once Thomas had carried the drummer-boy safely into the tent, Thomas took Boy's hand.

'Stay here and wait for Bonnie; but if the orderlies are told to retreat you must go with them. Do not go onto the battlefield. Understand? Bonnie will find you after all this is over. Promise.'

Boy nodded vigorously and Thomas ruffled his hair in a quick farewell. As Thomas made to leave he pointed to the transport wagons and said to the orderlies, 'There are still a few wounded behind those.' Thomas shook a few coins out of his pocket, gave some to Boy and some to the orderly. His basic Christian duty towards the dying Fallowfield done, Thomas remounted Fearless and rode off.

Thomas had often used to wonder what Boy might have seen in Badajoz; whether he'd seen Fallowfield himself loot the dead, turning over the women to pull off their necklaces and trinkets. Fallowfield had certainly changed for the worse since Badajoz, his infamous temper even less under control and he more contemptuous than ever of what people thought. Thomas now told himself he should have known Fallowfield would never have heeded his warning. He would have shot the boys in front of Thomas rather than back down, and when he fell Thomas had felt a surge of relief. No more looking over his shoulder.

But as he rode back to his lines to report to Lieutenant Haywood that none of the missing were to be found, he saw the frightened face of the young French officer turn into Michael's face, his hands turn into his mother's hands cupped around Michael's head, and Boy become Hannah in a bloody shift shivering with cold.

A single wound in the back. Although Fallowfield had taught him well, would that have been enough to finish it? A firing squad would have made sure.

~

By late afternoon the Regiment was still moving towards the right flank in short redeployments, halting at every stage, edging closer and closer towards the centre of the battlefield, to the rear of the infantry. As they gradually moved further towards the centre, Thomas could make out a desperate battle between their own infantry and the French artillery and cavalry ahead of them. The infantry, in squares so far away the men were no bigger than specks, surrounded by cavalry constantly attacking them, were being shelled by heavy artillery fire. The infantrymen were throwing out their dead from the squares, closing ranks, methodically defending themselves against each punishing assault, whilst yet more French cavalry swooped down through the narrow gaps between the beleaguered squares.

And still they waited for the Prussians.

Thomas felt strangely calm. It was as though he inhabited another body, as though he, Thomas Cowper, was no longer a man but some unknown creature surveying the scene below him with not an ounce of passion or even fear. It was as though these were not his comrades and the French were not the enemy. It was an uncomfortable feeling. It was not a feeling he wanted to cultivate.

He turned to look at his reformed and much depleted squadron. He remembered Salamanca and Garcia Hernandez, where the horse he'd rescued the previous night had broken the enemy square, when he'd told himself time and time again he'd been saved for a purpose. Not for his own sake. Not even for Grace's sake. But for a higher purpose. He had been spared so that he could exercise his skill in leading what men he had back into battle, so that he could bring as many back as he could. He studied the ground ahead and told himself not to think of Freer. Freer was alive. He told himself Freer was still alive. He looked to his right towards the grand Chateau of Hougoumont, still besieged by the French and wrapped in flames and smoke, though musket and rifle fire was being returned from the Chateau strongly enough to suggest a continued resolution to oppose the enemy. But the French seemed as determined as he'd ever seen them, even when they'd been fighting on their own lands beyond the Pyrenees. The troops facing them were some of Wellington's best, and yet the French seemed undeterred and willing to sacrifice themselves.

As Thomas turned back towards Haywood, he heard him exclaim, 'What the deuce are they doing, sending cavalry in with no supporting artillery? Are they mad or do they think themselves invincible, attacking our squares without guns or infantrymen, risking their best men and horses for nothing?'

Haywood pointed with his spyglass to the French cavalry, now charging at formations of British infantry drawn up so securely that there seemed no hope of breaking the squares.

Thomas could only think of one reason. 'They must think us beat already. Why else would they do it, sir?'

Haywood grunted. 'Could be good news for us then.'

Thomas studied the land to the front and to the rear. The ridge to the rear offered both safety and danger.

'Sir, I think perhaps we should get ourselves ready in case we're called upon to clear some of those escaping through onto the ridge.'

'Just what I was thinking, Cowper.'

As Thomas and his fellow serjeants prepared the small company of men left to them for further battle, Haywood assured them that at last the Prussians were coming. He'd heard tell they'd been seen only a short distance away. An emissary had already arrived to tell Wellington of their march and their imminent arrival.

Littlethorpe was not impressed. 'I thought they were just up the bloody road.'

Thomas thought there was little point in wasting anger on the Prussians. 'What a road it must have been though. You know what these roads are like, almost as muddy as this battlefield, I'll wager.'

They were soon too busy to care. Some French cavalry had slipped past the Allied squares to surprise the infantry from the rear. But they had reckoned without the well-placed dragoons, who had a bird's-eye view of their plan.

Within moments of Thomas hearing the command to attack whip along their lines, he'd rallied his men. Horses and men alike knew exactly what to do. Pick them off hand to hand; take revenge as best you can; clear the ridge and send the last of them crashing down the hill back towards their own lines.

But in spite of their success in doing this, it seemed as though they could do nothing to stop the swarms of French still marching across the valley below them. Surely their centre could not hold for much longer under such attacks. Thomas feared they would yet again be covering a retreat. But to retreat under these circumstances would be such a waste, achieving so little whilst losing so much. Thomas felt his spirits drop; but then Haywood passed on the order they'd been hoping to hear. 'Tell the men to keep holding firm. The Prussians are here. On the battlefield.'

By about seven the 36th had edged towards the extreme right flank, taking up their positions behind Maitland's Guards, placed ready to cover their rear until retreating men could reach the shelter of the great forest behind them. Maitland's Guards Brigades were lying on their stomachs to avoid the artillery fire and yet still the columns of French marched on. Somebody whispered they were the Imperial

Guards, the men that Napoleon sent in as soon as he sensed victory.

Thomas looked across at Maitland's Guards still hidden from view. With the French columns advancing like battering rams towards the infantry lying prone to protect themselves, how could they possibly check such a powerful force alone? And so the French advanced in close columns, cheering and confident of victory until they moved up the slope towards the summit.

Yet still Maitland's men held their positions until just before the French reached the last twenty yards of the deep-set bank, when Wellington gave the order 'Arise'. It was enough to terrify the most battle-hardened soldier to see these men appear like spirit creatures from behind the bank, their muskets loaded, ready to pick off the leaders of each column as they approached; and when Maitland's soldiers stood as one and opened fire together the Imperial Guards took to their heels quicker than any enemy Thomas had seen before.

So as soon as the order was given they were off in pursuit, and with horses rested and restored they galloped over the sunken road, over the heaps of the dying and dead, and bounded further and further across the valley until they were finally able to silence the French guns.

Thomas glanced up at the bleeding evening sky like a wounded god careless of all before him. This was not a field of the dead. It was a city of the dead, its occupants lying at every street corner, where even the still living had been abandoned to the careless brutality of their enemies. At this stage of the battle there would be no quarter expected or given.

~

Ordered to halt, Thomas rubbed his eyes, whether from exhaustion or disbelief he could hardly tell. They had galloped this time not to rescue their own but to destroy the French, who had seemed completely invincible at the start of the day. But, by now, with the sky so dark and the woods masking any faint traces of light, it was useless to continue. Both men and horses were quite blown. They'd been pushed to their limits not once but twice; the infantry holding their places like a wall, the cavalry like waves finally scattering the enemy. It didn't bear thinking about too much. He turned in the saddle. Difficult to see, but the straggling and depleted line behind him was unrecognisable as the band of men he'd inspected with Haywood that morning. He hadn't seen Freer since the first charge to rescue the Union Brigade and as for his other fireside friends, perhaps only one of them had survived, for, covered in gore and mud, the soldier riding towards him was unmistakably Littlethorpe.

'We're not bloody stopping now are we?' he hollered.

Thomas waved him wearily to a halt.

'The Prussians are to take over the chase. We are to fall back, collect prisoners, secure their rear and follow when we can.'

Littlethorpe spluttered with half-hearted indignation.

'So Blücher turns up hours after he promises, cuts through a couple of reserve forces and then gets to parade through Paris like he's won this whole bloody battle, does he?'

'Littlethorpe ... We couldn't even be chasing rabbits for our supper right now, could we?'

Thomas glanced again at the men closest to him. Hunched over, practically asleep, their horses still breathing heavily, the men needed to take care of their mounts before they collapsed with exhaustion.

They'd have to find somewhere to bivouac for the night and tend to the horses as best they could before finding somewhere to rest their own heads. Thomas found himself running through his checklist of orders. It was as though he'd never given them before. It was almost as though everything he'd ever known had been left behind on that field.

Soon their advance party returned to report that Haywood deemed it safe enough to camp out by the great observatory the French had commandeered the day before. With the 36th 's commander-in-chief and other officers missing, Lieutenant Haywood was one of the few officers left more or less unscathed. Thomas quickly moved through the clusters of pickets to check that the horses had been wisped down before being tethered for the night. Aside from the guards, most men were now asleep, rolled up like babies in blankets by their horse's head, none of them knowing whether they'd have another battle to face tomorrow, and hardly caring that they'd survived today's. Thomas knew it would be useless to look for Freer and his other friends tonight, or Webster and Pennington for that matter. As soon as it was light he would return once more to the city of the dead.

56

In the Woods

Sunday 18 June 1815. Woods near to Mont St Jean

By morning Louise felt she'd been a silly goose, bursting into tears like that last night. Bonnie had gathered up kindling and they were soon building a fire. Bonnie announced they were to get themselves dry and then set themselves to find out the whereabouts of the 36th. This seemed an excellent plan and Louise was in better spirits as she stirred the porridge and broke off some hunks of bread. Around her the forest was quiet. Perhaps all was well. Perhaps they'd soon be sitting round a campfire again. And there'd be dancing, she'd sit on Will's lap, his hands crossed against her belly, their child. By the time she'd persuaded herself that it was all a false alarm and that Boney had no intentions to hurt her new husband, Bonnie returned with grim news. The French had been drawing up their troops all night on the Charleroi to Brussels road in front of Wellington's armies now on the ridge, blocking the road to Brussels. 'And they say Boney won't be having it. They say Boney's never ever been beaten in battle, only by the Russian snows.'

'There's always a first time,' Louise asserted.

'Aye, and a last time too.' Bonnie sat down by the fire.

Louise had never before seen Bonnie on the brink of despair. Bonnie scrubbed her own face clear of tears.

'A galloper said you could see Napoleon's army stretching back along the road for miles like a swarm of ants marching straight towards them.' Bonnie took a deep breath. 'He'll surely know the place like the back of his own hand.'

The phrase suddenly jogged Louise's memory. It was the self-same one Will had used to her before he left. 'But Will said …'

'Said what?' Bonnie interrupted.

Louise sighed and started again. 'Will said that Wellington has mapped all the places around Brussels and he and his officers know them like the back of their own hands. Wellington will have already worked out the best place to take a stand against Boney.'

'Your Will said that?'

'And Thomas. Haywood tells him all sorts.'

Bonnie squatted down by the fire, which had now taken hold, and Louise passed her some porridge.

Bonnie tried to smile. Louise could see now she too was frightened but was better at hiding it. So would the two armies fight, or not?

Bonnie pulled out a rosary from her pocket.

'Being Sunday, perhaps we can pray for them and maybe we'll be heard, it being a holy day and all.'

'I suppose …', Louise wondered what Will would make of Bonnie Murphy praying for him, ' I suppose we should do something.'

Bonnie sank to her knees. 'Well, then, let's ask your English God and my Irish God what they can do about it.'

'Aren't we the same country now?' asked Louise.

Bonnie brushed some crumbs off her pinafore.

'Same king, same army, different God. Not the same country.'

~

By lunchtime, occasional gunfire could be heard in the distance. All thoughts of the women moving to Brussels were now put aside. The baggage trains had set off earlier to clear the road for what seemed to be an inevitable retreat. Bonnie, now loaded with extra supplies acquired with no questions asked from the Commissariat's wagons, wondered if they should sit tight.

'I have a map too,' she said and produced a sketch drawn by the pinch-faced baggage master. 'This is Mont St Jean where our troops are and this is where Napoleon is and … we are where?'

Louise squinted at the map. 'Perhaps it's the other way up,' she ventured. 'See … look, there are the trees we're in.'

Bonnie pulled a face.

'So where is this Mont St Jean from here?'

Louise suddenly felt less faint and pointed at the map. Not entirely useless after all. She and Bonnie and the half-dozen or so other women now straggling into position, would be at hand for whatever was required. 'Whatever was required' was how the officers put it when talking about the women's right to camp out and wait for battles to end.

It seemed as though the whole morning would pass with very little attention paid to the business of warfare. But towards noon gunshots could be heard in the distance, followed by the most tremendous cannonade. Bonnie exclaimed that it was like no noise she'd ever heard before, and she'd been at Salamanca and at Vittoria. Boney was an artilleryman, she explained to Louise, and he'd have made sure that his biggest guns were carried with him.

But not to worry; Wellington and the men knew how to deal with big guns. They'd be hiding safe somewhere behind that ridge, just where they're supposed to be. Horses too. Wellington, unlike some, wasn't given to wasting his troops. That's what Dermot says. You live on a small island and you waste not, want not.

Bonnie scraped out the last morsel from her porridge dish before wiping it clean. 'It's dirty work. It's dirty work being a soldier's wife,' Bonnie pronounced and settled down to light a pipe of tobacco.

Louise took out her knitting. The baby would be born in the autumn when there was a chill in the air. He'd need a jacket. Yes, she felt that this baby of theirs would be a son, though now she wasn't so sure she wanted a son. A son might follow his father into the army and be lost to his mother forever. She tried not to think of it. Why no, her Will had been through many years of war and had survived them all. Why shouldn't he survive this battle too – just because she was here, knowing about it, fretting about his safety? She offered up another not-quite prayer. She had been distracted earlier by Bonnie's mutterings as she'd tugged at her rosary. Louise didn't want her own message to be diverted by delays through the great roll call of saints that Bonnie had invoked to keep watch over her Dermot.

By early evening, now shredded into slivers of anticipation and worry, Louise felt her throat rasp with the taste of gunpowder and saltpetre. The noise of the guns surely must have been heard in England, so loud was the sound; whilst in between the cannonading the bandsmen's music and the men's shouts drifted faintly on the wind. Bonnie was striding about under the trees, looking amongst the leaves to see if she could find any of last year's beech nuts, which she was gathering up in her apron. The mule waited patiently, his halter tied with a rope firmly round a tree. There was no need; for he, aged and ragged, had walked the lengths of so many wars that he ignored it all.

~

The Regiment's women sat round the fire; half-a-dozen or so. Bonnie's talent for fire making was legendary. Amongst the wet carpet of last year's leaves she'd found half-branches of beech wood and had coaxed another fire into life, so now all the women were feeding it with whatever they could find, staring into its flames.

'We should have a plan,' announced Bonnie. 'We should know what each one of us can do and arrange to do it.' Bonnie had the authority of a veteran's wife. 'There'll be injuries, no doubt. I have blankets we can use to drag the wounded from the field.'

'What about the dead?' asked one of the women.

Bonnie remained matter-of-fact. 'Of course they must be buried and there'll be bandsmen and orderlies to see to that, but we mustn't be distracted from searching for our own men by looting and plundering.'

'You mean we can't loot?' Another woman snorted at the very suggestion.

Bonnie looked at her sternly. 'Only in so much as it'll help our men.'

Louise was more worried about how she would ever find Will if women like these got their hands on him.

'But how will we ever find our own if they've been plundered and stripped?'

Bonnie began to parrot the bandsmen's orders she'd obviously heard many times.

'We are not to assume our men are dead. Firstly, we will seek out the company and find out if they have muster rolls taken during the battle. Anyone not accounted for must be assumed to be still on the field or possibly gone to the rear. If we are satisfied they are not at the rear, then we have to find out where the fiercest actions took place and therefore where they might have fallen.'

Bonnie put another beech branch on her fire and waited for it to stop spitting, 'So you see, we must help each other. Even if our own men are safe we must help each other to find those who aren't. Is that agreed?'

Louise nodded, but she could tell that the others weren't impressed by this notion of co-operation. If their men were alive, they could take the opportunity to plunder and make some money, or to secure loose horses ready for selling. Why waste their time attending to others who were beyond saving, or at least so badly wounded they'd never soldier again?

But Bonnie wouldn't take no for an answer. 'This battle's bigger than any of us have ever seen before. Napoleon himself is here and one day he'll destroy us all if we don't act to preserve as many as we can.'

The idea of saving their men for yet more battles seemed to have little appeal either. The women started to drift away. Bonnie Murphy must have lost her senses, talking about co-operation, supporting each other, Louise heard them muttering. 'Doesn't she know that this is just the place where each of us must look out for herself?' said one.

Louise looked into Bonnie's face and saw her worries had worn her down. Bonnie Murphy, the great survivor, the hardened looter and plunderer from enemy and friend alike, seemed to have heard something in the gunfire she'd never heard before. She was fearful of defeat, fearful of the death of her man. Louise wondered if Bonnie too felt herself to be alone in this great grey forest, whose leaves blotted out the sky but not the noise of destruction.

Louise took her hand. 'Yes, that is a good idea, Bonnie. We'll help each other, you and I. Like you've helped me so far, like you've always done.'

Bonnie grunted. 'I gave them a chance. I gave them the chance to realise this is different; that we'll need each other.'

'You did all you could, Bonnie,' Louise said, as the gunfire began to fade into the night. She took the mule's halter in her hand and turned to her friend. 'I think we should move closer, don't you?'

Holding the sketch map, Louise put her newly found skills into practice and led them safely out of the woods towards a more terrible scene of slaughter than either could have imagined.

57

The Pickings

Overnight 18-19 June 1815, Mont St Jean battlefield

The road and field verges were choked with wagons, mules, and soldiers scarcely able to walk. Made ghastly by the light of the three-quarter moon, the wretchedness of those wounded and dying men struck fear into Louise's heart. There was no sign of mounted cavalry, but Bonnie soon picked out a small group of men with ragged and bloodied blue uniforms slowly making their way towards the surgeons' tents perched on the ridge by a large farmhouse.

'Dragoons,' Bonnie shouted, forcing her way past every obstacle in her path towards them.

'Any of you seen the 36th or know where we can find them?'

'Halfway to Paris, it's to be hoped,' replied their Corporal. 'Boney's men have made a run for it.' He pointed down the main road, its paving scarcely visible for the fallen bodies of men and horses.

Louise couldn't believe it. 'The Tyrant is defeated?'

The Corporal nodded wearily. 'We've got him on the run; well, maybe on the walk, like us lot. Nobody's moving very fast round here tonight. I suppose you might catch your fellows up if they've stopped for the night.'

'On the other hand ...' the Corporal explained that they'd been in Vivian's brigade on the left flank and had had a good view of Vandeleur's brigade's first charge. 'The 36th and the 16th made a very fine run on the guns; saved the arses, excuse my language, of the heavy brigade.

'If you're looking for brave soldiers I reckon there'll be a fair number lying in front of the guns on that ridge over there.' The Corporal gestured towards the centre of the battlefield, pointing at a tangled heap of guns in the distance.

Bonnie turned to Louise. 'They rode straight at the French lines? Mother of God, if we don't get down there before first light we won't stand a chance of finding them, alive or dead. They'll be stripped naked as newborn babes with nothing between them and their Maker. Mother of God, may it please you, guide us to Dermot Murphy and Will Freer, your most loyal servants.'

Louise protested, 'But Bonnie, we don't even know that they're still on the battlefield. They could be riding after Boney right now.'

Bonnie put her hands on her hips. 'And if they are, how are we going to catch them up and find out? No, we have to search where all the dragoons have fallen. We have to be sure Dermot and Will aren't left without help or a decent grave if it comes to that.'

Louise hated talk of graves. 'Won't the bandsmen and orderlies get to them as soon as us by first light?'

Bonnie threw her hands up. 'How many thousands are out there? Just look around you, Louise.'

Bonnie's face screwed up with enough determination to defy death itself. 'We're their best hope ... their only hope.'

Bonnie turned and headed straight towards the French guns, Louise trailing behind with the mule, as they forced a narrow passage through the column of wounded still snaking slowly back up the hill.

'Hang on tight to that beast whatever happens,' Bonnie had instructed.

The moon faded in and out of the clouds as the women now struggled over bodies, the mule too jibbing at the dead horses tipped over like chess pieces. About half-way down, where the fallen seemed to be mainly French, Bonnie dropped to her knees and began to pick over the officers' corpses. 'Over here, Louise. Quick. Give me a hand.'

Louise froze. She hated the idea. Besides, they were here to find their own men, weren't they? She shook her head. 'But what about Dermot and Will?'

Bonnie, now slashing through the tough outer uniforms, scarcely looked up. 'Believe me, we'll need all the money we can find. One way or another. Besides ... if we don't take it, somebody else will.'

Louise retrieved her scissors and began to unpick the seams. 'If we don't stay too long.'

Bonnie Murphy, the greatest plunderer of them all, sighed. 'Just ... just long enough to take what we'll need.'

Louise, gagging at every burst intestine and headless corpse, began to retch but told herself to look to the slitting open of the officers' jacket linings, then feeling carefully for coins and watches. Although reluctant to interrupt her steady invocation to some Almighty or other that her Will might yet be spared, she bent her head and whispered a short prayer over each body.

Bonnie though, lost in a rhythm of her own, was rolling over each officer in turn, methodically cutting and prising out money and precious trinkets straight into her bag. Watching from a distance, Louise thought she looked like a gleaner bending low over the few standing stalks of rye left against the ditch sides. It was as though sustenance for the following year was still to be found amongst the stubble of the dead.

When Bonnie decided they had enough booty she called across to Louise to join her, and so, with mule, tabour, pipe and various spare cloaks, flagons and other necessities, they made their way slowly down into the valley and towards the opposite slope, looking for English blues. It was almost first light by the time the two women reached the spot where many of the Union Brigade's Greys had fallen. Their loose horses were already being gathered up by the locals equipped with long pieces of rope. Their women too had already got to work on the corpses, stripping them naked and throwing all that was useable into large straw panniers.

Louise scanned the breaking waves of bodies ahead, desperate to pick out the Light Dragoons' familiar blue uniforms before the scavengers removed all traces of clothing, rendering French and English alike in an undulating lake of nakedness.

Suddenly, Bonnie, somewhat ahead of her, shouted, 'Louise. Over here!'

Bonnie had discovered blue uniforms ... English dragoons. She knelt down to tug at the bodies lying higgledy-piggledy next to their dead horses.

'We must divide this part of the field between us. You take over there.'

Louise found it hard to tug and roll the men onto their backs and then just leave them unrecorded, unremarked. Her hands were now sticky with blood, and though more accustomed to the smell of death, she was slowed further by her baby riding high against her diaphragm, making her every breath laboured.

Grabbing the mule, Bonnie now moved further up the field, the mule treading over the dead more delicately than Bonnie. All seemed to be a mass of blue except for some big grey horses and the scattered red splashes of the heavy cavalry. But French blues and English light-cavalry blues still mingled confusingly in the growing half-light of the dawn.

'Look for the nag tails,' Bonnie instructed Louise. It was one way of navigating towards the English dead, who would have fallen beside their own horses. Carefully, the women turned over each blue-jacketed body as they came to it. But sometimes the dying horses thrashed about so much that the women didn't dare get too close.

When she found one of the 36th dragoons, a man she recognised, stone dead, even Bonnie's nerves seemed to waver. She called Louise over.

'May your soul rest in peace. By the Holy Mother and Jesus Christ. We can't be burying you today, my friend.' She quickly emptied his pockets and boots of the small trinkets and saved them in a separate bag from her other booty. Then she closed his eyes and crossed herself.

Louise stopped briefly to comfort another acquaintance from the 36th but Bonnie was anxious not to delay any further.

'Louise. You mustn't stop now unless it's Dermot or Will.'

'I shan't be a moment.' Louise found the soldier's canteen and offered him the remaining grog. She thrust his sabre into the ground, perched his shako on its hilt, and whispered, 'Do you know where Dermot Murphy and Will Freer might be?'

It wasn't a question she expected an answer to. The dragoon could scarcely speak.

'Here …' he said. 'Here.'

By now Bonnie was slightly ahead. Louise reluctantly left the wounded dragoon and moved away. She felt he must know more, and if she stayed longer, he would surely remember where his Troop Serjeant-Major and Corporal might be.

Suddenly she heard a great shout as Bonnie fell in triumph upon another of their dragoons. It was Dermot, run through in several places, with gaping wounds, but still alive.

'Louise! Over here, Louise!'

The women quickly applied some of the bandages they had with them to staunch his wounds.

'And just what d'you think you're doing here?' Bonnie scolded. 'We've been out looking for you all night, you useless fella, giving us a fright like this, while we're after dragging your tabour across half of Flanders.

'And Louise's here, looking for Freer and all. You haven't seen Freer, have you?'

Dermot was half-insensible and incapable of speech, except for making a noise that Bonnie interpreted to be her name.

'Yes, I'm here,' she said. 'Where the hell did you expect me to be?'

Bonnie turned to Louise.

'You'd best be looking for your man now. But first, help strap Dermot on my back. I'll leave the mule for you.'

Louise couldn't help marvel at the strength of the woman as Bonnie insisted she should keep mule and tabour and pistol.

'As long as you promise you'll be returning Murphy's tabour to him.'

'But won't you be needing that pistol?'

Bonnie handed over a pistol and powder cartridges she'd plundered earlier.

'There'll be more than you wanting that mule.'

Louise feared the pistol would be of little practical use but took it anyway; then Bonnie strode off across the field towards Mont St Jean, carrying Murphy upon her broad back.

Louise, now in charge of animal and weapon, felt very alone but quickly resumed her search. Suddenly she heard pistol fire. In the distance she saw bands of blue-coated soldiers moving amongst the dead and wounded. One soldier walked over to a wounded horse and dispatched it quickly and efficiently. But then, to her horror, she realised he had turned his attention to the injured. Striding amongst the bodies, he was stopping to pick out wounded men, putting his pistol to each man's head as coolly as he had done with the horses. The other men in his party were doing likewise. The French, she thought; the French are back.

She looked around in alarm to see if there were any English soldiers on the field tending to their own dead and wounded. There were small parties behind her which she hoped were English, but she couldn't be sure. She stopped to see if there was any way to avoid being caught in the middle if they fired. The troops in blue moved closer and closer. Louise knew there was no way she could escape, and her pistol would be useless against this band of men. She couldn't have been more conspicuous with her mule, the tabour slung across its back. They would surely come for her next. As they approached she could hear their voices on the wind. It wasn't unlike the Flemish she'd begun to understand whilst in the Dender Valley. The sentences were harsh and guttural; some words could almost be English. These men weren't French. They must be the Prussians she'd heard tell of. So they were on the same side. But perhaps they'd think she was French. Could they tell the difference between a Frenchwoman and an Englishwoman, and would they spare her even if they could tell? As they gained upon her she realised that they were shooting their own soldiers. They were culling their own men. They'd occasionally pause when coming across a less seriously injured soldier, and if he could walk the man was helped to the edge of the road and left there for the wagons. But Louise could see that badly wounded soldiers were quickly turned over, their wounds examined, and, if all seemed hopeless, shot.

Yet Louise, looking around the field, began to see that final shot as a kindness. Just so long as they didn't take it upon themselves to shoot Will before she found him. She quickened her pace, reasoning that perhaps they'd leave her alone if they saw she wasn't interfering with their own work. She hoped too that, as they weren't securing many of their own wounded, perhaps they'd not take the mule from her.

But what if they considered her a rival in plunder? Then they might show her no mercy at all. Louise wondered how she might signal to them that she was merely a wife. She looked around, searching for a likely corpse, a British soldier light enough for her to try to lift and haul across her mule. She smiled as the Prussians came closer. One of them walked over to her to help her pull the body onto her mule before, she supposed, wishing her farewell. And so it was that Louise wandered around the battlefield looking for Will, signalling honest intentions to the Prussians, with the corpse of perhaps another woman's husband lashed across the mule's back.

Suddenly she noticed, in the distance, an infantryman, apparently unhurt and standing upright as though on guard. She clambered as fast as she could towards him and saw that he was guarding the body of Captain Webster. To her relief, she realised Webster was still alive, though much cut about. But he and the infantryman were desperate for water. Louise turned back to the mule, its reins tied loosely around her wrist to keep it from wandering, and took one of the small field canteens she and Bonnie had plundered earlier. She filled it from the larger flagons suspended across the mule's neck and ran forward to the soldier, who took the first swig and then passed it to Louise.

'You realise this is a senior officer of the 36th?'

The infantryman nodded.

'So you know you'll be well rewarded if you take good care of him.'

As she gave the half-delirious Webster the water, he seemed to recognise her, touching her hand as though he wanted to say something.

'Sir,' she ventured, 'this good soldier is here to watch over you till the orderlies come, but have you seen anything of Troop Serjeant-Major Freer? Would you know of his whereabouts at all, sir?'

Webster struggled to speak. 'Would have saved me, if he could have... '

If he could have. Louise's heart skipped a beat.

She knew Webster was saying that if Will had escaped unharmed, he would have come back for him and taken him from the field. She knew Will too must be lying somewhere, perhaps close by, unable to help either himself or his Captain.

She spoke again briefly to the infantryman. He promised to stay there until the orderlies arrived to remove the officers, when he'd claim his just reward for watching over a Captain just about alive enough to show his gratitude.

Louise, with renewed determination, began to search, circling outwards from where Webster lay. She'd gone about thirty yards, noticing that the morning light was playing more strongly on the soldiers' faces, when she saw Will's horse, Libby, with her distinctive white socks. She paused, hardly daring to go closer. The horse was dead, lying across the prone bodies of two dragoons. She moved closer. The first soldier she reached was lifeless; the second, his leg trapped by the horse's leg, might still be breathing. But by now Louise knew not to trust her own eyes, for if she stared at a corpse long enough, her own breathing sometimes seemed to animate the dead man. The one who perhaps was alive had ginger hair, she convinced herself, but it was hard to tell under the thick mud caked everywhere. She managed to turn the soldier's face gently towards her. It was Will. She shrieked with such force that Will opened his eyes. Louise gently ran her fingers across his cheek. She looked at his leg trapped under Libby's, his body twisted away from her. It would surely need two people to move him.

'Will. It's Louise. Listen to me.'

Will groaned and closed his eyes.

'Will! It's your Louise.'

She had to get her Will away from there. Maybe she could persuade the orderlies who'd soon be coming for Captain Webster to help. She fingered the money, the watch Bonnie had said they'd need. She'd no time to lose. She'd managed to escape the Prussians; but local men and women, their homes destroyed and robbed by these armies, were now returning to repay the compliment. She shouted across to the infantryman and showed him the fine gentleman's watch. He ran his hand under his throat to decline the offer; he could be sure of a bigger reward for saving a Captain, Louise thought grimly. She would have to find her own way.

Will was shivering. She unrolled the cape she'd taken from an officer's horse and quickly covered as much of him as she could. Then she searched Libby's saddle attachments to retrieve Will's field spade, and with this and her bare hands began to dig out the muddy clay from under his leg, keeping Libby's body supported on the bordering earth. Louise could see that Will's leg was broken, but not so badly that the bones were sticking through the skin. This was a good sign; fractured bones were better broken in just one or two pieces, never splintered. It's a good sign, she told herself; he'll live. She seemed to have been digging for an age, but at last Will's fractured leg was no longer trapped by Libby's. She placed her arms under his armpits and hauled him clear. The pain woke him again, and she saw that there were more wounds to his arms and body, mostly now staunched but probably the cause of his great weakness. She knew that next she must try to splint his broken bone. With what, though? His carbine was still in its holster on Libby's saddle. She strapped it hastily to his leg with her petticoat torn into strips. She felt her strength was about to run out, but she knew she had to get away right now, get Will onto their mule before it too fell victim to the groups of looters now fanning out across the battlefield.

She tipped off the other soldier's corpse. He had served her purpose. Now, lugging Will as though he were a sack of corn, she slowly pulled both him and the mule closer to the infantryman guarding Webster. She took out the watch again and this time the soldier, now sure of his bigger reward, came over, examined the handsome timepiece and helped Louise haul and strap Will onto the mule. She quickly gave Will some of the brandy from one of the hip flasks she'd taken earlier. In spite of his weakness and pain, he had to be woken just enough so that he might ride, however slumped, with his leg strapped firmly to the carbine resting against the mule's sturdy body. They had a long journey ahead, up the hill to the surgeons' tents.

As Louise turned away into the pale northern light, she could just make out Bonnie, with Murphy still strapped to her back, striding through the advancing groups of peasant women who were working through the lines of dead soldiers, stripping them of everything useful or valuable, taking in a very different harvest from their devastated fields.

58

Dog

19 June, The Observatory, Mont St Jean

They would have to decide what to do with their dead, but opinions were divided. There were scarcely enough men left in the Regiment to provide burial parties as well as undertake picquet duties, hunt for prisoners and secure the Prussians' rear. The survivors were unsentimental.

'Let the orderlies and the women deal with the dead.'

'Aye, for if we don't capture the French still on the run we could be dead and all by the end of tomorrow.'

'Oh, just let the damn Prussians get on with it.'

'And then for sure there'll be no prisoners left for us to find.'

'Or anything else, once the Prussians have got their hands on it.'

Thomas, too, knew that the Prussians, like the Spaniards Wellington had sent home from France, wouldn't flinch from inflicting vengeance upon the French, whether civilians or soldiers. Their homelands had been devastated by a triumphant French army long ago and now it would be their turn. Everybody knew that Blücher himself had threatened to burn Paris to the ground at the first opportunity.

Haywood and Thomas looked at each other. Thomas ventured, 'There'll be very little left for us or our horses once the Prussians have been ahead of us, sir. We shall need our Commissariat wagons more than ever.' Haywood nodded. 'You're right, Cowper. It would be foolish to go on too far ahead of the wagons. We may as well wait a little longer till they're ready.'

Thomas could see that Haywood, like himself, was in a state of exhaustion where thoughts and words would scarcely connect. He'd clearly been waiting for Thomas's opinion.

Thomas took a deep breath. 'About the stretcher and burial parties, sir.'

Haywood looked distracted again. 'Do you think that if we send our own men to collect our dead with the bandsmen and orderlies, they might become despondent and lack heart for further fighting?'

Thomas shook his head; he desperately wanted to find Freer, at least.

'To know that we won't abandon our wounded will surely give the men some cheer, sir. Perhaps we should send a small party to the battlefield to help the bandsmen secure those still alive, and possibly an officer with a small escort could go ahead to Brussels to see if any of the officers have been taken there already.'

Haywood nodded. 'Make whatever arrangements you think fit, then, and I'll see about one of us going to Brussels.' As Haywood rode off, Thomas mentally apportioned the available men to the various tasks.

Littlethorpe would certainly be bold enough to search out and capture prisoners if under the steady hand of a suitable Corporal. But who? He looked around him. There'd been no sign of Ashby, Byrne or Murphy since their first charge to support the Union Brigade. And who would direct the bandsmen to look for their dead and wounded? They'd need somebody steady and methodical – and scrupulous – to scour the battlefield. Someone who wouldn't spend too much of his time distracted by plunder. Someone who cared enough about his fellows to give them a decent burial and to make notes as to which dragoons were dead or alive. Perhaps he should take charge of that. As for guard duty, any one of them would be glad to be staying where they were. But who among these exhausted men could be relied upon to be vigilant?

Suddenly two of the newest private men came running towards him. 'It's Littlethorpe, Serjeant.'

Thomas heard the panic in their voices and quickly followed them. He soon saw why. Littlethorpe had drawn his sabre and was cursing and slicing at every tree that stood in his way as he twisted and turned through their forest camp. He seemed oblivious to everything else. Thomas loaded his carbine in case Littlethorpe's anger moved from trees to people and asked the new recruits if they knew what had set Littlethorpe off on this path. 'It was after we told him about the dog,' one said.

'You mean Dog, the little terrier that's been following us since Portugal?'

Being new recruits, these two were not familiar with Dog's long and faithful service within the Regiment.

'Yes, that one, I suppose.'

'What about Dog?' Thomas didn't want to hear what they were going to tell him, for it could only be bad. Dog's unerring sense of where the Regiment was to be found was the stuff of legend amongst the men. It seemed that so long as Dog knew where to find them, they could never be lost. And Littlethorpe and Dog were inseparable.

Apparently, when Dog hadn't arrived at the bivouac, Littlethorpe began to pace through the lines, waking everyone up, asking if and when they'd seen Dog. Eventually he'd found these two privates, who'd told him that a French lancer must have noticed Dog running with their troop during their charge to support the heavy cavalry. They'd seen him deliberately spear Dog, shaking his body off onto to the ground before himself being cut down; and yes, the two dragoons were quite certain it was that same little terrier they'd seen about camp.

'That's when he started to curse, Serjeant.'

'And slash at the trees. So we thought it best to get you, Serjeant.'

~

Thomas approached Littlethorpe slowly.

'I heard about Dog.'

Littlethorpe, sobbing in between curses, continued to slash at whatever was in his way.

'Why kill a bloody dog? What harm could the creature do?'

'Because Dog was our dog. That's why.'

Littlethorpe hacked at the trees even more violently, shouting, 'Maria, and now Dog! Gone!'

Thomas wished he could release his own anger so freely.

'You do right. Give these damn trees hell.'

Thomas sat out of Littlethorpe's way with his carbine cocked, until the wretched man had slashed and sliced the last sapling into shreds, thrown his sabre down and marched away, alone, into the darkness. Only then did Thomas let his eyes close; but it seemed only moments before Haywood came back.

'It's agreed,' he said. 'The men are to take turns between duties and rest today until the wagons are closer and provisions delivered. But you and I, and a guard, are to make our way to Brussels to establish the precise whereabouts of officers and other wounded men already taken there. We can take letters, but we leave in half an hour.'

Half an hour. Thomas cursed. What he wanted to do now was to stay and look for Freer. But he had no choice.

He sought out a Corporal and told him to gather some reliable men to spread the word that Serjeant Cowper would take any letters written in the next half-hour to Brussels, to the army postmaster there. It would be his chance too to write a letter to Grace, but once Thomas had taken out his pencil and bedraggled notebook, he found himself tongue-tied. What could he possibly say about the last few days? Nothing could convey the horror to someone who hadn't been there, this city of the dead and dying; it was as if all the citizens of Leicester, every last one, had been cut to the ground.

~

June 19th, Mont St Jean, Flanders

Dearest Grace,

I write in haste, as I leave for Brussels to secure this in the post as soon as I can, for almost certainly, by the time you read this, the newspapers will have reported upon a great battle here at Mont St Jean. There have been many lost, friend and foe. We have still to count the cost of our victory, but for now we are to follow the Prussians, who are driving back the French, including Napoleon himself, to the walls of Paris. There may be more battles ahead, but is to be hoped that the Prussians' great vigour in pursuit will persuade the French that Napoleon's day is over. In the meantime I send my love and hope to receive your response to my last letter very soon. It is nothing short of a miracle, I think, that we are able to send and receive letters, even if months elapse. It is the one thing that has always sustained me in good heart.

With the greatest of love, Thomas.

It was at this point, as Thomas went about the camp collecting the other brief notes the men had managed to write, that he came across Littlethorpe again, sitting white-faced, his back against one of the trunks he'd slashed.

Thomas crouched down next to Littlethorpe. He looked a broken man, quite unlike the Littlethorpe Thomas had known for the last four years. Not a man he could entrust with the capturing of prisoners.

'Littlethorpe?' Thomas touched his shoulder lightly.

Littlethorpe looked up. 'Can't believe the bastards killed Dog.'

How the hell could he grieve for Dog rather than for half the troop who'd been killed or wounded? But Thomas suddenly understood that for all Littlethorpe's apparent camaraderie with his fellows, once Maria had been shipped back with the other Portuguese women, Dog's simple affection and loyalty had been the Private's only sustenance: and now Dog was dead.

'I'll put those two young fellows who saw it happen into the burial party. I'll ask them to look out for Dog as well.'

'Get him a decent burial before some bastard has him for supper.'

Thomas patted Littlethorpe's arm.

'Dog was a good soldier. Saved our stomachs with his rats many a time.'

'Aye, he did that.'

Thomas was reluctant to leave Littlethorpe unsupervised, so he ordered the Private to join Haywood and himself to act as their guard on the way to Brussels.

~

As the small party of 36th Dragoons approached the ridge where the French had based themselves in the old inn, the road dipped until, at the bottom of the slope, Haywood, Thomas and Littlethorpe finally took their leave of the couple of corporals and half-dozen troopers who were to make up the stretcher and burial parties. It was where the fighting had been fiercest. It was where they'd expect to find most of their dead and injured.

It was now Haywood's turn to be thrown off course. They'd stopped by the baggage train assigned to the 36th to discover that Haywood's servant had not only abandoned everything he couldn't carry off but had also released Haywood's two setters to run loose on to the battlefield, and they had not returned. Haywood's anxieties about his lost dogs prompted Littlethorpe to mention Dog, and before Thomas knew it, Haywood and Littlethorpe were not only praising the loyalty and good nature of such animals but also cheering each up by telling as many affectionate stories about the creatures as they could decently recall whilst riding through the midst of such carnage.

They would have to ride across country, as all the roads to Brussels were blocked further on with vehicles trying to make their way there. They were able to reach the summit of the Allied ridge at Mont St Jean itself, but as they turned off the road, Thomas could have sworn he saw Louise Freer in the distance.

59

Brussels

Brussels was in turmoil, with deserters scurrying into hiding, wounded soldiers dragging themselves onto the roadside hoping to find help, and fine ladies in carriages stopping to assist the officers. Every household in the city seemed to have turned out its servants to help in some way, whilst the convents and schools were crowded with men and officers in urgent need of amputations, for splinters of shot and shreds of uniform had been blasted into their wounds, rendering them putrid. Haywood was anxious to tour the convents first, where he expected to find the most seriously wounded officers. There seemed little way discovering how the less seriously wounded were faring, for those officers were now scattered among all the noble houses of Brussels.

Thomas had seen amputations before, of course: officers given rum, the enlisted men biting on a block of wood; yet few screamed or protested at the pain. But he'd never seen quite so many men deprived of their limbs, or about to be, as bones had been fractured beyond any hope of recovery. Some men appeared intact, yet Thomas could see the deep puncture wounds made by the French long swords penetrating so far into the body that even if the bleeding were staunched the man wouldn't survive. Haywood had asked Thomas to bring with him as many of his healing herbs as he could carry.

On the second day, as Haywood searched elsewhere for officers, Thomas and Littlethorpe toured the overcrowded cloisters looking for any rank and file. To their delight, they found Byrne and Ashby in the first convent they visited. Both had been wounded early on and the less badly injured Byrne had helped Ashby back to the rear, from where they'd been taken back to Brussels on wagons just before all the roads became completely jammed.

Byrne, although clearly in pain, was of a mind to talk and, as Thomas administered a poultice to his wounds, he told them about the bands of deserters fleeing back to Brussels and claiming Wellington was finished. People then rushed to leave in a great fright, getting in the way of the returning wounded.

'As though you should believe bloody deserters.' Littlethorpe spat in disgust on the floor.

It was a hard couple of days in Brussels, with little to show for their efforts: two officers found likely to live, three not, six dragoons dying, three might perhaps survive; Ashby still uncertain, with a leg wound that threatened gangrene.

But on the second day, just as Haywood joined them and agreed it was time to return to the Regiment, one of the orderlies came running across to them, holding an unmistakeable 36th shako, complete with sphinx.

'Just come in. One of your serjeants. Half-dead. A queer business; he'd been brought in from the rear, well away from the action but lying right next to a dead Netherlander. Lucky man. Only one shot but it just missed his heart. Must be one of your fellows though.' He waved the shako again.

Thomas's heart fluttered. At the rear? It had to be Fallowfield ... But only half-dead?

Thomas tried to look at the matter dispassionately. Just missed his heart. Half-dead. It wouldn't take much to die from that kind of wound.

As Haywood began to follow the orderly across the courtyard back to one of the inner rooms he signalled Thomas to follow, bringing his healing herbs with him.

'Just need to check my stock first, sir.' Thomas excused himself and quickly hid most of his stock before Haywood returned.

'Well, damn me if it isn't Serjeant Fallowfield … in rather a sorry state, I might add. You had better come and show these nuns what to do with those potions of yours.'

Thomas wondered it he dared refuse. He knew Haywood didn't like Fallowfield either. 'If he's that badly injured, sir, perhaps I should save the last of my medicines for those more likely to benefit.'

Haywood sighed. 'It's a question of doing our basic Christian duty by the man, Cowper.'

It wasn't what he wanted to hear. Thomas followed Haywood across the courtyard, handed over a meagre portion of what he claimed to be the last of his healing herbs and whispered some basic instructions to an elderly nun. People said that even the dying could recognise people's voices, and Thomas already felt himself to be damned.

~

There had been no sign of Freer, but just before they left they heard some good news. Both Pennington and Webster had been found and after the most strenuous treatment by surgeons in Brussels both were still alive. With no sign of serious putrefaction around their wounds, there was every hope they would both recover.

As Thomas, Haywood and Littlethorpe left Brussels the stream of traffic into the city seemed scarcely less than before. Wagons loaded with the wounded were still arriving; but Haywood, having arranged for the clerks to keep a tally of their own soldiers, was anxious to rejoin the 36th, now in pursuit of the French.

Cutting across country, they were able to make good time back towards Mont St Jean. Surgeons' tents remained pitched all along the road to Waterloo, but on the battlefield itself the stink of the dead had driven away all but the hardiest of looters and plunderers.

~

Louise must have been keeping a watch on the road outside the rows of cottages, looking for blue uniforms, for even before they saw her she called out to them to stop. Thomas feared the worst and braced himself to hear of her loss and her sorrow, but as she walked towards him he could see she was smiling; well, almost smiling. That could only mean one thing. Freer was alive. He's alive, Thomas repeated to himself over and over again. Freer is alive.

Thomas made no attempt to stop his tears flowing as he heard her news.

Will's bones had been pulled back into place and were now strapped. His loss of blood had been serious, but not critical; and his wounds as yet showed no sign of gangrene, though this remained a risk until they were fully healed; and he was carrying a slight fever, which was causing the surgeons some concern.

Haywood smiled and said he had a good hour's business at Wellington's headquarters, and suggested to Thomas that he should go back with Louise to spend some time with Freer. Littlethorpe too excused himself and said he'd give the lads in the burial parties a hand; besides, he wanted to know if they ever did find Dog.

As they reached the cottage, Louise led him into a low-ceilinged room where Will was lying on one of the makeshift beds.

'Will. It's Thomas.' Thomas laid his hand over his friend's.

Freer grasped Thomas's arm and tried to raise his head. 'Not dead yet, eh.' But the effort of talking was too much and he quickly closed his eyes again. Soon he was deeply asleep.

Louise stood up. 'We must go while we can.'

Thomas stayed seated. He'd come to spend time with Freer, not go visiting.

'Go? Where?'

Louise tugged at his sleeve. 'I promised Bonnie I'd go back as soon as I could.'

~

Bonnie and Boy were bivouacking in the woods over the hill. When Thomas and Louise arrived they had just finished digging Murphy's grave. As they stood, all four of them, by the mound of earth now piled high with last year's beech leaves and Boy drummed the last beat of their farewell on Murphy's tabour, Bonnie murmured, 'Well, my darling man, I'll be off now to find my next soldier, with only your tabour and a few of my pickings from the battlefield for a dowry.' And with that, she gathered up her belongings, took hold of Boy's hand and followed Thomas and Louise back to the cottages.

As they drew near to the cottages Thomas saw Haywood and Littlethorpe riding towards him. Thomas ducked through the doorway and took a hasty leave of Freer, who was awake again.

'I'll see you again soon, my friend. We've both known many a man recover from worse wounds,' he said, grasping Freer's hand.

Freer nodded. 'Look after Louise and the baby, eh?'

Thomas squeezed Freer's hand. 'Course I will, but you'll be doing that yourself soon enough.'

Once outside, Thomas reached into his sabretache and fetched out the rest of his herbs together with some comfrey and beech leaves which he gave to Louise to make up a poultice. Then, turning to say his farewells to Bonnie and Boy, Thomas bent towards Boy's pale face, ran his fingers through his hair, and whispered to Bonnie, 'Whatever you do, if Fallowfield should by some miracle survive, keep Boy out of his way. So long as that man's alive, Boy will never be safe.'

Bonnie looked puzzled but nodded. 'Don't you be fretting now. When has arse-face ever got the better of me, eh?'

Louise came out say her goodbyes and reported that Will had fallen asleep again, but Thomas still couldn't find it in his heart to leave without a last farewell.

As soon as he entered the cottage Freer opened his eyes. 'Write, write to me when the Tyrant is truly beaten.'

60

The Road to Paris

Riding cross-country again, Haywood, Thomas and Littlethorpe set off south for the French border, Thomas and Littlethorpe taking turns to keep watch overnight in case of enemy stragglers.

Thomas began to wonder if he should write a further letter to Grace. He felt the need to tell her Freer had survived. Not that he recollected telling her that he'd feared Freer was dead, so perhaps it wasn't sensible to write about something she had no suspicion of.

Maybe when he reached Paris, when they knew whether Napoleon would stand and fight or flee; that would be the time to write, to ask Grace again: would she accept his proposal of marriage now, when peace seemed to be in sight? But first he must broach the subject with Haywood. He'd have to have support if he was to obtain permission from a senior officer. Perhaps he'd ask him that night. That might be a good moment, when they were sitting snug around the campfire, with Littlethorpe a little distance away keeping watch.

'Sir, I was wondering. Do you think Napoleon will abdicate or continue to put up a stiff resistance?'

Haywood poked the fire a couple of times, considering his answer. 'Now that's a good question to ponder, given he will want to prevent the Prussians destroying Paris. We can't know, of course, whether the Prussians will carry out their threats but Blücher's a rum character, rough in his manners, although a good friend to Wellington, and …' Haywood sniffed, as though unwilling to admit the point,'… therefore to us. So it may be that Wellington's usual good sense will prevail and he'll be able to persuade Blücher it would be unwise to risk enraging the entire French nation by setting its capital on fire.'

Thomas hardly dared venture his next question.

'Then do you think, sir, we shall see peace before the end of the year?'

'Who knows? Perhaps Bonaparte will abdicate or the French will declare themselves sick of fighting. Are not we all sick of fighting?' Haywood pulled his jacket straight.

Thomas saw his chance. 'Though there are some of us, sir, who would be prepared to stay in the army – so long as we were permitted to marry – rather than be discharged and not be able to earn an honest living.'

Haywood sighed. 'Indeed. Yet if peace ever does come, I rather expect to have to go on half-pay myself, unless I manage to secure a position in the colonies. Without Napoleon to fight, regiments will be disbanded, mark my words.'

'But we may have to wait for some time before we know what our fate will be, sir?'

Haywood blew his nose. 'The one lesson I've learned over the last few months is that to wait too long for anything may be too late.'

Haywood looked into the fire, deep in his own thoughts. Thomas had learnt recently that of the brave breakfast party that had made so much merriment before Quatre Bras, two officers had been wounded and six killed; only Haywood himself remained unharmed. It was a grim toll.

Haywood looked up from the fire. 'None of us will be quite the same fellows we used to be … after this business.'

Thomas wondered if his own face looked as careworn as Haywood's.

So Haywood and Thomas bivouacked in a small copse near the border with much still unspoken between them. Almost inevitable between an officer and his serjeant, Thomas reflected. His request to marry would have to wait till another day. But it was that night that brought him the first indications that he too would never be quite the same fellow he used to be. It started with the nightmares and finished with the voices.

61

Revenge Can Be Sweet

The nightmares began with the shooting of Fallowfield and ended with the slicing open of the head of the young French officer. The voices began and ended with his mother, Michael and Hannah; Hannah screaming, Michael and his mother shouting, and Thomas climbing the apple loft ladder.

Thomas woke. Littlethorpe was moving; it was time to take his turn on the watch, but whatever he did the voices followed him every step of the way as they rejoined the Regiment gradually edging its way to Paris. By the beginning of July, with victory still not certain, everyone's spirits seemed as low as Thomas's.

Still expecting to be required to support the Prussians, they crept even closer towards the French rearguard. Both sides were then obliged to observe the practical courtesies of flags of truce so they could attend to their necessities; but with the French clearly unreconciled to defeat, the British troops took care at every halt made to move their light artillery units to their front.

So it came as no surprise when Haywood, newly promoted again to Acting Captain, announced to his troop, 'I have bad news: the Prussians have been defeated on the very outskirts of Paris. So we may well have to fight again on to the end … the bitter end,' Haywood uncharacteristically added, 'until our great victory at Mont St Jean, or Waterloo, as we now hear that engagement is called, is secured.'

Thomas knew Haywood well enough to detect the weariness in his voice: he was clearly not relishing the prospect of having to fight another great battle or perhaps stand by helplessly whilst the Prussians, who were still much roused, inflicted their revenge upon French civilians.

So none of them had been expecting the Prussians to win a great battle only a few days later. Haywood was smiling for the first time in weeks. 'The French are retreating and Wellington expects negotiations to open shortly for their complete surrender.'

Thomas could hardly believe it. None of them could, but when the good news finally sank in all became giddy and desperate to celebrate. But how? It was Littlethorpe who provided the answer. They had stopped for the night beside a great mansion set in a vast estate. Rumour had it that it had been the Navy Minster's official residence, but now there was little left to see as the forward troops had already destroyed its interior.

So Thomas and Littlethorpe decided to inspect its grounds instead. Suddenly Littlethorpe, who was just ahead, yelled 'Just look at that bloody great thing.'

Thomas hurried to join him. Littlethorpe was pointing towards a pleasure boat, tricked out like a miniature man-of-war, bobbing at anchor off an island in the middle of an enormous lake.

Littlethorpe whooped with delight. 'Time to show the buggers we still rule the bloody waves and all.' He shouted to one of the artillery lads who was just behind them. 'Come on, Crowther, show us what you're made of.' He began to sprint towards the water, the young lad following, his knapsack bouncing almost off his shoulders. By the time

Thomas reached the shore, Littlethorpe and his companion had already stripped off and were swimming out to the boat, Littlethorpe holding the knapsack high above the water.

By now a crowd had gathered to watch as both of them boarded the minister's miniature vessel. Scrambling everywhere before lighting the fuses, Littlethorpe and Crowther ran back onto the island, hands high in the air, Littlethorpe shouting.

'For Lord bloody Nelson and every other bugger killed by the crapauds.'

Soon the soldiers lining the lakeside were swearing, cheering and laughing as the ship, now well ablaze, drifted across the water, until the dying embers faded away into the night. Thomas watched; all seemed satisfied that proper revenge had been taken – but without the dreadful consequences of another Badajoz.

Thomas, for just a moment, felt at peace; if only it weren't for his dreams, the new and the old terrors which came uninvited every time he laid down his head to sleep: Fallowfield not yet dead, the French officer resurrected, the stink of blood and gunpowder making him gag, Thomas in the apple loft, Hannah screaming, his mother shouting, Michael falling.

62

The Bridge to Paris

Thomas leant back against one of the sturdy pines encircling their campsite and breathed in their scent. He read over his letter to Freer one more time. Was he being unduly pessimistic?

July 6th, 1815, Neuilly

My dear Freer,

It would appear the Tyrant is truly beaten, though I fear Napoleon's men still seem reluctant to accept their defeat. When Paris was about to fall, about thirty or so of us were sent to watch the bridge across the Seine, where we could see, on the other bank, French troops massed with double abattis, sharp as sabres, ready to block our progress. The French eventually sent a flag of truce, so that they might water their horses in the river. This took some time, so officers from both sides, including Haywood, stood chatting together on the bridge. Then one of the French officers, a fellow with a harelip, quite unprovoked, took out his horsewhip and attacked an elderly French gentleman dressed in old-fashioned clothes and with long powdered hair, who had edged too close to them. Haywood and I quickly moved forward to put ourselves between the officer and the old man now lying helpless on the ground. I placed my hand on my sabre hilt ready to protect Haywood as I thought the officer might well strike him too. Fortunately one of this man's fellow-officers seized the horsewhip before he could use it again. What harm was the old man doing, other than to remind the officer of the old ways? Who knows, my dear friend? Who knows?

Thomas recalled the old man's face, the way his eyes pleaded as the officer raised his horsewhip to strike, and tried not to remember that other officer and his bewildered brown eyes as Thomas wielded his sabre downward straight through his skull.

63

The Field of Mars

July 1815, Paris

That should have been the end of it. But Thomas wasn't sure that the officer with the harelip was ever going to forget his public humiliation. It was the second time since then that they had seen him following their troop into the city.

The 36th were camped in the woods between the main road into Paris and the Seine and rode into the city itself every third day, taking their turn to remind its citizens that the Allies, not they, were in command. Their destination was the great square by the royal palaces down a broad avenue lined with chestnuts. It was called the Champs Élysées, Haywood pointed out gloomily, in honour of some mythical paradise for dead heroes. It was in the great square itself that the French officer had taken to circling round the edge of their troop, keeping his distance but unmistakably watching their every move.

After another day of this, Haywood, by nature a cheerful person, declared they should ignore the French officer, shake off all gloomy thoughts and enjoy the fruits of their victory. Haywood would consult Captain Webster's notebook, which he had been obliged to leave behind after Waterloo, and visit as many of the city's notable sights as and when their other responsibilities allowed.

'You'll have to come, of course. Can't have the likes of that man stalking us without the two of us looking forward and aft.'

Haywood too had, at last, acquired a horse of his own to replace his charger, lost at Waterloo. Thomas had tried to counsel him against it but he'd made use of one of the many traders who, thick as thieves with some enterprising soldiers, were making a considerable profit selling ownerless British mounts to those officers in need of a new horse. It was a fine-looking but nervous creature whose skittishness, Thomas thought, did not bode well for its rider.

Still, Thomas was pleased to see Haywood in a more expansive mood, though not quite back to his usual self; but then, as Haywood himself had said, none of them would ever be quite the same fellows again.

'I don't know whether these Parisians realise just how close they came to having the whole damned city burned to the ground. It was only Wellington who dared talk Blücher out of it. Doesn't possess a single gentlemanly bone in his body, our friend Blücher, I'm sorry to say.'

Thomas nodded, but thought this a little ungenerous of Haywood, who didn't have a good word for the elderly general with his great moustaches and whoring and gambling ways, even though he and his men had most likely saved them all from destruction.

Thomas smiled at the thought of Haywood being rather more impressed by Napoleon. They'd already visited several monuments dedicated to the Emperor and his army. They'd begun by inspecting the triumphal archway positioned between the royal palaces close by where the Allies assembled their own troops, built to commemorate his victories of 1805 … the same year he'd enlisted, Thomas recalled. A whole lifetime ago.

'Modelled on an ancient archway in Rome, it says here.' Haywood peered at Webster's notebook and then at the carvings. 'Never been myself.'

Likewise, in another huge square, Haywood, consulting Webster's guide yet again, pointed to a tall stone column. 'It's a copy of one in Rome. Erected by Napoleon to celebrate the Austerlitz campaign.'

Thomas grimaced. He recalled Dickenson on East Blatchington cliffs announcing the death of Pitt and the collapse of the Allied Coalition after their defeat at Austerlitz. How invincible the Tyrant had seemed then.

'If only we British soldiers had such wonders of architecture built in our honour,' Haywood would exclaim at every monument. But what had impressed Haywood and Thomas most so far were the army establishments on the far side of the Seine: the Military School, situated on the Field of Mars and the nearby Army Hospital, with a church as grand as St Paul's.

Of course, two cavalrymen from the Allied Army of Occupation weren't going to risk inspecting them more closely, especially when being followed by a French officer holding a grudge.

64

Our Lady

The summer heat was easing at last and, thanks to Haywood's excursions, Thomas now knew Napoleon's capital in some detail; though he was taking less pleasure in the endless reviews and victory parades, especially as they had had the strictest of orders not to flaunt their victories. Thomas thought this a strange instruction, for they were soon to be reviewed by the monarchs of Europe in the great Royal Square with all the pomp and ceremony that occasion would entail.

'And if that's not flaunting our victories, my name's not Thomas Cowper,' he whispered to Fearless.

Haywood's new horse too had clearly taken a dislike to such displays for during the last review Haywood had only just been saved from being tipped straight into the river by Thomas and Fearless, who managed to divert the creature away from its intended path. Thomas soothed Haywood's wounded pride. 'They say that horses' battle scars can't always be seen, but are as painful as any sabre cut.'

'Second, or maybe third time you've saved my life, Cowper,' Haywood muttered.

'That's my job, sir.'

Haywood looked him up and down. 'You know, Captain Webster said a damned odd thing to me just before we left for the Netherlands. Don't let Fallowfield act as an officer's cover serjeant. Whatever you do. Seemed quite emphatic about it.'

Thomas sighed. Maybe he should explain. 'There was much talk, sir, before you joined the Regiment, that Serjeant Fallowfield had been less than diligent in his duties at Salamanca.'

Haywood nodded. 'I see. Well, I'm exceedingly grateful for your diligence, Cowper.'

'Thank you, sir.'

So it was that Thomas took Haywood's charger in hand and gradually restored her steady disposition. If only he could forget the horrors of that day as easily.

~

They weren't to be disbanded. They were to stay on in France as part of the Army of Occupation. For three years or more. Thomas would be unlikely to see England again for some time. He fretted. If only Grace would reply. He would ask her to come to France. But it wasn't until the last gasp of summer, when they were about to take up their posts yet again in the great square by the Champs Élysées that the first batch of letters from England finally arrived. Recognising Grace's hand, Thomas seized the letter from the pile.

~

August 12th 1815

Dear Thomas,

I received your welcome letter today. I was relieved to hear you are safe and that the War is over at long last.

All of Melton and its villages have been relieved too to hear of Napoleon's exile far away to the middle of a great ocean.

There has been talk of little else, and great admiration of how bravely our troops have conducted themselves. Since the news reached us, there have been bonfires, pageants and dancing all summer long.

Thomas frowned. If only the troops had had the opportunity and inclination to celebrate in such innocent ways.

Master Andrew has been at home visiting his family for the last two weeks and has enthralled us all with tales of our soldiers' brave deeds. Indeed he has determined to mark the event and has devised a bold plan to turn some of his father's parkland into a representation of the battlefield of Waterloo itself.

Thomas read the sentence again. No. He was not mistaken.

He intends to plant trees in copses being true to the exact formations and locations of the French, British, and Prussian troops, making use of the different colours and foliage of the trees.

Thomas recalled meeting the young Captain briefly during their stay in Brussels; he was a staff officer there. His scarred face and finger stumps bore witness to his old injuries from Corunna but he had gone out of his way to help them, especially after he'd recognised Thomas as being one of his father's former estate workers.

But what about his proposal? He quickly scanned the letter to its end instead of savouring every line as he would once have done.

~

Thomas pulled himself together enough to trot Fearless over to Haywood. Reining her in, Thomas ventured to ask, 'Sir, may I have your permission to leave my duties here for a few hours? I have to attend to a pressing matter which has just been brought to my attention.'

This wasn't strictly accurate, but near enough to the truth for Thomas to feel he could look Haywood in the eye.

Haywood was puzzled. 'Can it not wait until tomorrow?'

Thomas tried to keep his voice calm. 'It's like you said once, sir; to wait too long for anything may be too late.'

Waiting for Haywood's decision, Thomas felt the moments stretching into an eternity as he wondered what he would do if Haywood said no.

Haywood's expression softened. ' Indeed. So long as you are back in time for our return to the Bois de Boulogne, you may take leave for the rest of the day.'

Thomas felt his knees tremble with relief. 'Yes, sir.'

Entrusting Fearless to the care of Littlethorpe, Thomas walked briskly across the square towards the Tuileries. He didn't know where he was going, but his instinct told him to get away, as far away as possible. He decided to walk towards the hay market. That would be far enough from prying eyes and any officers he might meet could be told he was going there on regimental business. But he wasn't in the mood to be questioned. Following the walls of the Louvre, he traced his route back towards the river, Grace's letter running ceaselessly through his head as though he'd committed every word to memory, the more to torture himself.

You can imagine too how the Hall has been. We have not been so busy in years with house parties and dramatic entertainments that have delighted our guests. I have been asked again to play in their theatricals in the great barn. Master Andrew has a good friend, a gentleman manager at one of the best theatres in London, and has asked him to attend.

I must break off writing now, Thomas. Miss Susan calls and I am required, but I shall resume as soon as I am able.

For the next hour or more, he wandered the streets of Paris. He followed the river where he could though sometimes he would dodge into a deep shuttered road close to the riverbank or cut down a twisting alley; but the old town with its narrow streets was no place for a lone English soldier to linger, especially when followed by a vengeful French officer. He decided to cross over the bridge to try and shake him off. Maybe he would make his way to La Tournelle after all; but just before he reached the left bank, drawn by the Seine's swirling waters, he stopped to reflect on the next part of Grace's letter.

August 14th 1815

I take up my pen again, Thomas, to give you news about both our families. Bailiff Strutt and my sister Sarah were married just last week. Bailiff Strutt is the kindest of men so I hope he will find happiness with someone who is not easily content. I know he thinks she is more of a straightforward woman than I know her to be, but Sarah long ago determined to marry well and as another had just refused him, she chose her moment carefully to offer him sympathy and succour.

But I must tell you now of other less happy news. I wrote before about the theatricals celebrating our great victory, which have also been enjoyed by all the workers on the Squire's estate. Your father found me after the end of the performance yesterday and told me that his young daughter by his new wife is gravely ill and is not expected to live. Poor Ruth; she is such a sweet, loving child. I fear your father and stepmother may not be blessed with living children.

Would his father recall the last time he'd buried a child? Thomas wiped away the tears that were beginning to run down his cheeks, and damped down a baser impulse to anger. He quickened his pace instead to reach the far bank of the river when he suddenly looked up and saw the towers of the great church. He remembered Freer back in Guilford asking him after his mother died; *what has God or the Devil to do with any of it?* Thomas started walking towards them like a man bearing a grudge.

But then, sensing someone was walking close behind him, he stopped and turned. It was the French officer. Remembering that Haywood maintained the officer's English was perfectly serviceable, and now he was within inches of the man perhaps he should speak to him directly; but what to say? Well, Thomas knew all about humiliation and defeat, how it felt to be pitied.

Thomas saluted the officer. 'Sir, my Captain and I have marvelled at how Napoleon honoured his soldiers. We understand how proud of him you are and how angry you are at his defeat. But we are soldiers, sir. We should not bear ill-will towards each other.'

The officer inclined his head and turned away. When Thomas heard the click of the officer's heels finally recede into the distance he started walking once more towards the great church.

~

He didn't stop again until he'd safely reached its three deeply incised archways. It was as substantial a bulwark as any fortification built to withstand a siege or attempted breach of its walls. God's very own fortress, he could imagine Freer joking.

And yes, some rows of figures above the doors were positioned rather like an infantry line, ready to fire … though most were lacking their heads. Guillotined, so Reason might prevail, he could also imagine Freer saying. But this time the joke would have been a grim one. Even Freer now said he feared a rational but uncompassionate man just as much as an irrational one. Thomas turned around and saw the officer with the harelip was watching him.

He moved closer to the entrance on the right and saw that the figures over the doorway were mostly intact. He peered closer and tried to make them all out. In the Peninsula, Webster had explained to him and Freer how this Catholic religion felt the need to be on praying terms with a variety of saintly intermediaries, who liaised between the individual and God, rather like staff officers. Neither of them had been impressed at the time but Thomas suddenly understood; he understood why men might feel the need to anchor their beliefs in stone. They might disappear otherwise.

I dare say you will be wondering why I have made no reference, so far, to your own proposal of marriage when you were leaving for the Low Countries.

The cathedral's dark interior beckoned him in like a shady grove in the midday heat. Thomas slipped through the doorway, dizzied by the rapid change between the day's heat and the cool, averting his eyes from the dancing rainbows thrown into the air. Trying to keep his eyes firmly fixed on the ground, he stumbled into an enormous carved frieze which, he realised, was depicting the life of Jesus. As he moved towards the section representing The Last Supper, he counted the number of disciples gathered around Christ, his last companions in this earthly life. So important. Friends. Like Freer. He suddenly recalled what Freer had told him years ago, and then Webster's painting in payment of his debts to Louise at the Receiving House. So this was Notre Dame Cathedral; the self-same place where Napoleon had crowned himself Emperor in front of the Pope! Thomas moved closer to the altar and stood before it, half-expecting to see the Pope himself emerge from the shadows. He wiped away a tear. So this was where it all began, when a saviour became an emperor and a Tyrant; when, Freer insisted the French had finally lost their claim to be the guardians of the Rights of Man.

It was only then that he noticed the huge white statue of the Virgin Mary, her arms outstretched in the agony of every mother who has ever lost a child, with the dead Christ lying across her lap.

Your offer of marriage is not something I would easily turn away. You know how fond I am of you, Thomas, our childhood being one of such closeness and happiness. But I realise now that I do not have the necessary character to become a soldier's wife and therefore if I release you from any sense of obligation to me, I feel sure you will find yourself a more suitable bride than I could ever have been. Also I too, like you all those years ago, will be leaving Burton. Master Andrew's good friend, whom I spoke of earlier, was most encouraging when he saw my performance during the theatricals and tells me that I would make a fine actress. He is, as I told you, the gentleman manager of a theatre that stages many reputable plays and he has offered me a position in his company in London; and so I shall soon enter a profession that will afford me as much interest as you have found in being a soldier.

Thomas moved further round, towards the door, and looked back once more at the dancing rainbows, and felt himself to be a long way from home. He saw the circle close again, his journey ending here, where it had begun, when Napoleon became Emperor, and he and Freer became soldiers. As for Grace, perhaps the mysteries were what she had always loved, the power of illusion, as she once called Master Andrew's theatricals.

Your letters were always a source of great inspiration and comfort to me, and now I know that you are safe, I feel free to accept this offer. There are many older actresses of good character in the gentleman's company and he assures me that my reputation will be preserved by their presence as chaperons.

I leave at the end of the week. I shall be able to give you an address in London, but the company undertakes a considerable amount of touring in the southern parts of England and correspondence is not delivered regularly.

Please accept my fondest regards and sincere good wishes for your future health and happiness.

Grace

He heard the frenzied beat of wings, felt their icy sweep shattering the air. He gripped his sabre hilt – and told himself such is the power of illusions.

He noticed a chapel gate left open. He knelt down before the small altar and placed his head in his hands and prayed for the relief of *the agony of every mother who has ever lost a child.* But then, as he recalled the image of the Virgin Mary, the dying Christ draped across her lap, he heard his mother's voice reassuring him, telling him he could let himself remember. It was time. He closed his eyes and in the chapel's fragmented silence he saw himself once again wrestling with Michael in the apple loft. He remembered being angry with him, angrier than he'd ever been … not over Grace, but over Hannah and what Michael had done to his own sister, just ten years old. But as they fought Michael tripped, tumbling straight down the ladder. Michael lay winded and dazed. And then Thomas saw his mother run over to push Michael's head straight back onto the ground yelling, 'You wicked, wicked boy. How could you do that to our Hannah?' As the images and voices crowded back, he finally let himself see his mother bending over her fallen angel screaming, 'Son of Beelzebub,' gripping Michael's head in her hands, dashing it time after time against the frozen earth until there was silence.

~

He tried not to remember Michael's bloodied face, and his mother's lamentations when she realised what she'd done; but the pain of every loss he'd ever felt now crowded in on him: his grandmother, his mother, his dead comrades. And now Grace. Not dead but lost to him. Forever.

Suddenly he saw Grace there, standing right next to him, smiling, reaching out. He tried to stand up, to shout, but the words wouldn't come. And then he heard distant bells. His mother was shouting, telling him to save himself from a procession of dark-hooded figures closing in on him.

He pulled out the small bag of soil hanging around his neck. He smelt the summer-dry ash-lined lanes, and winter-deep, waterlogged tracks, dipping over the horizon across the high fields of the township of Burton Lazarus. Home. Once upon a time. In the great shire of Leicester, when he and his grandmother roamed fields and woods looking for herbs that would heal bodies and souls.

Thomas felt his grandmother's arms pulling him up from the stream bank back onto the lane, he holding tight the ramsons and feverfew he'd climbed down to fetch. He felt her hand upon his shoulder and turned to smile, but she wasn't there. It was Freer, who was reaching out, moving him gently away from the cliff edge.

Thomas shifted his weight and lifted his eyes towards the chapel ceiling and found himself floating, floating away from his old self, his head bobbing up and down in Blatchington horse ponds, his eyes fixed on the blue sky, counting the clouds drifting slowly into the distance, leaving all behind him. Then he heard Littlethorpe shouting, Dog yapping; felt the warmth once again of that last campfire in the Dender Valley, and remembered the song he'd chosen to sing.

I seek for one as fair and gay,
But find none to remind me
How sweet the hours I passed away,
With the girl I left behind me.

He stood up. It was time to rejoin his company on the Champs Élysées. They were his only family now. He walked slowly out of that great dark space back into the light.

Notes

The War

The French Revolutionary and Napoleonic Wars lasted from 1792 to 1815, with a short lull after the 1801/2 Peace of Amiens. Britain's involvement began in 1793. Our 19th century ancestors called it the Great War. It consisted of a complicated series of campaigns waged against France by a total of seven coalitions of different allied forces. Britain was also at war with the United States of America on land and at sea from 1812 until early 1815.

My story opens in March 1805, just after the height of the 1804 invasion scares when Napoleon's army of over 100,000 men was stationed at Boulogne, and concludes just after the Battle of Waterloo in June 1815. Even after Nelson's defeat of the French fleet at Trafalgar in October 1805, the British continued to fear invasion and the coast of southern Britain was protected by all manner of fortifications, an early-warning system established by a network of telegraph stations and constant patrols on land and at sea.

By 1808 Napoleon dominated most of Europe, but the imposition of his brother Joseph on the throne of Spain led to an uprising by the Spanish people. A British expeditionary force was launched and after a number of false starts, including the disastrous retreat from Corunna in 1809, the British and Portuguese, led by Arthur Wellesley (the future Duke of Wellington), fought the six-year-long Peninsular

War in parallel with various Spanish military units. Based in Portugal, the Anglo-Portuguese army was supplied and reinforced by the British navy.

The campaign in the Peninsula tied down valuable French troops and culminated in the invasion of France across the Pyrenees, which contributed to Napoleon's 1814 abdication. After Napoleon escaped from Elba in 1815, he gathered a vast army around him as he travelled through France to Paris. British and Prussian soldiers were sent immediately to the Netherlands to assist in their defence and waited for Napoleon's next move. His Hundred Days campaign ended, in effect, with his defeat at Waterloo on June 18th 1815, though, in practice, hostilities did not conclude until the formal surrender of Paris in early July. The second restoration of the Bourbon king, Louis XV111, was on July 8th 1815.

Cavalry units

My 36th Light Dragoons is a fictional regiment, although inspired by an actual one. A couple of other fictional regiments are referred to in the text but otherwise I have called regiments and historical figures by their original names.

The regiment would have been led by a Lieutenant-Colonel but on active service a cavalry regiment was frequently brigaded with another regiment under a brigade commander.

Light cavalry regiments were usually made up of ten troops with approximately ninety rank-and-file men in each troop, though regiments were frequently not up to strength. It was usual for two troops to provide a depot squadron at home and the others to form four active service squadrons of two troops each.

Captains were responsible for leading their individual troops consisting of subaltern (junior) officers – lieutenants and the even more junior cornets, a senior non-commissioned officer, a troop serjeant-major (after 1813), together with serjeants, corporals, and chosen men (lance corporals) as well as private men (privates).

Hopefully most of the military terminology is self-evident in context but the following are possibly less easily fathomed:

A sabretache: a large leather satchel/pouch worn by cavalrymen.

The Forlorn Hope: the band of soldiers who take the lead in an assault, but who have little realistic prospect of survival.

Locations and maps

UK. See map:

http://upload.wikimedia.org/wikipedia/commons/2/2e/UnitedKingdomCitiesandTownsOMC.png

The novel opens in Burton Lazarus, a small village outside Melton Mowbray in Leicestershire, in the East Midlands. My main character enlists in Leicester, is trained as a cavalryman in Nottingham, moves to Romford in Essex and thereafter spends most of his home service patrolling the south coast, from East Sussex to Kent with occasional tours in and around London. His regiment embarks for the Peninsula from Portsmouth in 1811. They spend the 1814/15 winter in Dorchester and Weymouth.

Approximate locations in relation to those places shown on the UK map:

Burton Lazarus (Burton Lazars), 2 miles south-east of Melton Mowbray
Deal, Kent coast, 9 miles west of Dover
Dorchester, 8 miles north of Weymouth
East Blatchington, part of west Seaford
Hampton Court, 10 miles west of central London
Hounslow Heath, 12 miles west of central London
Hythe, Kent coast, 14 miles west of Dover
Romford, 14 miles north-east of central London
Seaford, East Sussex coast, 12 miles east of Brighton
Stathern, 10 miles north of Melton Mowbray

Europe in 1812. See map:

http://upload.wikimedia.org/wikipedia/commons/f/f5/Europe_1812_map_en.png. The thicker line around countries indicates the French Empire and its allies.

The Iberian Peninsula. See map:

http://upload.wikimedia.org/wikipedia/commons/c/c0/Peninsular_War_battles.PNG

The regiment is based briefly in Lisbon and nearby Belem but then spend some of the campaigning seasons in and around the Spanish northern border fort of Ciudad Rodrigo and the southern one of Badajoz. They make occasional forays into Spain with a victory at Salamanca and a defeat at Burgos, both in 1812, until their break-through campaign, including the battle of Vittoria, in 1813. They eventually cross the Pyrenees into the south of France in 1814. After the battle of Toulouse, Napoleon's abdication is confirmed in April 1814.

Europe in 1815. See map:

http://upload.wikimedia.org/wikipedia/commons/a/ac/Strategic_Situation_of_Western_Europe_1815.jpg

The Waterloo campaign. See maps:

http://upload.wikimedia.org/wikipedia/commons/7/77/Waterloo_Campaign_map-alt3.svg

- Quatre Bras and Waterloo (the battle site is at Mont St Jean) are in present day Belgium about twenty kilometres south of Brussels.
- The location of the 36th Light Dragoons on the Waterloo battlefield. I am indebted to David Beckford and Andrew Bamford for the illustration.

Shetland
Haroldswick
Lerwick
Sumburgh
Foula
Fair Isle
Stonybreck
Orkney
Stromness
Kirkwall
Atlantic
Ocean
Outer
Hebrides
(Western
Isles)
St Kilda
Cape Wrath
Durness
Thurso
John o' Groats
Wick
Kinlochbervie
Stornoway
Ullapool
Carrykinloch
Lewis
Harris
Skye
Dingwall
Nairn
Inverness
Brandenburgh
Fraserburgh
Peterhead
Aberdeen
Stonehaven
Braemar
Banchory
Fort Augustus
Mallaig
Fort William
Killiecrankie
Brechin
Montrose
Inner
Hebrides
Mull
Oban
Killin
Perth
Dundee
St Andrews
Fife Ness
Crieff
Stirling
Kirkcaldy
North Berwick
Jura
Helensburgh
Dunfermline
Falkirk
Edinburgh
Paisley
Glasgow
Islay
Mull of Oa
Hamilton
Clyde
Peebles
Irvine
Ayr
Kilmarnock
Tweed
Newtown St. Boswells
Hawick
Campbeltown
Girvan
Mull of Kintyre
Berwick-upon-Tweed
Coleraine
Limavady
Derry
Strabane
Ballymena
Antrim
Magherafelt
Carrickfergus
Omagh
Cookstown
Belfast
Dungannon
Lisburn
Lurgan
Portadown
Enniskillen
Armagh
Newry
Newcastle
Kilkeel
Dumfries
Stranraer
Carlisle
Penrith
Workington
Whitehaven
Grasmere
Morpeth
Ashington
Tyne
Newcastle upon Tyne
Sunderland
Consett
Durham
Hartlepool
Middlesbrough
Darlington
Whitby
Scarborough
Isle of
Man
(UK)
Douglas
Barrow-in-Furness
Lancaster
Kendal
Thirsk
Ripon
Flamborough Head
Bridlington
Ireland
Blackpool
Preston
Bradford
Leeds
York
Kingston upon Hull
Wakefield
Spurn Head
Grimsby
Irish
Dublin
Anglesey
Holyhead
Formby Point
Liverpool
Salford
Manchester
Doncaster
Sheffield
Rhyl
Llandudno
Bangor
Chester
Caernarfon
Lincoln
Trent
Skegness
Stoke-on-Trent
Derby
Nottingham
Lichfield
Melton Mowbray
King's Lynn
Norwich
Great Yarmouth
Wolverhampton
Birmingham
Leicester
Peterborough
Newtown
Coventry
Rugby
Ely
Lowestoft
Aberystwyth
Worcester
Northampton
Bedford
Cambridge
Ipswich
Cardigan
Severn
Hereford
Milton Keynes
Bishop's Stortford
St David's
Gloucester
Cheltenham
Luton
Colchester
Newport
Oxford
St Albans
Chelmsford
Swansea
Cardiff
Bristol
Swindon
Reading
LONDON
Southend
Bath
Thames
Canterbury
Ilfracombe
Guildford
Tunbridge Wells
Maidstone
Dover
Folkestone
Lundy
Barnstaple
Bridgwater
Taunton
Salisbury
Winchester
Horsham
Calais
Hartland Point
Southampton
Brighton
Crediton
Lyme Regis
Exeter
Poole
Cowes
Chichester
Hastings
Eastbourne
Beachy Head
Weymouth
Ryde
Portsmouth
Tintagel
Exmouth
Newquay
Tavistock
Torquay
Bournemouth
Truro
St Austell
Plymouth
Isle of Wight
Camborne
Penzance
Falmouth
Bill of Portland
English
Channel
Land's End
Lizard Point
Isles of
Scilly
Alderney
Channel
St. Peter Port
Guernsey
Sark
Le Havre
Islands
(UK)
Jersey
St. Helier
France
North
Sea
km
0
50
100
61°
60°
59°
58°
57°
56°
55°
54°
53°
52°
51°
50°
49°
-8°
-6°
-4°
-2°
0°
2°

The Peninsula War.

Battles, principal cities and rivers.

ATLANTIC OCEAN
NORTH SEA
UNITED KINGDOM OF GREAT BRITAIN AND IRELAND
KINGDOM OF NORWAY
KINGDOM OF SWEDEN
KINGDOM OF DENMARK
K. OF PRUSSIA
DUCHY OF WARSAW
EMPIRE OF AUSTRIA
CONFEDERATION OF THE RHINE
EMPIRE OF FRANCE
KINGDOM OF ITALY
KINGDOM OF NAPLES
KINGDOM OF SICILY
KINGDOM OF SARDINIA
KINGDOM OF SPAIN
K. OF PORTUGAL
MEDITERRANEAN
Balearic Islands
Corsica
Bohemia
Hungary
Transylvania
Galicia
Moldavia
Wallachia
Bulgaria
Serbia
Bosnia
Slavonia
Albania
Macedonia
Thessaly
Morea
Ionian Islands
Volhynia
Podolia
Kurland
Livonia
England
Paris
London
Madrid
Vienna
Berlin
Rome
Naples

Europe 1812

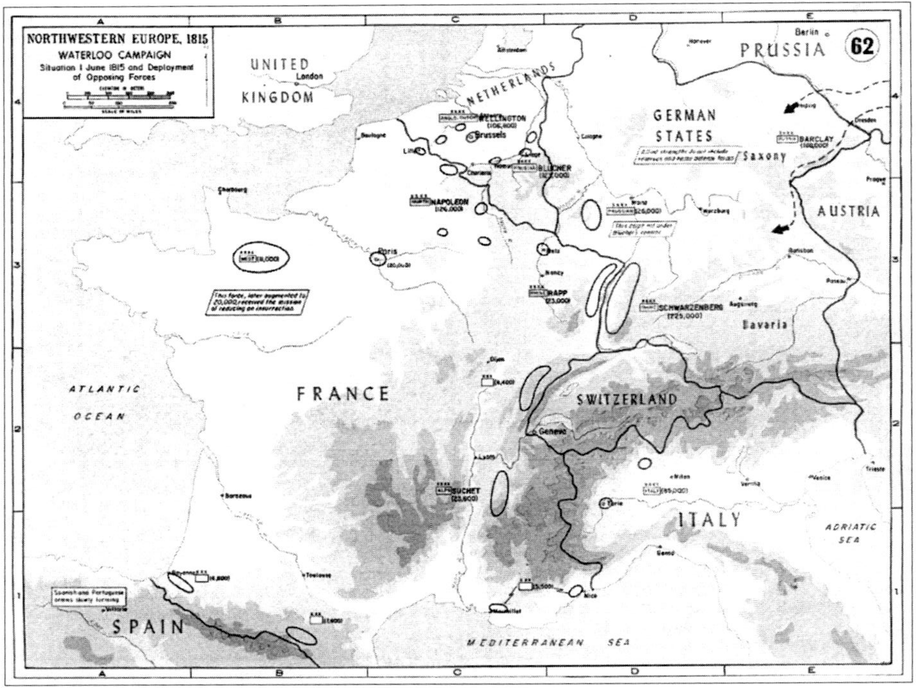
NORTHWESTERN EUROPE, 1815
WATERLOO CAMPAIGN
Situation 1 June 1815 and Deployment of Opposing Forces
62
UNITED KINGDOM
London
NETHERLANDS
WELLINGTON
(106,000)
Brussels
BLUCHER
NAPOLEON
(126,000)
Paris
GERMAN STATES
PRUSSIA
Berlin
BARCLAY
Saxony
AUSTRIA
Bavaria
SCHWARZENBERG
RAPP
(23,000)
FRANCE
SWITZERLAND
Geneva
SUCHET
(23,600)
ITALY
ADRIATIC SEA
ATLANTIC OCEAN
MEDITERRANEAN SEA
SPAIN
Nice
Europe 1815

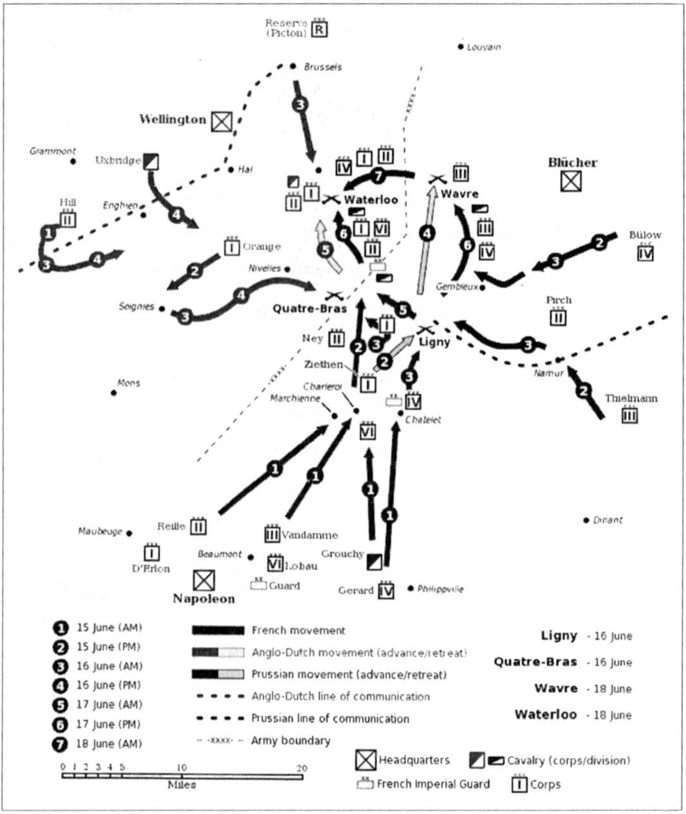

The armies, 15th to 18th June 1815

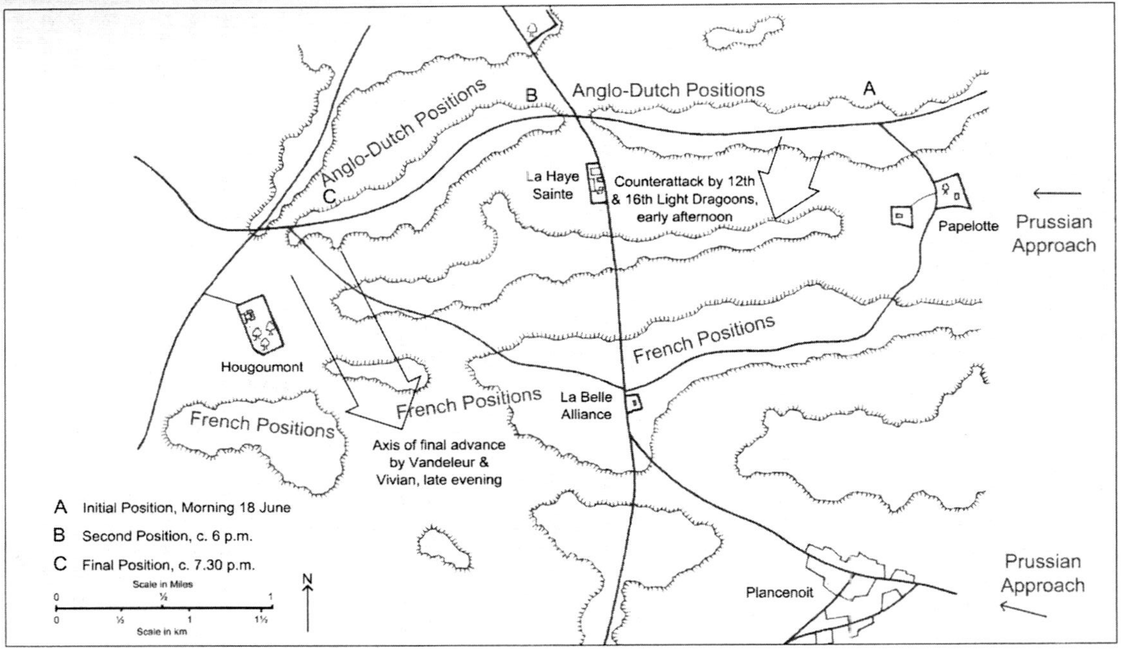

Map 6: The 12th Light Dragoons at Waterloo, 18 June 1815

Acknowledgements

With all my love to Trevor, Anna and Alice, who must feel they've lived with the writing of this book for almost as long as Britain was at war with Napoleon.

Many people have contributed to the book's completion. In particular, I would like to thank: Carole Bromley for getting me started and her ongoing support, advice and encouragement; Diana Stainforth, from The Writers' Workshop, for her helpful reader's report; Martin Riley for his incisive comments about story and structure; Peter Coleman for his formidable editing and proofreading skills.

I would also like to thank all those from my writing workshops and book group who have read extracts along the way and especially those who read my penultimate draft: Carole Bromley, Penny Davies, James Elliot, John Gilham, Doreen Gurrey and Julia Terry.

I must also thank Janet Senior and Alex Gordon for their great hospitality during so many of my research trips; Nicholas Henshall, who demonstrated how to fire a Brown Bess musket; Jill Peters for her shared interest in our great-great-great grandfather; Jane Kasam and other friends for keeping me anchored in the present century.

I am indebted to David Beckford and Andrew Bamford[1] for the illustration showing the involvement of the fictional 36th Light Dragoons in the cavalry actions at Waterloo.

---

1 Andrew Bamford: Gallantry and Discipline, the 12th Light Dragoons at War with Wellington ISBN: 9781848327436

I am grateful to the staff at The National Archives, local record offices, bookshops and libraries in every town my soldiers found themselves in during the course of their wanderings.

Finally I wish to thank the staff at Endeavour Press (e-book release) and at York Publishing Services (paperback production).